UNSETTLED AFFINITIES

UNSETTLED AFFINITIES

Reinhard Bendix

Edited by
John Bendix

with epilogues by
John Bendix and Rudolph von Thadden

Transaction Publishers
New Brunswick (U.S.A.) London (U.K.)

Library of Congress Catalog Number: 92-43184
ISBN: 1-56000-101-1 (cloth)
Printed in the United States of America

Library of Congress Cataloging-in-Publication Data

Bendix, Reinhard.
    Unsettled affinities / Reinhard Bendix : edited and with an epilogue by John Bendix
    p. cm.
    Includes index.
    ISBN 1-56000-101-1 (cloth)
    1. Social groups. 2. Community. 3. Germany—Politics and government—1945- I. Bendix, John, 1956-. II. Title.
HM131.B3994   1993
305—dc20
                                                              92-43184
                                                                  CIP

To Jane, Karen, Erik, and John

Contents

Acknowledgments

Several friends and colleagues have given me the benefit of their critical scrutiny: William Bouwsma, Gordon Craig, Dietrich Goldschmidt, Philip Selznick, Brian Stock, Rudolf von Thadden, and Conrad Wiedemann. I thank them for their time and their thoughtfulness.

The West European Center of the Institute of International Studies, University of California, Berkeley has supported this project with a financial grant. I should add that the Department of Political Science at the University of California, Berkeley has allowed me to avail myself of its facilities even after my retirement in 1986. I have also benefited from the support of the Wissenschaftskolleg zu Berlin during my stay in 1987–88 and subsequently.

I wish to dedicate this book to my wife and my children and to acknowledge the stimulation of students and colleagues during my career.

Introduction

Our affinities are unsettled—and unsettling, personally, socially and politically. From birth on, each of us goes through a personal life cycle, buffeted about by circumstances and uneasily suspended between the risks of individual opportunity and the psychological support we seek from others. All of us stand at the intersection of many social groups such as the family, a social club, the occupation we pursue, or the ethnic and national affiliation into which we were born. Each of these groups or communities exists by distinguishing between those who belong and those who do not. Yet each community also aspires to serve mankind, wherever it is believed that all of us are part of the universe created by one God. The coexistence of group identity and humanitarian aspiration is one ethical paradox of the human condition, the paradox of universalism. Another is the coexistence between diversity and unity within each community, the paradox of unity. Ever and again, the political task arises, how to deal with the scarcity of goods and the inequality of life chances so that personal and social goals can be achieved to a degree of satisfaction that is sufficient for the maintenance of life and community. This book explores the ethical paradoxes of personal affiliation, social universalism, and political unity in Western civilization.

Words like *sufficient* or *maintenance* or *degree of satisfaction* point to the contentions that jeopardize but need not destroy the person, the community, and the political order. As the Austrian writer Hugo von Hofmannsthal has reminded us, "The main difference between living people and fictitious characters is that the writer takes great pains to give the characters coherence and inner unity, whereas the living people may go to extremes of incoherence because their physical existence holds them together."[1] The point is well taken, even if somewhat exaggerated. Groups are held together by the in-group/out-group distinction and by the territorial and institutional base of their political life, even where much contention prevails. In cases of individual incoherence, persons are held together, however precariously, by their efforts to make sense of themselves and of the world in which they live.

Accordingly, I begin the book with the personal background that has led me to write this account of group formation and the political order in Western civilization. A scholar who writes about "unsettled affinities" can be more clearheaded if he comes to terms with the affinities in his own life. By explaining why they ask the questions they do, social scientists can contribute to the diminution of needless controversy that arises when the same evidence is approached with different questions in mind. This will not settle arguments over methods and interpretation. But where different results are reached, we should make sure that the same issue has been considered. Two people can hardly agree on the same answer, in scholarship or anything else, if they do not ask the same question. In this limited sense scholarly self-scrutiny can make a positive contribution to the search for truth.

These studies are concerned with basic aspects of the human condition: the distinction between those close to us and those at a distance. We live in a world of limited resources and unequal life chances in which struggles over distribution are inescapable.

Note

1. Hugo von Hofmannsthal, *Selected Works*, Bollingen Series (New York: Pantheon Books, 1952), 370.

Part I

Personal

1

Intellectual Emigration from Hitler's Germany

Two Generations of Refugees

Each life is a history of affinities through which we find ourselves and are "defined" by others. For me, life began in Berlin, the capital of Germany, in the second year of World War I. I grew up in the sheltered world of a middle-class family, whose German-Jewish identity did not become clear to me until Adolf Hitler came to power in January 1933. The imprisonment of my father and my dismissal from the Gymnasium followed shortly thereafter. The standard "explanation" was that suspects like us had to be put into "protective custody" against the righteous wrath of the people. The people could not be expected to suffer further from the continuation of our activities. The implied threat was that we would be lynched and the authorities would have to take the necessary precautions to protect us. The impressions of that experience at the age of seventeen, and of emigration from Germany to the United States at twenty-two (in 1938), being separated from my nation's culture and finding my place in another, have not been diminished by the passing of half a century.

The escape of German-Jewish social scientists from Hitler's dictatorship in the 1930s affected me in a particular way. Eduard Heimann (1889-1967), professor of economics at the New School for Social Research, saved my life by arranging for my immigration affidavit in 1938. A colleague of his, Adolf Lowe (1893-), another economist at the New School, had been my sister's teacher at the University of Frankfurt and became a fatherly friend to me, albeit a distant one. Both men were younger contemporaries of my father, who was born in 1877. Among the generation of their children, I belong to the group of those who completed

3

their secondary education in Germany (or nearly so in my case), but did their university work in the United States. Other refugees who completed either their primary or secondary education after emigration were less affected by the German background of their parents.[1]

Since I did my academic work in America, it was inevitable that I stood at some remove from the older academic emigrants who had begun their careers in Germany. But my experience allowed me to reflect on this intellectual emigration as a whole, particularly its German-Jewish aspect.[2] Many German-Jewish intellectuals denied that their Jewish ancestry made any difference except for the way Nazi discrimination had abused it. How then is this underarticulated subject a part of the sense that these academic emigrants, and I among them, made of their experience? In attempting to answer this question, I should note an exception. Hannah Arendt had a Jewish upbringing, was involved in Zionist affairs, and had a lifelong concern with Jewish issues. My impression is that she was an exception. The great majority of the intellectuals among German-Jewish refugees were either agnostics or had reduced their Jewish heritage to a bare minimum. Nevertheless, they were greatly influenced by a German-Jewish symbiosis that shaped their outlook and mine, though it is about to fade as we pass from the scene.

That symbiosis was a part of our unsettled affinities, however much the Jewish element was neglected or denied. Like my parents, these German-Jewish refugees did not convert, but neither the synagogue nor Jewish observances played any part in their lives. They thought of themselves as political refugees from Germany. But they were also members of a pervasive German-Jewish subculture on which they reflected rarely, if at all. This subculture manifested itself in frequent quotations from the classics, from the ancients to the moderns. In part, this practice was a generational phenomenon. But German Jews cultivated it with a special intensity, because it represented a personal acquisition by which they qualified themselves as German citizens. It should be remembered that the legal emancipation of the Prussian Jews in the early nineteenth century had done nothing to eliminate the social and political discrimination against them. Accordingly, they felt compelled, if only subconsciously, to prove themselves worthy of equal consideration as citizens.[3] This preoccupation (*Bildungsbeflissenheit*) represented a subculture shared by most German-Jewish intellectuals who fled Hitler's Germany since 1933.

In what sense did the group of German-Jewish academics reflect these conditions of their earlier lives, even in exile? The educational preoccupations of a discriminated minority are a response to the pressure of having to prove themselves worthy as citizens, in a manner beyond formal legal equality. In the eyes of many Germans, intellectualization set the Jews apart. To compensate for social and political disadvantages, the Jewish outsider often overestimates the importance of intellectual dimensions. He engages in the search for truth among equal knowledge seekers, recognizing no bounds and hence running the danger of presumption in the name of mind or spirit. From here it is only a short step to the perspective of the stranger, whom Simmel defined as a man, who comes today and stays tomorrow, and who tends to remain an outsider in his views of the society in which he lives. This experience is by no means confined to German-Jewish intellectuals. It is a common frame of mind among social scientists, but it may help to account for the notable success in the United States of the intellectual emigration from Hitler's Germany.

Between 1933 and 1939 there were about 800,000 German refugees. Only a small fraction of them were academics. Compare that with the number of refugees in the world in 1989-90, estimated at some 14 million. During the twentieth century as a whole the approximate figure is ten times that number. Yet several conferences were held in 1983 and 1984, commemorating the fiftieth anniversary of the emigration of German intellectuals, suggesting the exceptional impact this tiny group of people made on their country of exile. But this statement only applies to intellectual emigrants of my father's generation whose agony of displacement was palpable despite their success. Because of the difference in age and experience I have noted, my own emigration at twenty-two was a liberating rather than a wrenching experience. After all, I had been dismissed from the Gymnasium in 1933 at seventeen, had worked in the interim under the steadily worsening conditions of Hitler's Germany, and had only begun my university studies in the United States after my emigration in 1938.

Therefore, as a participant, I am very conscious of belonging to another generation than those refugees who had received their academic training in Germany before 1933, and who had a good start on their careers before their emigration. At fifteen, in 1931, my father had taken me to a meeting of religious socialists in Berlin, at which Eduard

Heimann, Adolf Lowe, and Paul Tillich were the featured speakers. When I actually met my benefactor, Professor Heimann, on my arrival in New York, I quickly sensed the generational difference despite Heimann's helpfulness and generosity. He was my senior by twenty-seven years.

What stands out in my mind is the intellectual continuity of scholars in Heimann's age-group despite the disruption caused by their emigration. In the United States, with its readiness to receive professionals from abroad, there was a widespread response to their ideas. Native competitors certainly put obstacles in their way. Experienced doctors and lawyers had to submit to new training and examinations, academics did not always find positions to their liking, free-lance writers and artists had to struggle for several years. But these obstacles were also overcome, and in notable instances the transition was smoother and the American response uncommonly positive and widespread. Nevertheless, a number of refugee scholars expressed their frustration at the lack of public response to their work in America.

In some cases this may have been a correct appraisal, but broadly speaking the opposite conclusion is more persuasive. By arriving when market and opinion research were in the ascendance, Paul Lazarsfeld influenced that field as he could not have done in his native Austria. In political theory, Leo Strauss developed an influence that has few parallels, and certainly none in his native Germany. In phenomenology, Alfred Schütz elicited a widespread response among American academics, not otherwise in touch with German refugee scholars. Hannah Arendt played an important role in the New York intelligentsia as well as in the often heated debates of the American Jewish community. At one time, economists like Gerhard Colm and Hans Neisser held important positions in the U.S. government. Members of the faculty at the New School for Social Research were active during the war in the Office of Strategic Services. One of them was Herbert Marcuse, whose writings were influential in the student movement of the 1960s. Finally, Horkheimer and Adorno probably had their greatest intellectual impact in the United States only after they had returned to Germany in the 1950s. These achievements are significant enough so that one may wonder why some of these refugees felt as isolated as they did.

Intellectual Controversies

The sense of isolation hardly applied to Paul Lazarsfeld. His emigration roughly coincided with the beginning of American market and opinion research. In Austria, Lazarsfeld had been a young collaborator of Charlotte Bühler, who trained him in statistics and social psychology. Though he had several publications to his credit, they became prominent in America only after his emigration because of his major impact on public opinion research. I want to consider Lazarsfeld and his followers, because their work highlights a basic intellectual dilemma that was accentuated among German refugee scholars, had a considerable impact in the United States, and also influenced my own work.

At a commemorative conference in 1984, Hans Zeisel, at seventy-five, was the only participant from that earlier generation of German refugee scholars. Zeisel had been a co-author of Lazarsfeld's early study of the unemployed in the Austrian town of Marienthal, and since the 1950s he had taught at the University of Chicago. As a lawyer and a collaborator of Lazarsfeld, he was affiliated with both the Law School and the Department of Sociology. He described his research in the sociology of law, in which he studied the behavior of juries under a variety of controlled conditions. At the conference, Zeisel was asked about his attitude toward the postulates of critical theory, the intellectual trademark of Max Horkheimer and Theodor Adorno at the Frankfurt *Institut für Sozialforschung* since the 1920s. It was contended that Zeisel's studies only provided a more or less interesting but inevitably fragmentary selection from the social structure as a whole. It turned out that Zeisel had hardly been concerned with "critical theory." Such theorizing was irrelevant, he maintained, because conflicting opinions circulated among lawyers concerning the behavior of juries, and these lawyers wanted to know which of the many opinions was probably the correct one. Zeisel added that as a lawyer and sociologist he was interested in the truth. He seemed unconcerned that this conception of truth differed from the one espoused by "critical theory." At this point the discussion turned to other matters.

However, the question is worth pursuing, because this little debate reflected the divergent purposes of knowledge, which have divided social scientists in Germany, the United States, and elsewhere throughout the twentieth century. As with other endeavors, the pursuit of knowledge leads to solidarity within one group, while it also leads to tension with others. Zeisel's legal colleagues were interested because his findings seemed to facilitate their professional work and that interest was sufficient to justify the "jury project." But truths about juries are easily disparaged without invalidating them. For juries are "only" part of the legal system, and that system is "only" part of a governmental structure, which in turn is part of American society as a superpower among other powers and all these together constitute a "world system." In this way, one gets from the parts to the whole, which can be labeled, according to taste, as capitalism, as world politics, as one type of legal system among many, or as a moment of world history. In each of these perspectives, Zeisel's studies appear as parts whose *real* significance can only be assessed in relation to the whole. This position implies a negative evaluation of *all* partial studies. For no empirical study can be compared with the alleged comprehension of the whole. I say alleged, because "the whole" is not a proper object of human knowledge, but of religious belief.

Only questions within well-defined limits can be answered by empirical research. Though there will always be debate as to how well-defined those limits should be, such limitations have proved themselves through the productivity of the research that is confined to them. It is the dominant mode of modern science. But this way of producing knowledge depends on a hope that cannot result from scientific inquiry itself. The hope is that the cumulation of knowledge can lead to the resolution of all conceivable questions, if not tomorrow, then in the long run. Scholars committed to this approach contend that other ways of seeking knowledge fail to clarify the questions posed and do not achieve reliable results. For thirty years Hans Zeisel has been concerned with limited truths about juries and jurors. Lawyers who deal with insurance claims are naturally interested in findings that show which kinds of jurors are inclined to award high compensation. Zeisel's inquiries have also elucidated the group dynamics of jury deliberations.

Whatever the merit of seeking answers to specific questions, empirical inquiry comes up against the uncertain prospect of its own long-term hope of resolving *all* questions *reliably*. The ideal of finding reliable answers is not compatible with the hope that all interesting questions are answerable in this way, or the claim that only reliably answered questions are worth considering. Nietzsche already polemicized against "scientism" as a delusion and disparaged its motivation as an inordinate craving for knowledge, a notion with many modern adherents. The purpose of these adherents is to search for "knowledge of the whole," an idea with an ancient religious lineage.

A Personal Perspective

My American training induced a pervasive skepticism about holistic approaches, but then my European background also made me skeptical toward empiricism carried to extremes. An example from the early years of Lazarsfeld's opinion research brought this out. Initially, that research had to be financed by contracts for commercial projects. Often the task was to construct questionnaires in such a way that both a practical and a theoretical interest could be satisfied. Yet any commercially oriented project could always be justified by its potential contribution to methodological refinements and its indirect payoff for more theoretically significant work. This familiar ambivalence provokes the critique that opinion polls dehumanize the people interviewed, degrade people by their quantification, and thereby subject them to a mechanical subdivision like other aspects of capitalism. Lazarsfeld's special contribution made opinion research academically respectable (instead of remaining confined to institutes of market research).

Conferences occasioned by the fiftieth anniversary of the intellectual emigration from Hitler's Germany made me confront the old question whether human understanding can encompass "the whole." Those who affirm this position appear to their opponents as "mere metaphysicians," whereas those who reject it appear to *their* opponents as "empty empiricists." Intellectual concern with the ultimate dilemmas of the human condition on one side, techniques of inquiry dealing as precisely as possible with the "facts of the matter" on the other. Presumably, "truth" lies somewhere between these extremes, though not necessarily in the middle. Rather, one ought to be mindful of human dilemmas even as one inquires into specific conditions, just as reflections on those dilemmas ought to grapple with what one can learn from empirical inquiries. For reflection unchecked by a concern with "finding out" runs the risk of idle speculation. These cautionary guidelines pertain to the search for "truth," a word that needs quotation marks because of its many philosophical difficulties. Nevertheless, I use the term in the naive sense that any search for knowledge presupposes a shared purpose among those who inquire.

Judgments about propositions diverge not only because of disputes over whether they are true. The contention between "mere metaphysicians" and "empty empiricists" also involves different, even contradictory purposes of their search for knowledge. If two scholars do not have the same purpose and question in mind, they are unlikely to find the same thing to be true.

These orientations divide the modern search for knowledge. Perhaps this is one reason why the refugee scholars from Hitler's Germany fit into American academic life as smoothly as they did. For generational as well as intellectual reasons, this helps to account for my sense of not quite belonging either to the intellectual emigration from Hitler's Germany or to the mainstream of American social science.

Many of the German scholars who came to America had considerable experience in Weimar Germany with the public application of social science knowledge. They may have been disappointed at their reduced American role in this respect, but in my eyes their participation was considerable. After all, my only political experience in Germany had been participation in *Neu Beginnen*, a small underground group in the first years of the Hitler regime. As a research assistant of Louis Wirth and Charles Merriam at the University of Chicago I witnessed the political participation of American academics at first hand, but to a recent immigrant like myself American politics at this level appeared utterly foreign. So, in contrast to some older German emigrants, I put most of my effort into teaching and research.

I also discovered that American immigration had put me on a different intellectual wavelength. Although I shared many of the interests of social theorists such as Hannah Arendt, Leo Strauss, and members of the Frankfurt School, I found myself put off by their tendency to seek answers for the ills of our time through reliance on the models provided by ancient Greek politics and literature. Only later did I discover that many of them had been students of Martin Heidegger, who used pre-Socratic philosophy in a similar manner. Still later I also discovered that the idealization of Ancient Greece had been an antimodern ideology in German philosophy and education ever since the eighteenth century. This idealization of the classics had found its echo in the Great Books program at the University of Chicago, which developed into a missionary enterprise later on.[4] I thought then, as I do now, that knowledge of the classics is an important part of our education, but that they are ill-suited as a fountainhead of answers for the dilemmas of our time.[5]

How did I find my own intellectual orientation as a young German immigrant who began his university studies in 1938 at Chicago, away from the self-reinforcing ambience of German-Jewish refugees in New York? At the University of Chicago the contrast between American empiricism and the European penchant for theoretical relevance was reinforced by the College Program of survey courses, initiated by Robert Hutchins. After my first two years as an undergraduate I had to declare a major and I chose sociology, because my earlier exploration as an adolescent bookworm in my native Berlin had pointed me in this direction. As presented at Chicago, expert knowledge often consisted of strictly delimited subjects, which seemed to become ever smaller in the interest of methodological stringency. At the time, the saying made the rounds among students that sociologists learned more, and more accurately, about less and less. The curriculum as a whole appeared as a juxtaposition of general survey courses and sharply focused studies of detail. It seemed to be left to the students to bridge the resulting gap.

My teachers in sociology agreed, at least superficially, that scientific rigor was indispensable. Their intellectual guideline was derived from a generalized and uncritical acceptance of natural science as a model, and at first I was quite attracted by this position. Research should begin with a clear statement of what one wants to find out, what kind of evidence should be assembled, and how this evidence could answer the initial question. If one did not know what one was after, one was not likely to find it. In this rudimentary sense all my teachers were partisans of impartiality, which meant that one should not prejudge the answer in the way one framed the question. I thought this exciting because only a short time before I had experienced enough partisanship under the Nazis to be ready for a more rational approach to seeking knowledge. But then what?

One cannot investigate everything in detail, nor would the effort be worthwhile, since we are always obliged to economize time and effort and hence make decisions at every important step. Otherwise, like Buridan's ass, we would starve to death among all those inviting haystacks. For the choices that have to be made, methodological stringency alone is not a sufficient criterion. In retrospect I have come to understand that I owe my interest in social and political history to this initial, negative reaction. On the positive side, social groups are a central focus of sociology and it does not make sense to interpret them exclusively on the "knife-edge of the present." Groups have more or less enduring attributes so that their present characteristics depend in part on earlier conditions, even though we will remain ignorant about their origins.

This historical awareness helped me to avoid the dead end of a strictly positivist orientation. But at the same time I came to recognize that several of the social scientists coming from Germany counterpoised this American positivism with a global theoretical approach. I became non-plussed when I discovered that the "holistic approach" of a Protestant theologian like Paul Tillich was shared by scholars like Leo Strauss and Eric Voegelin, by Hannah Arendt and the group around Max Horkheimer, even though these scholars for most of their careers did not profess any religious conviction. In the 1940s I became aware of their strong tendency to surround themselves with groups of disciples rather than students. I considered this a misuse of teaching in a secular context, though they had probably taken this tendency from their German university professors and carried it with them into exile. I recognized only later that my early spontaneous reaction against this practice originated in my deep distrust of religious simulation under the guise of academic scholarship. Despite my agnosticism, I dislike intellectuals who act as if their "holistic view" entitles them to a higher cultural and moral standing.

Finally, I want to characterize my "elective affinity" with Max Weber, which I acquired only in the United States. Weber proved to be decisive for my work as a sociologist. When I became a student at the University of Chicago I had to come to terms with the social determinism that was part of the faith in science among American sociologists. Here I found much needed support for my "European doubts" in Weber's balanced view of the individual and society. Weber represented to me an anti-utopian view of the social world, which remained open to its possible developments nevertheless. His definition of action emphasizes in equal measure the propensity of individuals to make what sense they could of their world as well as their propensity to respond to the expectations of others. His definition of class and status do the same for the pursuit of gain and the striving for prestige and power over others. His definition of morals encompasses an ethic of conviction and an ethic of responsibility. Indeed, conceptual oppositions like these appear in his writings with such frequency that I have come to think of them as the theoretical core of his work. This approach is, of course, very old and not confined to the Western tradition.

Weber provided us with two interpretations that became particularly important to me. One of these consisted in a comparative historical perspective, which to me is not only a method, but implies a basic conception of man and society. Every human achievement, every social fact or development allows a conceptual formulation only through emphasizing certain attributes while neglecting or excluding others. To borrow a Marxian phrase for my purposes, every formulation contains within it the seeds of its own destruction. Social scientists should not be satisfied with the observation of any particular fact without regard for its cultural, chronological, or other limitations. Sooner or later, what was previously excluded conceptually will be seen as important, with the result that new constellations come into view. This notion may be reminiscent of Hegel's dialectic, but one must remember that Weber explicitly opposed Hegel's approach. For Weber, sense or meaning are attributes of human action, not a construction of Spirit or Reason manifesting itself in history. This theoretical starting point is as incompatible with "empty empiricism" as it is with "mere metaphysics."

I was also attracted by the anti-utopian implications of Weber's use of conceptual opposites. Fascism and communism are two versions of a utopian mentality. However different they are ideologically, both started from the idea of the total manipulability of man and society. If racial identity or the organization of production are the ultimate determinants of history, then control over these fundamentals implies that man can direct history. The consequences of these two utopias have been so abhorrent that I developed a basic distrust of their underlying intellectual claims. Weber's conceptual oppositions provide a safeguard against utopian tendencies without devaluing the concern with alternatives. Such thinking is indispensable, because the world as we find it is deeply flawed. But, for all that, it is not the worst possible world. Hence, distinctions between democracy and one-party dictatorships, between a technology employed for good or for morally degrading ends should be considered carefully. They should not be dismissed because apocalyptic visions can make them appear as equally flawed aspects of modernity.

Utopians set so high an aim for the future, that nothing existing at present seems worth preserving. If every human condition shows drawbacks and, therefore, provokes tendencies in other directions, then utopia can be defined as a society without deficiencies and hence without alternatives. Weber's whole work shows that such a society cannot be a realizable human goal. True, he also mentions that striving for the impossible is sometimes necessary in order to achieve the possible. But principled utopians demand the impossible as the *only* feasible way in a totally irrational world. This excess tends to jeopardize the possible and to counteract what is valuable in the utopian critique.

Unfortunately I do not possess the theological sophistication that would enable me to place this approach in its proper context. But my interpretation of Weber is more than a position "halfway" between empirical narrow-mindedness and holistic presumption. Unwittingly, I may have caught a distant echo of religious beliefs. The Jewish idea of God refers to an incommensurate absolute that has no name and, for fear of idolatry, must not be named, but which is a constant reminder of human limitation. I take an example from Gershom Scholem's essay "Creation out of Nothing and the Self-Embrace of God." Scholem analyzes parallels between Jewish and Christian mysticism in the Middle Ages and quotes the following passage from a German theology of the fourteenth century:

> The peculiarities are capable of being apprehended, known and expressed, but perfection is for all creatures beyond apprehension, knowledge or expression. For that reason one calls perfection 'nothing' for it is not of a creaturely kind. A creation cannot know or comprehend perfection, nor is it capable of naming it or thinking about it.[6]

If my secular conclusions derived from Weber's work have an "elective affinity" with Judeo-Christian ideas, then this may be mere coincidence, or it may derive from some intellectual influence beyond my comprehension. This open question reflects the uncertainties of the world as I have found it, standing on the margins not only of German-Jewish and American culture but also of different generations of intellectual emigration from Hitler's Germany.[7]

Emigrants are marginal by definition and it may be true that my marginal position among German-Jewish refugee scholars and my American colleagues helps to account for the contemplative character of my work as a scholar and teacher. If every human achievement (including every intellectual formulation) comes at a price, as I have argued, then obviously this applies to myself. The price of contemplation is not the failure to take a stand, but detachment from the world of action and decision making except in scholarship itself. I have felt throughout that

I had to pay that price in a world torn by wars of nerves, arms, and words, in which universities for all their flaws *can* be institutions of detachment, a point worth reiterating after more than two decades of attempts to destroy that detachment by political agitation.[8] It is one thing to acknowledge that there is no science or scholarship without presuppositions. It is quite another to claim that efforts at detachment on behalf of reason are both futile and politically pernicious.

Notes

1. For details, see Reinhard Bendix, *From Berlin to Berkeley*, (New Brunswick, NJ: Transaction Publishers, 1986).
2. There were non-Jewish refugees from Hitler's Germany as well, but I do not consider them here.
3. This sense of having to prove oneself influenced even orthodox Jews as David Sorkin has shown in *The Transformation of German Jews, 1780-1840* (New York: Oxford University Press, 1987), passim.
4. The movement was also notable for its zealotry. Cf. Alan Bloom, *The Closing of the American Mind* (Chicago: University of Chicago Press, 1987), passim. Bloom was a student of Leo Strauss, whose peculiar influence is analyzed in Stephen Holmes, "Wahrheiten für Wenige," *Merkur* 44 (July 1990), 554-69.
5. In this respect I have learned much from Stuart Hampshire's *Morality and Conflict* (Cambridge: Harvard University Press, 1983).
6. Quoted in Gershom Scholem, *Über einige Grundbegriffe des Judentums* (Frankfurt: Suhrkamp, 1970), 74-75.
7. For a biographical discussion of this marginality see my essay "Emigration als Problem geistiger Identität," in Ilja Srubar, ed., *Exil, Wissenschaft, Ideologie* (Frankfurt: Suhrkamp, 1988), 23-36. This volume contains the papers of the conference I have referred to in this discussion. Cf. also my "Geistige Gegensätze deutsch-jüdischer Sozialwissenschaftler in ihrer Emigration," in Ehrhard A. Wiehn, ed., *Juden in der Soziologie* (Konstanz: Hartung-Gorre Verlag, 1989), 323-38 for an earlier version of this chapter.
8. This restates a position first articulated in Reinhard Bendix, *Social Science and the Distrust of Reason*, University of California Publications in Sociology and Social Institutions, vol. 1 (Berkeley: University of California Press, 1951), 41-42. See also Reinhard Bendix, *Force, Fate and Freedom* (Berkeley: University of California Press, 1984), 125-27.

2

Embattled Reason—a Report

Half a century ago I was a junior member of the intellectual emigration from Hitler's Germany. Since then I have had an academic career, largely at the University of California in Berkeley, from which I retired in 1986. What has been the intellectual result? Since the answer is contained in my teaching career and a good many books and articles, I want to provide a "road map" to my work, both as a summary for myself and as an aid to others. What has been written and documented at length can be put more briefly, and near the end of an academic career it seems appropriate to do so.[1]

Conditions of Seeking Knowledge

The first impulse of my intellectual career arose from my father's critical approach to judicial decision making in Weimar Germany. He was skeptical of judges who used the law to cling to their monarchical sympathies despite their oath to a Republican constitution. They would render their decisions with "impeccable" logic and yet express their political prejudices and social conceits. Marx and Nietzsche were forerunners of this skepticism, which, under the influence of Wilhelm Dilthey, my father transformed into an individualistic and philosophical direction. Only a general impression of my father's endeavor reached me during my adolescence. That impression came into focus when he urged me to read Karl Mannheim's *Ideology and Utopia*, originally published in 1929. He helped me with this difficult text and brought me to understand in some proximate way that in the interest of honesty, the life of the mind has preconditions worth examining. I pass over the details of this initial and rudimentary insight in order to turn to my experience at the University of Chicago, not as I encountered it at first, but as I look at it in retrospect.

American sociology presents itself as an empirical social science that is divided by a fundamental controversy over the proper object of cognition. On the one side one finds analyses of life histories and of ethnic or occupational subcultures, which emphasize empathy; on the other side one finds demography and opinion surveys, which emphasize statistics and the ideal of "hard science." Both sides profess a common empirical interest, but opinions concerning matters of substance and method diverge. In looking back I realize that I circumvented these intellectual alternatives by making *reflexivity* the starting point of my work. In the history of the natural sciences since the Greeks, reflection always started with the distinction between subject and object. That tendency has only come into question with modern physics, Heisenberg's principle of uncertainty, which states that one cannot measure the location and velocity of electrons at the same time. Hence, the observer must decide on which object he wants to focus his attention.

In the history of the social sciences this questioning of the subject-object distinction was a problem from the outset. Hans Barth has traced the questioning of human rationality from Bacon's theory of idols in the seventeenth century to Freud's concept of the unconscious in the twentieth.[2] When I summarized Barth's results in 1951, I concluded that the development of the social sciences frequently consisted of ever more probing insights into the unwitting sources of human error and ever more drastic efforts to eradicate error. One copes with Francis Bacon's idols by more circumspect reflection, with Destutt de Tracy's ideology by the reform of education with Karl Marx's false consciousness by revolution, and with Sigmund Freud's repression by psychotherapy. Our idea of the remedy needed to correct the sources of error has become ever more drastic, because the development of social thought has made us more knowledgeable about the sources of human fallibility.[3] Robert Merton has criticized this starting point by saying that the paradox of the liar (Zeno's "a Cretan says all Cretans are liars") may be a logical paradox for mathematicians and logicians, but that scientists sidestep it without jeopardizing the productivity of their research. Therefore, social scientists should do the same.[4]

I disagree with this conclusion for three reasons. First, errors in the search for knowledge about society are themselves an object of social research, because without vague and false assumptions about man and society we would live in a different world from the one familiar to us.

Errors and illusions are an integral part of the social life we try to understand. Second, recent work in the philosophy of science makes it appear probable that research in the natural sciences also starts from more or less arbitrary assumptions. Some of these are obviously compatible with the familiar productivity of scientific research. Scholars need to consider that errors and illusions are *not* a part of nature as they are a part of society. Third, Merton starts from the hope that the social sciences can and will develop as successfully as the natural sciences, if only they would similarly bypass the paradox of the liar. That way they proceed empirically by the hypothetical-deductive method.[5] I do not share this hope and am consequently more skeptical toward "natural science" as a model for the social sciences. In particular, I do not consider the discovery of social laws a desirable goal. Such laws, even if they are discovered and until now they have not been, would have to be relatively empty of content. A good example would be Simmel's idea of the "negativity of collective behavior," according to which mass solidarity is most readily achieved in opposition to a common enemy. To be sure, I am no legislator for the social sciences and in the American context there is no danger that social scientists will cease on my account to model themselves on the "natural sciences."[6] I have thought it useful to try a different approach precisely because these efforts to discover social laws continue.

There are no sciences without presuppositions. The art of asking questions is one of them. One cannot find answers without asking questions, and only the same question can yield the same answer. Hence, agreement on propositions depends upon a shared purpose of cognition. The pursuit of knowledge also involves the hope that by posing a question one can find an answer. Sometimes even our assumptions and expectations regarding the same general problem diverge and lead to different conclusions. Merton's hope and my skepticism represent two views concerning the purpose of cognition. I call such views images of the human condition, which each of us brings to the pursuit of knowledge about society, just as different ideas of nature underlie the physical sciences.

Philosophers tend to regard the starting point I have proposed as relativistic, and they consider such relativism untenable on logical as well as moral grounds. Logically, one can accept the multiplicity of intellectual systems only if one views this multiplicity as unconditionally true and morally binding. To do so would be a contradiction in terms, because one cannot assert relative and absolute ideas of truth and morals at one and the same time. Yet this is what happens when one declares that there are as many truths and moralities as there are cultures and subcultures so that every single truth and morality is relative. I submit that social scientists are as little troubled by this paradox as natural scientists are by the paradox of the liar. Social scientists do not have to solve a logical problem in cognition and ethics. Their task is, rather, to analyze the multiplicity of truths and moralities as they find them. They could not do this if at the same time they were to strive for the unity of truth and morality.

Two further observations are appropriate. The people who share a common culture are not disturbed by the fact that there are many truths and moralities. On the contrary. They adhere to their own culture all the more persistently, while they reject other cultures. From a universalist standpoint such ethnocentrism is a misfortune; from the standpoint of a social scientist it is a fact he must consider.[7] Relativism presents philosophers with a logical problem. However, the philosophical assumption of only one truth or ethic presupposes the possibility of apprehending the whole. How can that be if all human cognition is limited? When Hegel stated that "the truth is the whole" he appealed to a religious tradition, that his own secularizing philosophy undermined. When social scientists recognize the multiplicity of truths and morals, they seek to advance our understanding and moderation, not the ethnocentrism that divides one group from another. Indeed, the universalism of knowledge seeks to limit the relativity of cultures. As I see it, the task consists in seeing both together: the elementary impulse and capacity to idealize truth and virtue which exists in all societies, and the fact that people of different cultures have different ideals of truth and virtue.

With every question posed, we associate the hopes implicit in our image of the human condition, but we articulate that implication only intermittently. This is as it should be, in order to get on with the pursuit of knowledge. For by throwing a critical light on the assumptions that underlie that pursuit, one may appear to obstruct the quest for knowledge. Every scholar starts with presuppositions, in order to find his answers. He cannot find answers, if he is continuously occupied with analyzing his own presuppositions. It is difficult to find a proper balance between a scholar's legitimate concern with finding the right answers and the equally legitimate but self-critical concern with understanding why these rather than some other questions matter.

Nevertheless, analysis of presuppositions has its utility despite the difficulties arising from it. Contrary opinions, interpretations and explanatory models recur endlessly. The critical self-consciousness of scholars will not change that. One can hope that a raised level of consciousness can reduce the large number of incompatible answers when questions are asked. Put differently: even with the same question different presuppositions are possible, and when this occurs, one should not be surprised that the answers diverge as well.

Scholarly work is beset by hegemonic drives, which can be constructive as well as destructive. Don Price has pointed out that every science insists on determining the questions it pursues and the methods it adopts. Even when scientists allow themselves to be influenced by purposes brought to them from the outside, they do so in principle on the condition that they decide on the way their project is to be framed. Research has only been successful where this self-determination prevails, which of course has pedagogic and institutional consequences as well.[8] This is the constructive side. On the other hand, there is the danger that scientific autonomy becomes a purpose in its own right and can lead to delusions about science and hence to results, which the self-limitation was supposed to preclude. Here also the principle of self-critical reflexivity can have salutary effects. A raised consciousness about the presuppositions of inquiry are especially important today when science has increased the human potential for good and ill at an unprecedented pace.

Theoretical Assumptions

Since World War II the idea of "system" has become popular in social thought. Systemic thinking was already widespread in such diverse fields as biology, ecology, economics, and computer science, before Talcott Parsons introduced it to sociology. Concepts like function, equilibrium, and evolution were closely associated with the idea of "system." Nevertheless, the application of these concepts to society as a whole is questionable.

The term *system* means the mutual interdependence of all factors such that changes in one factor inexorably entail changes in all the others. Such interdependence is regulated internally within certain defined limits, the social system as a whole is differentiated by clear boundaries from other social systems. The analogy to the concept of the body is apparent and has been employed in various ways since antiquity. The great age of the idea suggests that it has religious as well as deep psychological roots. Yet the systemic model seems to me unsuitable as the basic metaphor of society. My reasons are that the three attributes of "the system" fail to take account of societies as we encounter them, either historically or at the present time.

Societies are loose structures so that the mutual interdependence of their different parts is relatively unpredictable. Societies also lack an equilibrating device like body temperature with specific upper and lower limits. When Durkheim contended that a "normal" rate of crime was "needed" so that the penalties imposed could maintain basic social norms, he failed to specify the meaning of this proposition. Merton has called the underlying conception of an intrasocietal equilibrium the cloudiest idea in the theory of functionalism.[9] The boundaries between different societies are permeable in varying degrees, in contrast to bodies that are clearly separated from one another. Today, the penetrability of boundaries by modern means of communication is one of the important reasons of political unrest. Censorship is one clue to the lack of integration in societies around the world, because it is imposed wherever a society seeks to protect its internal divisions against further disruptions from the outside.

How, then, can we study social change if societies lack integration and at any one time comprise many countervailing tendencies? Since change means that after a given interval of time a social structure is different from what it was before, we are obliged to "simplify and exaggerate" those differences conceptually, in order to study change. This is one reason for the recurrent use of Max Weber's ideal types despite the many critiques leveled against them. For example, it has been customary in recent social thought to contrast tradition with modernity. One should regard this practice skeptically, but as long as one wants to speak of change, it will be difficult to avoid it altogether.[10] In the presence of flux, all conceptual distinctions are artificial but some are indispensable for the pursuit of knowledge.

Take the evolutionary idea that in the long run all societies pass through the same stages of development, a sequence which, regardless of what basic factors are assumed, is most often associated with the idea of progress. One can, of course, speak of progress in particular fields, provided the criterion used is clearly stated. Science and technology provide ample evidence that today men can know and do more than they could earlier. This "more" presupposes the ideal of advancing knowledge and control over nature that is not universally shared. The argument over the balance between progressive and regressive consequences of knowledge will continue. Regardless of how this assessment is made, change does *not* always occur in the form of a ceaseless flux as in Heraclitus's metaphor of not being able to step in the same river twice. All change is the end result of cumulative antecedents, but cumulation alone will not account for the breakthroughs that occur from time to time, just as all the water in a glass is not sufficient to account for the last drops necessary to cause an overflow. Because of these breakthroughs I cannot accept the idea of a sequence of stages through which all societies will pass sooner or later. That idea founders on the fact that breakthroughs in one part of the world permanently alter the international environment in which other parts must develop from then on.

Max Weber's theory of cumulative tendencies toward technical rationality in Western civilization is in these terms a theory of successive breakthroughs. Weber has analyzed types of rationality in many contexts and hinted at them in many others. If tendencies toward rationality in one field after another have introduced something new, like the emergence of monotheism in the Near East, or the development of Roman law, or the spurt of Western European discoveries from Copernicus to Newton, then the different parts of the world are affected unevenly. In this respect pioneering countries exert "demonstration effects" on follower societies, which must decide between emulating or rejecting these models and usually end up with some unstable mixture between the two. There are many contexts in which this phenomenon can be explored.

How can we analyze this world history of uneven developments without taking sides, like preferring economic advance over backwardness and equating that difference, at least implicitly, with progress? This question supposes that we can distinguish between observers and participants, that scholars can and should hold their preferences in abeyance. Of course, they participate in their own society, but in their professional capacity they participate by their partisanship for scholarly detachment. By contrast, "ordinary" participants often lack both the interest and the ability to take such a detached position.

The scholarly observer turns to the world in a well-controlled manner in order to understand and/or control it, basing himself on values like knowledge and assumptions like the orderliness of nature. These values and assumptions differ from personal preferences, as Max Weber emphasized. The moralist also turns to the world, but he does so in order to attain the good life in the highest sense of that term. He also takes account of the way things are, but for the sake of perfecting the soul, not in order to gain knowledge. True, in ancient Greece the idea that knowledge is virtue gained a temporary ascendance; the Greeks possessed a unified cosmological foundation of causes and norms. Since that classical model has receded, there have been these two, more or less incompatible, tendencies: one oriented toward an understanding of causes, the other toward the comprehension of norms. "The intellect of man is forced to choose,/ Perfection of the life, or of the work," as W. B. Yeats put it. "Perfection of the life," or of the Great Chain of Being, is an object of contemplation. By contrast, "perfection of the work," or, in the present case, of worldly knowledge, is an object of inquiry. Inquiry depends upon the distinctions men make, not upon the spiritual unity to which they aspire.

Much clarity would be gained if scholars preoccupied with normative questions were to articulate their own religious roots instead of disguising them through recourse to ancient moral philosophy. The distinction between the "heavenly ought" and the "mundane is" cannot be eradicated by denouncing the sciences, which are based on a partial separation of these realms. It is morally questionable to criticize the lower realm of science from the standpoint of a higher perfection, when the critics of science benefit from its results. True, it would also be better if scientists themselves were fully conscious of the moral presuppositions of their research and of the moral burdens arising from its results. For we may speak of such burdens whenever scientific findings go beyond the capacity of a society for moral and political decision making.

In sum, society is not an organism in the sense of a biological system. Hence, we must presuppose that social structures are only loosely or weakly integrated. The ideal types, which are indispensable for scholarly studies in the social sciences, "simplify and exaggerate" the evidence so that they present social structures as more integrated than they are. Since studies of social change must operate with a "before-and-after" comparison based on ideal types, we face a dilemma. How is one to avoid ideal types that exaggerate the social integration of the earlier and the later social structure? I believe that, despite great differences in detail, the answer is found in the recurrence of the same themes in the history of social theory.

These themes can be characterized in summary fashion by the Kantian formula of the "asocial sociability" of man. Many reasons have been given to account for this "asocial sociability," and the phenomenon itself is widely accepted and has consequences of its own. Social theory needs a double emphasis on man's sociability and on his propensity to go it alone, a desideratum that probably accounts for the frequency of dichotomous concepts like community and society, private and public, or the self and the other. This recurrence becomes understandable if one is mindful of Goethe's aphoristic wisdom that "every condition has its burdens, the confined as well as the unrestrained."[11] To be sure, the social scientist wants to know which difficulties go together with which confined or unrestrained conditions. He must bear in mind that every concept must exclude more than it includes if it is to be useful. Similarly, an analysis of different cultures and historical constellations should be examined not only in terms of what each pattern achieves but also what difficulties are associated with that achievement. In this way one can protect the ideal types indispensable for studying social change against the moralizing that lurks behind their unavoidable exaggerations. Such an intellectual safeguard also reflects the interactive uncertainties of the social process.

Comparative, Sociohistorical Inquiries

My first comparative studies reflected the impact of the Hitler regime from which I had escaped. I wanted to know how the German catastrophe had come about. That question resulted in an unpublished historical investigation of social teachings in Germany during the eighteenth and nineteenth century. My doctoral dissertation dealt with higher civil servants in the United States, which allowed me to make a largely implicit comparison with German civil servants.[12] A third, more substantial investigation prompted by the Hitler experience was a comparative study of managerial ideologies in the course of industrialization.[13]

This last study was still prompted by the "German problem" and the experience of emigrating to the United States. In a comparison between

"East and West, then and now," I analyzed English and Russian industrialization in the eighteenth and nineteenth centuries. Then I examined problems of industrial management in the German Democratic Republic before the East Berlin uprising of 17 June 1953 and in the United States up to the early 1950s.

One must consider economic enterprises when one wants to understand the modern world. Their productivity has made us "modern" and could not have been achieved without an exercise of authority. Call this statement a basic assumption. No one engaging in social science research can proceed without a supposition of this kind. My initial question was whether the Russian and the Western European tradition differed in the exercise of organizational authority during industrialization. How did English and Russian industrial enterprises differ from one another and how had they changed over time? My finding was that in the two countries the self-image of the entrepreneur or manager as well as the upper-class image of the worker had differed for a long time, but that both had been entirely transformed in the course of industrialization.

The idea of the exclusive authority of the proprietor and entrepreneur had been replaced on the one hand by the organizational expert, and on the other by factory directors in close collaboration with Communist party functionaries. At the same time, the Western idea of the worker had been transformed from a subordinate in England to a person responsible for his fate in the American struggle for survival. In the East, the idea of the worker had changed from that of an untrustworthy servant to that of workers as "people" nominally in charge, but actually the victims of a one-party system and its mass propaganda.

In 1956, I did not articulate as clearly as I would now that both transformations had their assets and liabilities. Early industrialization was ruthless, in England as well as in Russia. The proprietor was an autocrat who did what he wished with his own people. However, the English proprietor was ruthless on his own account, while his Russian counterpart cringed before those above him while maltreating the workers in his employ. In retrospect one can see that individualistic ruthlessness was an asset for later economic developments, while hierarchic ruthlessness was a liability. That hierarchic ruthlessness was part of an autocratic society in which censorship gave literature a special political impetus entirely lacking in England. Workers were cruelly exploited in England as well as in Russia. The English worker was forced to fend for himself, while the Russian worker remained personally subservient to his master. That distinction did nothing to relieve either worker from his misery. But evidently misery, like autocracy, can be of different kinds. In Russia it led to relations between the "people" and the intelligentsia eventuating in revolution, while in England such a coalescence did not develop except in the minds of Marx and Engels.

By the mid-1950s sociohistorical comparison had become my principal approach. That interest has become widely shared, though in my view too often in a manner that makes the comparative method a variant of causal analysis. I consider it instead as an exploration that is a necessary preliminary to such analysis, much as Max Weber treated sociology as a preliminary step toward causal historical analysis. My preferred model is the selection of one general problem like legitimate authority, citizenship, or the experience of backwardness. Then analysis focuses attention on how two or more social structures in their different historical contexts have resolved the issue. These contexts are very complex. As J. S. Mill pointed out, the general theorems of social science "cannot be made very complex without so rapidly accumulating a liability to error as must soon deprive our conclusions of all value."[14] Here, the emphasis on assets and liabilities shifts from historical to intellectual constellations or frameworks. It is a very old idea that, for every question and concept we formulate, we pay the price of excluding much more than we include. Kenneth Burke's modern version of that idea is worth repeating:

> Any performance is discussable either from the standpoint of what it *attains* or what it *misses*. Comprehensiveness can be discussed as superficiality, intensiveness as stricture, tolerance as uncertainty—and the poor pedestrian abilities of the fish are clearly explainable in terms of his excellence as a swimmer. A way of seeing is also a way of not seeing.[15]

After World War II we witnessed an era of decolonization, the spread of communism culminating in the Chinese revolution of 1949, as well as the worldwide issue of "modernization." In this context I asked myself why the proletariat, despite the sweep of communism, had not played the "world-historical" role Marx had predicted. This question led me to the problem of national citizenship. If the English proletariat in the most industrialized country of the world had not become radicalized, how then is its social integration to be interpreted? How and to what extent had groups previously excluded from political participation been integrated in the body politic? My question was confined to the working class.[16]

The analysis suggested a shift of focus from lower-class protest to the protests and concerns of other excluded groups and the more encompassing issue of nationalism. In England, the integration of the industrial work force and other disadvantaged groups was achieved only in the course of conflicts over a prolonged period of time. In Ireland, these religious and ethnic-political disputes continue down to the present. In countries less institutionally stable than England these integration processes were still more difficult. Here again assets and liabilities go together, because inclusion as well as exclusion exacts the price of unanticipated consequences.

Accordingly, I turned to a third set of questions. Over time, societies develop markedly different social structures and with them different capacities of integrating groups previously excluded from the body politic. To understand such structures one is obliged to go far back in history.[17] My first purpose was a comparative analysis of basic concepts like kingship, aristocracy, and representation in order to show what historical diversities hide behind such apparently simple terms. For example, Russian tsardom as well as English kingship came to terms with aristocratic or municipal striving for independence. The terms in which these medieval autocracies did so differed, and led to divergent patterns of political accommodation. Accordingly, the general terms that we use to communicate—kingship, aristocracy—often obscure rather than reveal the structural differences to which we want to refer.

Skepticism in the use of terms is therefore a methodological "must" because it highlights what meanings the words we employ exclude as well as include. That skepticism is discouraged when social scientists use language carelessly, creating neologisms and multiplying near synonyms. In my view, American sociologists exhibit too little awareness that the same term can have many meanings which often change their implications over time. That mutability goes unrecognized in academic departments that model themselves on some simplified notion of the natural sciences and treat courses in the history of ideas as an expendable luxury. When single words like kingship can refer to very different social and political structures, it is counterproductive to use them as if their meaning was unequivocal. That error is unavoidable where the history of ideas is neglected.

My second purpose in *Kings or People* is suggested by the subtitle "Towards a Mandate of the People" for the second part of the book. After characterizing historically differentiated social structures of kingship and aristocracy, I examined the nationally differentiated processes of mobilization associated with the idea of a popular mandate. I focused attention on the relationship between relative backwardness and intellectual mobilization in different political structures. In this context nationalism has apparently played a much larger role in the nineteenth and twentieth centuries than the simultaneous movements of the working class.

My last completed project before this present book contains a biography of my father and an analysis of my relations with him.[18] This turn to the personal was prompted in part by the legitimacy crisis of modern science. The very productivity of the natural sciences poses the question to what extent they can cope with the multiple side effects of their results. At the beginning of my career as a social scientist in 1951 this worry had led me to the "perverse" idea that it was just as well for the social sciences not to produce as much usable knowledge as the natural sciences. "They can do less harm and less good."[19] Accordingly, social scientists must cultivate a more contemplative mode than natural scientists because participation in society involves the scholarly process more directly than participation in nature. That is one reason why I regard reflexivity as a methodological "must."

The biography also continues my scholarly work. I wanted to satisfy myself that I was able to analyze the case best known to me in a scholarly manner and despite my obvious personal involvement, it was quite literally a test of "embattled reason." Then I also wanted to use this case study of my family as a means of interpreting the manifold refractions of our time represented by the position of outsiders, the precarious position of individualism, and the conflict of generations. This self-critical study exemplifies the intellectual self-awareness that I consider one basis for scholarly work in the social sciences.

The present study continues in this mode, examining the preconditions of our world in Ancient Judaism, early Christianity, early science and industrialization, the French and the Bolshevik Revolutions, to which I have added a case study of Germany. While the beginnings and the trajectories of these movements diverge, all of them involve the paradoxes of unity and universalism with their worldwide repercussions. Indeed, all of them have involved the paradox of reason that is attained at the price of distinguishing between an elite of those who know and those outside that inner circle who hope to benefit from its special gifts.

Judaism, Christianity, science, industrialization, the ideas of the French and the Bolshevik Revolutions, as well as the unsettled affinities of Germany in the center of Europe remain embattled to this day. To understand that embattled position seems to me a contribution scholars can make to the cultivation of moral awareness.

Notes

1. This report is based on two volumes of my essays entitled *Embattled Reason* (New Brunswick, NJ: Transaction Publishers, 1988, 1989). It is added here for those readers interested in a more comprehensive statement of the standpoint from which this book has been written.
2. Hans Barth, *Truth and Ideology* (Berkeley: University of California Press, 1976). The German original was published in 1945. In the introduction to this English edition I comment on Barth's work.
3. Reinhard Bendix, *Social Science and the Distrust of Reason*, University of California Publication in Sociology and Social Institutions, vol. 1 (Berkeley: University of California Press, 1951), 1-42.
4. Robert Merton, "The Precarious Foundations of Detachment in Sociology," in Edward Tiryakian, ed., *The Phenomenon of Sociology* (New York: Appleton-Century-Crofts, 1971), 188-99.
5. Reinhard Bendix, "Sociology and Ideology," in ibid., 173-87. See also my comments on Merton's critique in ibid., 200-1.
6. For a critique of this model for the social sciences see Richard Bernstein, *The Restructuring of Social and Political Theory* (New York: Harcourt Brace Jovanovich, 1976).
7. This coexistence between particularism and universalism is the main theme of chapter 3.
8. Don Price, *The Scientific Estate* (Cambridge: Harvard University Press, 1967), 105.
9. Emile Durkheim, *The Rules of Sociological Method* (Chicago: University of Chicago Press, 1938), chapter 3 and Robert K. Merton, *Social Theory and Social Structure* (Glencoe, IL: The Free Press, 1949), 52.
10. See Reinhard Bendix, "Tradition and Modernity Reconsidered," in *Embattled Reason* (New Brunswick, NJ: Transaction Books, 1988), chapter 12 for a more detailed discussion of this point.
11. J. W. Goethe, *Die Wahlverwandtschaften* (München: Deutscher Taschenbuchverlag, 1986), 183.
12. Reinhard Bendix, "The Rise and Acceptance of German Sociology" (M.A. thesis, University of Chicago, 1943) and *Higher Civil Servants in American Society, a Study of the Social Origins, the Careers, and the Power-Position of Higher Federal Administrators* (Westport, CT: Greenwood Press, 1974, originally published in 1949 by the University of Colorado Press).
13. Reinhard Bendix, *Work and Authority in Industry, Ideologies of Management in the Course of Industrialization* (Berkeley: University of California Press, 1974, originally published in 1956 by John Wiley & Sons).
14. John Stuart Mill, *A System of Logic* (London: Longmans, Green & Co., 1911), 587.
15. Kenneth Burke, *Permanence and Change* (New York: New Republic, 1936), 70.

16. Reinhard Bendix, *Nation-Building and Citizenship* (Berkeley: University of California Press, 1977). This second edition is an expansion of the original one, published by John Wiley in 1964.
17. Reinhard Bendix, *Kings or People: Power and the Mandate to Rule* (Berkeley: University of California Press, 1978).
18. Reinhard Bendix, *From Berlin to Berkeley* (New Brunswick, NJ: Transaction Books, 1986).
19. Reinhard Bendix, *Social Science and the Distrust of Reason*, University of California Publications in Sociology and Social Institutions, vol. 1 (Berkeley: University of California Press, 1951), 42.

Part II
Social

3

Definitions of Community in Western Civilization

We speak of a community when those belonging to it distinguish between themselves and strangers, foreigners, or nonresidents. People, not scholars, decide who belongs to the community and who does not. We know of no community that encompasses all mankind. Yet those who define their community in terms of inclusion and exclusion nevertheless espouse ideals of humanity. This paradox of social particularism and universalism may be due to the rise of monotheism in Western civilization. All men and women are God's children (universalism), but the distinction between "us" and "them" (particularism) has pervaded our history throughout.

The ingroup-outgroup distinctions have helped to shape the history of Western civilization. The examples that I have chosen are ancient Judaism, early Christianity, Renaissance science, the Industrial Revolution, the French Revolution, and the Bolshevik Revolution. In each instance, how people define their communal affinity affects their view of themselves and their relations with others. The complexities of these historical configurations are well known. Yet the ways in which communities can be constituted are limited. I highlight the principles of community-building in Western civilization in the hope that scholars of other civilizations will find the approach suggestive for their own studies.

It is probably impossible to define community in unequivocal terms. Social scientists may use such polyvalent terms too frequently, but it would be unwise to do without them. Community has the rudimentary meaning that people belong together by consciously distinguishing themselves from others. My purpose is to follow the changing ideas of community over time and to explore some of their implications.

The scholarly emphasis on Western civilization must have an intellectual warrant if it is to be free of parochialism. In his collected essays on the sociology of religion Max Weber summarized this argument by asking

> to what combination of circumstances the fact should be attributed that in Western civilization, and *in Western civilization only* [my italics], cultural phenomena have appeared which (as we like to think) lie in a line of development having *universal* significance and value.[1]

He enumerated many of the fields that have been marked by the kind of rationalism peculiar to Western civilization, including science, music, painting, sculpture, architecture, printing, scientific, or administrative specialization. These provided the bases of political, technical, and economic developments, estate societies, states based on constitutions and enacted laws, and, last but not least, modern capitalism. Weber also explored other kinds of rationalism in China, India, Islam, and elsewhere, both to understand these civilizations better and as a means of coming to terms with what was unique to the West.

As a model of a nonparochial study of Western civilization this set a landmark. But I have found Weber's focus on rationalism troublesome, even on his own terms. In specific cases, he always emphasized how problematic each kind of rationalism was. The Protestant reformers were preoccupied with theological doctrine and pastoral care, yet by the psychological implications of their ideas they unwittingly promoted the pursuit of gain. Yoga practices induced nonrational states of consciousness, but were based on intricately elaborated rational foundations. In my view the idea of a rise of Western rationalism is in some doubt, when each instance of rationality has complex nonrational preconditions as well as unanticipated and contra-indicated consequences.

For these reasons I shall concentrate on one aspect of Weber's purpose that remains undisputed. Certain distinctive cultural achievements originated in Western civilization, among them monotheism, a science based on measurement, an individualism based on faith, invention, imagination and the pursuit of gain, the emergence of the modern state with its constitutionalism and the rule of law, the development of nationalism, and what I call, for want of a better term, the communitarian backlash among intellectuals. Some of these developments also occurred in other civilizations. In combining all of them, the Western European continent achieved comparative material advantages that, through overseas explorations since the fifteenth century, culminated in an unprecedented outward thrust that put the rest of the world in a position of relative backwardness. The redefinitions of community, which I trace here from ancient Judaism to the French Revolution, help to account for this outward thrust, while the Bolshevik Revolution can be considered a communitarian backlash from the European periphery. I should add that in each case ideas and definitions were the work of the few who relate to the many in unsettled (and unsettling) ways.

Basic to the human condition is a feeling of individual helplessness and the desire to mitigate it by associating with others, whether in religious or in secular terms. But to associate with others in some enduring fashion one must define the terms in which the people belonging to a community participate in it.

Ancient Judaism

Jewish monotheism may be regarded as the first major turning point in Western history.[2] Monotheism prevailed only after prolonged struggles against polytheistic beliefs and practices such as the Baal-cult or the dance around the Golden Calf. Judaism adapted the old idea of a special relation between a transcendent power and its worshipers who must perform certain actions to gain the desired blessing. But by defining the human community under God in a new way, Judaism replaced the crowded pantheon of the past with the idea of the one God, to whom all other gods were so many abominations. Moses and the prophets rejected the idea of widely diffused amorphous powers. Now all transcendence was embodied in one God, whose mysterious designs and omnipotent will were evident throughout nature and in all human affairs. In lieu of easy access to places of worship by all people prepared to perform the required ablutions and sacrifices, there was now an exclusive group of believers, marked off from all nonbelievers by circumcision and adherence to an elaborate daily ritual.

The idea of the Covenant between the God of the Old Testament and "his chosen people" has universalist elements as well as particularistic ones. Yahweh has universal attributes: he is the Creator, the Judge, the Just and Merciful, the Avenger of Wrongs, the Lord of History who emerges from the unknowable to reveal himself. Yet for the Jews this universal revelation came as a historical and particular experience. Their community was blessed by release from its Egyptian bondage as well as by a series of other miracles. The Covenant revealed to Moses on Mt. Sinai blessed the Jews, as no other people were blessed before or since. Paradoxically, this particularistic monotheism was combined with the idea that God has created the universe out of nothing, and that his omnipotence and omniscience are both certain and incomprehensible. The Covenant with the Jews is concluded upon Yahweh's initiative, a part of his unfathomable wisdom that infinitely surpasses this transaction between the one God and his people. In 5 Mos. 32:8, God distributes the land and separates the children of men from one another, but then determines the borders between people in accordance with the number of Israel's children. Such references to people as a whole and to the children of Israel oddly combine the universal with the particular. Humanity appears like a secondary part of God's creation in comparison with the commands of the Torah, which are enjoined upon the Jews alone and, through their religious practice, distinguish their community from all others.

The Five Books of Moses (the Torah) embody the true shrine of all synagogues, for they contain the Convenant of Sinai and hence the foundation of Judaism. Copying the Torah, reciting from it, and providing for its safekeeping are governed by the strictest rules. Memorization, interpretation, and recitation of the Torah are the main tasks of the scribal scholars, who have been at the core of orthodox Judaism down to the present. These scholars always begin their efforts with the ever more accurate understanding of the written word, the main justification of their work. But beyond this they also develop an oral Torah, which undertakes to deduce and unfold the legal, historical, ethical, and homiletic truths, the declarations and facts implicitly contained in the written revelation. In this way, revelation appears not as something that occurred once and for all, but rather as something endlessly creative, which must be understood and rethought again and again. God's creation in its glorious diversity can only be fathomed in this way. If in the process contradictions appear, so be it, for these contradictions merely manifest the limitations of the finite mind in relation to God's infinite wisdom. Jewish tradition gives particular emphasis to the holy text, while the oral lore of the commentaries enhance both understanding and celebration. God's revelation to his people must be read and interpreted with the exacting attention of the devout recipient of the Truth. Revelation and commentaries are coequal parts of the tradition, each illuminated by the other. In this way total humility before the written word is combined with an extraordinary facility of dialectical inventiveness,[3] often labeled "Talmudic" by hostile critics. Since text and commentaries are believed to be divinely inspired, successive generations of scholars constitute an elite, which preserves the eternal presence of the Sinaitic revelation and in so doing maintains the tradition of the Jewish community at large.

Gershom Scholem has observed that the humility before the divine text is based on the assumption that everything in God's creation is already contained therein. But this humility is combined with the presumption that the full truth can be obtained only by shaping the old text into a meaning that accords with truth as the scholar sees it. As Scholem states, the commentator always has a bit of both humility and presumption, a combination that provides a clue not only to the culture of Judaism, but to the nature of intellectuality more generally.

This cultural configuration of Judaism goes together with its attendant principles of exclusion, which the pious regard as enjoined upon them by God. The Jewish definition of community is based in practice on circumcision, ceremonial admission of adolescents to the circle of worshipers, endogamous marriage, food taboos, and some 600 other rules enjoined upon the orthodox believer. This definition is also expressed by the specific injunction of Deuteronomy (23:19–20) concerning economic relations:

> Thou shalt not lend upon usury to thy brother; usury of money, usury of victuals, usury of anything that is lent upon usury; Unto a stranger thou mayest lend upon usury; but unto thy brother thou shalt not lend upon usury; that the Lord thy God may bless thee in all that thou settest thine hand to in the land whither though goest to possess it.

The Old Testament also contains the injunction that "thou shalt love they neighbor as thyself" (Mos. 3:18), but the passage refers to the neighbor among "thy people," not the stranger. True, the invocation of the Lord God as the creator of the universe refers to "all the people of whom thou art afraid," but the very next verse speaks of their destruction (Mos. 5:7, 19–20). Perhaps these are efforts to remain true to the universalism of God the Creator despite the monotheistic particularism of the Jewish people as an "elect nation." But in practice, ethical dualism provided the mainstay without which the Jewish community and its contribution to Western civilization would not have survived two millennia of persecution.

This dualism resulted in a religious paradox. A small group of believers rested its faith on a Creator who established a Covenant with his "chosen people." That left the remainder of humankind in religious limbo. Judaism is not a missionary religion. Conversion to Judaism requires extensive reeducation as a precondition of participation in the religious community. As a result, Jews have paid the price of social exclusion and its cultural repercussions.

Early Christianity

Christianity emerged through protracted struggles, both against Jewish monotheism as its immediate rival and more broadly against pagan unbelievers. The New Testament (1 Pet. 2:9) refers to Christians as a royal priesthood, a holy nation, a peculiar people, much as the Old Testament had done with reference to the Jews. But whereas the Jewish community distinguished between solidarity among kinsmen or neighbors and hostility or moral indifference toward strangers, Christianity introduced the idea of a community based on faith alone, even to the extent of disregarding family obligations. For the text adds to the passage just mentioned that the Christians "in times past were not a people, but are now the people of God." Faith rather than kinship defines the community of believers.

In his letter to the Galatians (3:23), the Apostle Paul writes that "before faith came, we were kept under the law, shut up unto the faith which should afterwards be revealed." In his view (3:24–26) "the law was our schoolmaster to bring us unto Christ that we might be justified by faith. But after that faith is come, we are no longer under a schoolmaster. For ye are all the children of God by faith in Christ Jesus." Hence, where faith prevails (3:28), "there is neither Jew nor Greek, there is neither bond nor free, there is neither male nor female, for ye are all one in Christ Jesus." Judaism had reinforced existing ethnic and cultural distinctions by committing each male child through circumcision to the community of believers. Christianity sought to overcome those distinctions through a community of believers whose faith made them equal in the Lord.

Since Jews and Christians constituted communities of the faithful, the distinction between them depended on what was meant by faith. Gershom Scholem states that the two religions differ most fundamentally in their respective concepts of salvation. For Judaism in all its variety, salvation can occur only in the full light of day, above all as an event in the public forum of the human community. Apart from that visible context salvation has no discernable meaning. For Christianity, on the other hand, salvation occurs only invisibly, in the spiritual realm of each individual's soul, a secret or inward transformation that has no necessary external manifestation. St. Augustine conceived of salvation as a mysterious process by which a community of the saved emerges in the midst of an utterly corrupted world. In his interpretation, biblical prophecies are concerned with each man's thoughts and actions, as they stand revealed before God's omniscient and ultimate judgment.

To the philosophers of Judaism, that approach transposed everyone's ethical conduct into a realm of inwardness, subject to all the vagaries of human emotion. As they saw it, religiosity in this inward sense may or may not occur as a corollary of ritual performance, though never in its absence. By contrast, Christian doctrine always considered its ideal of inward faith as a decisive advance over a concept of salvation that remained bound up with ritual in strict accordance with received law. But just this "deeper" conception of what Christians interpreted as rituals emptied of meaning, appeared to Jews as a liquidation of religious and divinely inspired law. To the philosophers of Judaism this notion of inward piety was merely hypothetical, an escape from the only way in which the messianic message could be manifested. It was not, as Paul would have it, a contrast between the discipline of the law and the vindication through faith, but rather a contrast between two conceptions of salvation, one through faith in the divine law and the other through faith in Christ as the son of God.

The difference between rabbi and priest belongs to this context. The reading of sacred texts is the obligation of every pious person, though inevitably some are more learned than others. The rabbi's years of study have qualified him as a spiritual leader, but for all that he is only a first among equals. Holiness resides solely in the word of God; it cannot attach itself to the person of the rabbi because of his studiousness and the authority derived from learning. By contrast, the priest possesses a spiritual authority regardless of his learning or other personal qualities. That authority derives from his ordination by the church. Originally, the church derived its authority from Christ and the "keys of the kingdom of heaven" he gave to St. Peter. In turn, the apostle gave them to the bishop of Rome, who has been followed by a long line of popes since the first century A.D. Accordingly, the priest derives his authority from this institutionally transmitted, but spiritual link with Christ. As a result, every action the priest performs in his official capacity is endowed with sanctity in which the believer partakes through his worship.

Judaism and Christianity represent two monotheistic ways of dealing with the Holy, and in so doing they provide models of constituting the human community in religious terms. Both creeds have fostered religious inwardness and esoteric learning and both are capable of deteriorating into empty formalism. But Judaism and Christianity define their respective communities in very different ways. Judaism does not encourage converts, pays the price of ethical dualism through its self-enclosure, and runs the risk of intolerance. Christianity encourages a worldwide mission, pays the price of ethical universalism through forcible conversions, and also runs the risk of intolerance. Whereas Judaism distinguishes the people under the law from those outside the law, Christianity distinguishes between believers in Christ and all nonbelievers. True, Judaism tended to reinforce the ethnic and cultural divisions among people, whereas Christianity sought to overcome them by its ethical universalism. Christians were then faced with the task of converting all unbelievers to the one true faith for the sake of their eternal souls while Judaism, partly no doubt in response to the military and political disasters befalling the Jews, became a self-enclosing religion that preserved its identity despite persecutions. Christianity was from the start a missionary religion and became a state religion by the fourth century A.D. However, its advance against paganism has been troubled by the use of force as an alternative to self-enclosure. Though Christianity encompasses all believers in the faith, its "universalism" must fall far short of encompassing all of humankind. For some two millennia, Judaism and Christianity have presented the world with the alternative between self-enclosure and missionary expansion.

Renaissance Science

Christian ideas concerning the "Great Chain of Being" emerged from the convergence between Greek philosophy and Catholic theology. In its intricacy, scholastic reasoning may be considered the equivalent of the "Talmudic" disputations over Jewish law. The speculations of Christian theologians were the immediate background for the development of modern science in the sixteenth century. Science, as much as Judaism and Christianity, had a major effect on the definition of the human community, though it did so through its transformation of material culture rather than a change in religious sensibility. Nevertheless, modern science also has a metaphysical foundation.[4]

Christian theology had projected the image of a created world in which God's designs are fulfilled, and in which for all their sins, mankind can hope for a future different from the past. Theologians distinguished between speculative and practical reason, the first concerned with what is unchangeable and eternal, the second with what is changeable and springs from experience. Speculative reason or contemplation of Truth, Goodness, and Beauty can have an enlightening effect on the whole person, leading to wisdom, which creates happiness in the soul of the knower. This view presupposes a belief in the God-created hierarchy of Being, which is a realm of perfection apart from the spell of common things. Since man was created in God's image, it was taken for granted that the world is intelligible to the human mind. That intelligibility derived from the idea that God had endowed all natural objects including man with a propensity toward perfection so that all things "seek after and desire" their own "fullness of being."[5]

The great pioneers of modern science did not set out to deviate from this position. Copernicus (1473–1543), for example, did not ask: Is the earth the center of the universe, or does the earth revolve around the sun? He asked instead: What motions should we attribute to the earth in order to obtain the simplest and most harmonious geometry of the heavens that will accord with our observations? In his dedication to Pope Paul III he declared that mathematics is written for mathematicians and that he would leave the judgment of what he had achieved "to the decision of your Holiness especially, and to all other learned mathematicians."[6]

Kepler was born in 1571, a generation after the death of Copernicus. He used the astronomical observation of Tycho Brahe who had dedicated his work to the "fullest knowledge of God through nature." By assuming nature's simplicity and unity, Kepler wanted to reveal the underlying mathematical harmony that caused the heavenly bodies to move as they did. Since the mind of the Creator had determined the number, size, and orbits of the heavenly bodies, the real world was not discovered by speculations about purpose, but by discovering the mathematical harmony with which God endowed his creation.

Galileo, the contemporary of Kepler, adhered to much the same outlook. But he combined his extraordinary scientific achievements with propagandistic and literary gifts, which brought him into conflict with the church. "The Bible was not written to teach us astronomy," he wrote in his attempts to separate the religious from the scientific realm, to the benefit of both as he saw it. God is as excellently "revealed in nature's action as in the sacred statements of the Bible" and it would be the part of prudence to allow for both. However, Galileo did not leave it at that. Instead he argued that the universe can be understood only by those who have learned the language of mathematics, which alone yields "demonstrated physical conclusions." No biblical citation must be allowed to interfere with them, for God has endowed man with reason and the evidence of the senses. Galileo did not question the enormous distinction that remained. God, he says, knows an infinity of propositions as a single intuition, whereas men must proceed by reasoning from conclusion to conclusion and can know only a few. Still, he also says that the few mathematical demonstrations we achieve have the same truth as that known by divine wisdom.

Although Galileo thought of himself as an obedient son of the church, he rejected the compromise formula offered to him by the church. According to that formula all knowledge of nature is hypothetical, a position by which the church fathers sought to reconcile the rise of science with the findings of their own Jesuit astronomers. In an overwhelmingly Catholic population, the church and these astronomers were the accepted interpreters of faith and knowledge. By rejecting the compromise offered by the church, Galileo opened a gulf between scientists and the public at large. What was at stake, however inadvertently, was a new definition of the human community. For Galileo, only measurable entities like size, number, and motion were instances of certain knowledge in contrast to the odors, colors, and sounds of external objects, which were unreal deceptions of the senses. If only mathematics reveals the true nature of the world, then the everyday observations of ordinary people are denied all genuine competence. Galileo was convinced that the real world, which lies behind what appears to us through sense impressions, can only be discovered through experiments and mathematical reasoning. As a populist, Galileo successfully enlisted the people's interest in science, but the long-run effect of his work was to distinguish sharply between scientists and ordinary folk.[7]

The most powerful impulse behind the scientific upsurge of the seventeenth century was the discovery of demonstrated conclusions that promised increased control over nature. What then was the community-defining impact of this new science? Science introduced a new division of mankind between the few capable of mathematical reasoning and the many who are not. Judaism and Christianity had also developed a division between the learned and the untutored, but one that involved contemplation based on the knowledge of sacred texts. A realm of perfection was believed to exist and contemplation of that realm was thought to be the highest kind of knowledge. By contrast, the scientific pursuit of knowledge involves the realm of common things. Not the perfection of God's creation, but the necessities and causes of nature are the object of inquiry. In the old view, God alone is great and man is wretched. In the new view, dignity belongs to man the knower as well. Francis Bacon wrote of the "kingdom of man," which is founded upon mastery over nature. In this realm of practical reason, knowledge can benefit *all* people who are concerned with the "benefit and use of life" (Bacon) rather than with the search for knowledge or the happiness of contemplation. Hence, the old universalism of religious belief was replaced by a new universalism. This new universalism of increasing the knowledge of nature by the few held out the promise of material benefits for the many.

But this was only one community-defining effect of science. The other effect concerns the community of scientists itself. The early scientific pioneers were ostensibly modest men and this has been true of scientists ever since. Francis Bacon denounced self-seeking in philosophy. He did not want to speak of himself but only of what was needed to advance science. To Thomas Sprat, the historian of the Royal Society, its members "have guarded themselves against themselves" and "by sobriety of debating and moderation of dissenting" they have escaped the prejudices arising from authority, social rank, and related obstacles to the unimpeded study of nature. Even Newton, who did not accept rivalry or opposition gladly, but whose achievements overshadowed all others, likened himself to a small boy at the seashore, who has discovered a few pretty stones, "while the great ocean of truth lay undiscovered" before him. Yet Newton became the subject of panegyrics: Halley declared that no mortal could approach divinity nearer than Newton, and Voltaire contrasted the enlightened genius of Newton with the notorious villainy of politicians and conquerors. Where one man had achieved so much, the promise of mankind became unlimited.

In this way, personal modesty was combined with the vaunting ambition of discovering truth and benefiting mankind. Images like an "America of knowledge" to be gained turned Columbus from a real person into a symbol that promised "the fertility of succeeding ages." That promise could be kept only if scientists barred all passions from their proceedings so that dispassion became the distinguishing virtue of the scientific community. An early expression of this self-defining virtue is contained in Sprat's *History of the Royal Society*. Following the English civil war and the restoration of the monarchy, the society was founded in 1660 and Sprat's book was published in 1667:

> For such a candid, and unpassionate company, as that was, and for such a gloomy season, what could have been a fitter Subject to pitch upon, than *Natural Philosophy*? To have always tossing about some Theological questions, would have been . . . the excess to which they themselves dislik'd in the publick: To have been eternally musing on *Civil business* and the distresses of their Country, was too melancholy a reflexion: It was *Nature* alone, which could pleasantly entertain them, in that estate. The contemplation of that, draws our minds off from past and present misfortunes, and makes them conquerors over things, in the midst of the greatest publick unhappiness. . . . *That* never separates us into mortal Factions; that gives us room to differ, without animosity, and permits us, to raise contrary imaginations upon it, without danger of *Civil War*.

Limited as this example is to gentlemen scholars who played an important part in the early modern period, it nevertheless tells a good deal about scientists as a special part of the human community.[8]

The unfettered inventor was thought to be wholly devoted to a calling that obliterated the self and its passions for the sake of enhancing truth and the welfare of all. Scientists were consummate individualists in their single-minded pursuit of knowledge, yet as such they participated in a common enterprise. The social distinctions derived from the rivalry among knowledge seekers went hand in hand with their shared participation in a community of peers; the team of knowledge seekers engaged in an endeavor for the common good. Perhaps never before in human history had individualism and communalism been combined so effectively with the virtue of increasing knowledge as a public good. Is it any wonder that intellectuals are forever searching for the perfect community in which individual striving at its most intense can be combined with the equally intense feeling of being at one with the community at large?[9]

The intellectual life of the sixteenth and seventeenth centuries was beset by a tremendous paradox. Science had removed the earth from the center of the universe. At the same time, scientists vindicated the "dignity of man" by putting physical demonstrations of human reason on a par with divine wisdom. Here is a literary summation of this paradox by Sir John Davies, a deceptively balanced poetic image written in 1599:

> I know my body's of so frail a kind,
> As force without, fevers within can kill;
> I know the heavenly nature of my mind,
> But 'tis corrupted both in wit and will.
> I know my Soul has power to know all things,
> Yet is she blind and ignorant in all;
> I know I am one of Nature's little kings,
> Yet to the least and vilest thing am thrall.
> I know my life's a pain and but a span,
> I know my Sense is mock'd with everything;
> And to conclude, I know myself a MAN,
> Which is a Proud, and yet a wretched thing.[10]

In retrospect, one can see that in fact man's pride and his wretchedness marked the two sides of the beginning of European modernity.

European explorations overseas showed how far men could reach but how little they knew. The Renaissance showed Italy's cultural efflorescence in the midst of political anarchy. The Lutheran Reformation showed a religion that put a premium on each individual's relation to God, but then placed the authority of the church in the hands of secular rulers, combining trust in the individual's conscience with distrust of the impulses controlling human action. The formation of early modern states showed that each step in the direction of centralized power and bureaucratic rule divided the human community between those qualified by rank or training for the exercise of authority, and those who were not. And the pride of kings was undiminished by the wretchedness of their subjects. These blatant contradictions were a harsh preparation for the modern world.

This discussion of three transformations of Western civilization—ancient Judaism, early Christianity, and Renaissance science—has had two interrelated themes. Ordinary people in groups or communities distinguish between those who belong and those who do not, but they do not do so by themselves. Typically, the ideas behind that distinction are the work of a few who relate to the many in different ways. The few are well known: the prophets and, later, the rabbis of Ancient Judaism; the disciples of Christ and, later, the bishops and theologians of the early church; and the late medieval scholars and craftsmen whose contributions were formalized and developed by the scientific pioneers of Renaissance Europe. The many are anonymous, but they follow the few in their religious or secular faith and practice. To be sure, learning divides the few from the many, yet both face the paradoxes mentioned at the beginning. Ever since the emergence of monotheism in the Western world people in their particularism and diversity have been moved by the unsettling idea that God and the world he created are one. It is unsettling because that idea runs counter to the divisions among us that constitute our everyday experience. It is unsettling also because the few who stand in the forefront of ethical universalism and scientific innovation cannot be of one mind. If they were of one mind, they would resemble God, which is to say they would transgress the limits of the human condition. Yet they try to do so again and again, giving rise to the spiritual tensions endemic to Western civilization, and perhaps to all human civilizations. With these themes in mind, I turn to the three revolutions of modern Western civilization: the Industrial Revolution, the French Revolution and the Bolshevik Revolution.

Individualism and the Industrial Revolution

Renaissance, Reformation, and Absolutism were phases in the development of "individualism" broadly considered. In his book on the Italian Renaissance Jacob Burckhardt noted many of the conditions since the fourteenth century that favored the growing emphasis on individual character. Other ages had had commanding figures, but the great artists and philosophers of the Renaissance developed a pride that tended to overcome the wretchedness of original sin, even though most retained their Christian faith. In his *Oration on the Dignity of Man* (1486), Pico della Mirandola wrote this paean to man's highest achievement:

> If you are a philosopher determining all things by means of right reason, him you shall reverence: he is a heavenly being and not of this earth. If you see a pure contemplator, one unaware of the body and confined to the inner reaches of the mind, he is neither an earthly nor a heavenly being; he is a more reverend divinity vested with human flesh.[11]

But pride in man's dignity was only one of many elements in the growth of individualism.

Humility before God was another. Luther's Reformation fostered an intensification of personal faith, extending individuality to all believers. No doubt pride played a role in the political developments of the early modern period in which all power was concentrated in the hands of the king. But royal power also led, however indirectly, to the internalization of emotions among aristocrats, who vied with one another for influence in court and in that context cultivated their manners rather than asserted their rights by force of arms.[12]

These and related developments came to a head in the individualism of the eighteenth century, though individualism is as ambiguous a term as community and evokes a cluster of related meanings, as general terms tend to do. Pascal observed:

> A town, a country-place, is from afar a town and a country-place. But as we draw near, there are houses, trees, tiles, leaves, grass, ants, limbs of ants, in infinity. All this is contained in the name of country-place.[13]

Through distance we can neglect the particulars and recognize "a whole" although efforts to define it fail. Yet when a child draws a house with simple lines showing a floor, walls, roof, windows, and a chimney, we instantly recognize what is meant, though we have never seen a house like that. The point of using comprehensive but ambiguous terms is to suggest affinities among related observations: we thereby highlight one complex unit while neglecting details that from this standpoint are irrelevant. My effort will be to delineate and distinguish two further types of individualism that developed in England and France in the eighteenth century.

In the mind of Karl Marx, these two types—the Industrial Revolution in England and the political revolution in France—became superimposed on each other.[14] His abstract model of a coming revolution resulted from turning the revolutionary events in France into a necessary consequence of the class conflicts in England. By now we know that the many revolutions of the twentieth century have not conformed to this model, which reduces political events to forces emerging from the organization of production. I shall speak instead of two forms of individualism and universalism in the intellectual development of the period, closely related but quite distinct and rather antagonistic. The English economic and the

French political development had quite different effects on the definition of community in the modern world.

Since the middle of the eighteenth century, the age-old pursuit of gain turned into capitalist entrepreneurship and its new methods of organizing the production of goods.[15] New arguments were used to show that everyone's single-minded pursuit of gain would benefit all. In the emerging industrial economy of England, individualism became a universalizing idea in that all adults were treated as separate, gain-maximizing persons. In its effects, the new industrialism divided the human community into rich and poor classes, breaking up an older inequality that had divided along patriarchal lines. In the context of industrialization, I consider domestic class relations first, and then turn to the division of the human community brought about by European expansion overseas.

Tocqueville observed that "no communities have ever yet existed, in which social conditions have been so equal that there were neither rich nor poor, and, consequently, neither masters nor servants."[16] In ancient and medieval times, human inequalities were an unalterable part of the cosmic order.[17] In a God-created world, all things have a purpose including the division of every society into rich and poor. Hence, priests typically called upon Christian believers to be contented with their station in life, whatever it might be. As a result, premodern treatises on "economics" do not deal with the *homo oeconomicus* and his pursuit of gain as a distinct activity that is to be judged solely by its material success. Instead, they see all economic concerns as part of estate or household management, in which instructions concerning agriculture, trade, and the keeping of accounts occur side by side with advice on the rearing of children, marital relations, or the proper treatment of servants. Technical and economic considerations were part and parcel of a moral approach to human relations. They belonged together in a world in which the household or estate typically constituted a unit of production, consumption, and family life, with moral and religious concerns animating all participants under the authority of a patriarchal master.[18]

The assumption of all ranks of society was one of service, which John Stuart Mill called the "theory of dependence":

> The lot of the poor, in all things which affect them collectively, should be regulated for them, not by them. They should not be required or encouraged to think for themselves, or give to their own reflection or forecast an influential voice in the determination of their destiny. It is the duty of the higher classes to think for them. . . . The relation between rich and poor should be only partially authoritative; it should

be amiable, moral, and sentimental; affectionate tutelage on the one side, respectful and grateful deference on the other.[19]

This worldview of the masters was matched by a worldview of the servants, which is much harder for us to understand.

We have been reared in an age in which the idea of service has been abandoned in the interest of freedom and individualism. But Tocqueville reminds us that "a sort of servile honor" went along with patriarchal tutelage:

> In the society of servants, as in that of masters, men exercise a great influence over one another: they acknowledge settled rules, and in the absence of law they are guided by a sort of public opinion: their habits are settled and their conduct is placed under a certain control. These men, whose destiny it is to obey, certainly do not understand fame, virtue, honesty, and honor in the same manner as their masters; but they have a pride, a virtue, and honesty pertaining to their condition. . . . Because a class is mean, it must not be supposed that all who belong to it are mean-hearted; to think so would be a great mistake.[20]

In other words, servants belonged to the estates and households of their masters, and as long as these views prevailed, masters and servants knew what to expect of one another. Naturally, relations between masters and servants, as well as relations within each rank, were also beset by the strife that seems endemic in the human condition. All the same, the *idea* of honor, service, and mutual obligation governed the lives of masters and servants.[21]

In the course of industrialization this patriarchal idea was replaced by the idea of individual independence. Ideals of obligation were denied in the name of self-interest and economic growth, individualism in yet another form. The root metaphor of emerging capitalism as an intellectual movement was that all men are alike in their desire to maximize their gains. Men also depend on each other, whether in market relations or enterprises. Yet if one required the help of others, one cannot expect that help to emerge from benevolence, as Adam Smith pointed out in 1776:

> He will be more likely to prevail, if he can interest their self-love in his favor, and show them that it is for their own advantage to do for him what he requires of them. . . . Give me that which I want, and you shall have this which you want, is the meaning of every such offer; and it is in this manner that we obtain from one another the far greater part of those good offices which we stand in need of.[22]

When this outlook was applied to employment relations, it led to a denial of responsibility on the part of the masters and the belief that only dire necessity could induce the servants to obey. Hunger came to be viewed as a salutary incentive.

Where this new idea of independence comes to prevail, employers *rely* on the force of circumstances that will compel workers to offer their services. For workers can expect nothing from the benevolence of their employers. If employers were to mitigate such external compulsion, they would only reduce the incentive to work as a last safeguard against starvation; workers had to accept the employment offered to them. We know that these ideas are still alive and well when we hear the president of the United States declare that the homeless people who spend their nights on the streets of New York do so by choice. As Edmund Burke wrote in 1795:

> Labor is a commodity, and, as such, an article of trade. . . . When any commodity is carried to market, it is not the necessity of the vendor, but the necessity of the purchaser, that raises the price. . . . The impossibility of subsistence of the man who carries his labor to a market is totally beside the question, in this way of viewing it. The only question is, What is it worth to the buyer?[23]

This new inequality was attributed to personal character, whereas the old inequality had been God-given, a shift to independence that put the responsibility for one's fate on the individual.

The successful entrepreneur possessed the requisite qualities, the poor in his employ did not. Yet the poor could "redeem" themselves by acquiring those qualities and thereby prevail in the long run. The new way of pursuing gain goes back to the Puritan virtue of being responsible to God for the way in which we use his gifts throughout our earthly existence. The moral liability of this position was the sin of pride and self-conceit. "The fortunate is seldom satisfied with the fact of being fortunate. Beyond this, he needs to know that he has a *right* to his good fortune." Though most intense during their religious phase, these ideas spread primarily when they became secularized and commonplace. "The idea of duty in one's calling prowls about in our lives like the ghost of dead religious beliefs."[24]

The transition from the idea of service to the idea of independence, from a patriarchal household—collectivism to an economic enterprise—individualism, has been a continuous process, with many of the old ideas "prowling about" even to the present day. Though the division of the human community between the morally superior few and the morally suspect many has a religious background, its main consequences during the nineteenth century were secular protests, as in the labor movements of the industrialized countries. John Stuart Mill ascribed English working-class reactions to various forms of mobilization. Literacy, newspapers, the preaching of dissenting ministers, the new mobility made possible by railroads and frequent job changes, increased participation in government through the franchise all played a part. Mill pronounced it as certain that, wherever these developments had occurred, the working classes would not again be subject to the "patriarchal or paternal system of government."

> The working classes . . . are perpetually showing that they think the interests of their employers not identical with their own, but opposite to them. . . . The principles of the Reformation [i.e., individual independence] have reached as low down in society as reading and writing, and the Poor will not much longer accept morals and religion of other people's prescribing.[25]

English workers certainly suffered severely from the deprivations of early industrialization. However, they had their pride, and they also wanted to benefit from industrial expansion on as equal terms as possible. That fact was recognized, however reluctantly, by Friedrich Engels in a letter to Marx, from 1863:

> The English proletariat is actually becoming more and more bourgeois. . . . For a nation which exploits the whole world this is of course to a certain extent justifiable. The only thing that would help here would be a few thoroughly bad years, but since the gold discoveries these no longer seem so easy to come by.[26]

The insight seems remarkable, however little it modified the author's hopes for a proletarian revolution. After some 120 years we should be able to make better use of it than Marx and Engels could, given their preoccupation with the miseries to which workers were subjected. They did not see the economic growth that went with the dark side of industrialization.

This omission led to the false prediction of a proletarian revolution in the industrialized countries as well as an incorrect assessment of the entrepreneurial belief in economic progress. Marx and Engels did not consider that English workers took pride in their country in the midst of their misery, and that this pride could be reinforced once conditions improved through economic growth. The ideal of independence had superseded the ideal of service, and on that basis the two communities of capitalists and workers eventually merged into one nation that distinguished itself from others. The process was aided by religious and educational leaders on the workers' side and by the ideologists of management on the side of employers.[27] Apparently, some sense of unity developed despite the clashes of interest and ideas that constituted everyday experience.

***

Modern imperialism enhanced that sense of unity when it continued the division between conquering and conquered countries that had divided the human community as regularly as the division between rich and poor. One can say perhaps that, by intensifying both, the individualism of the Industrial Revolution put its own stamp on these age-old divisions between "us" and "them." One can distinguish between a northward and eastward thrust of Western Europe inspired by Christianity, the westward thrust of numerous Asian people, and since the fifteenth century, the counterthrust of Western Europe that was subsequently magnified by commercialization and industrialization.

In the early Christian era mankind was divided between a Europe of Christian believers and the heathen rest of the world. As the Christian missions gained momentum, they spread from their Near Eastern origin to the rest of Europe, its first phase culminating in the Christianization of Russia in the tenth century. This European mission was followed by the Crusades to the Holy Land from 1096 to 1270.

These outward thrusts of Western Europe were superseded by a westward thrust of Near Eastern and Central Asian forces. In the seventh and eighth centuries, Arab conquests ranged from the Middle East to North Africa and Spain, coming to a halt only in 732 A.D. at the hands of the Frankish ruler Charles Martel. In the thirteenth century, the Mongolian conquest of Russia culminated in the destruction of Kiev and the invasion of Hungary in the 1240s. In the fifteenth century the Turkish attacks on Western Europe started with the destruction of the Byzantine empire in 1453 and the occupation of the Balkans, beginning with the conquest of Athens in 1458. The end of this Turkish occupation may be dated between 1716 and 1718, when the Habsburg empire achieved major victories. However, the repercussions lasted much longer, ranging from the Russo-Turkish war and the Greek struggle for independence in

1828–29 to the present division of Cyprus, the recent expulsion of Turks from Bulgaria, and the outbreak of the Gulf War in 1991.

The first phase of the counterthrust of Western Europe began with the reconquest of the Spanish peninsula from its Muslim overlords, which lasted some four centuries (1063–1492). The second, prolonged phase consisted in holding actions against the Turkish enemy in southeastern Europe. At sea, efforts to circumvent the Ottoman Empire were undertaken by finding a westward way of reaching India and a southern one by rounding the Cape of Good Hope. These overseas explorations of the fifteenth and sixteenth centuries demonstrated the increasing scientific and technical potential of Western Europe. For they depended on improved methods of navigation together with the increased firepower and mobility achieved by canons mounted on sailing vessels.

This centuries-long background should be kept in mind, as we now turn to the redefinition of the human community brought about by European expansion overseas. In the early modern period, that expansion combined science, exploration, plunder, slavery, and religion. I have mentioned the first two earlier. Their combination with plunder, slavery, and religion is exemplified by the plenary indulgences (1452–55), which Pope Nicholas V granted to Prince Henry the Navigator (1394–1460), the initiator of the first Portuguese colonization of the West African coast. The pope empowered Prince Henry to make the ocean navigable as far as India, where Christians were said to be settled already and could come to the aid of the West against the Muslim enemies of the faith:

> At the same time, he will bring under submission . . . the pagans of the countries not yet afflicted with the plague of Islam and give them knowledge of the name of Christ. . . . We, after careful deliberation, and having considered that we have by our apostolic letters conceded to King Alfonso, the right, total and absolute, to invade, conquer and subject all the countries which are under rule of the enemies of Christ, Saracen or Pagan, by our apostolic letters we wish the same King Alfonso, the Prince and all their successors, occupy and possess in exclusive rights the said islands, ports, and seas.[28]

As the Ottoman threat diminished, the rationale of this position lost its force, but the reasoning behind Western expansion continued to draw upon this historical background.

Gradually, the impulse behind overseas explorations and annexations shifted from the fear of Islam to rivalries among the European states. The first phase of these developments may be dated from the Portuguese conquest of the Moroccan stronghold (Ceuta, 1415) to England's defeat of the Spanish Armada in 1588. One can date a second phase of European resurgence between the reign of Queen Elizabeth (1558–1603) and the Glorious Revolution of 1688, because in this period the main area of economic development and seaborne conflict shifted from the Mediterranean to the Atlantic. By the end of the seventeenth century England was well on her way toward world hegemony.

The idea of the British empire was inspired by four national achievements that prepared the way for the development of imperialism and its ideology. England had secured her liberties by putting the nation, as represented by Parliament, on a par with the Crown. England ruled the sea by providing impregnable naval protection for her seaborne commerce and had risen to prominent status among the great powers of Europe. Finally, the union of the Crowns of England and Scotland was expected to become a union of the kingdoms and their people. Thus, long before the Industrial Revolution, England had rallied her forces for an outward thrust in all directions. In all this, the main trends we have followed persisted: individualism in all its guises, and, now on a world scale, the division of the human community into a metropolitan power of the few and vast areas of subject territories and populations.

These material achievements furthered England's overseas expansion and left their mark on the great minds and humble scribblers of the age. John Milton's spiritual ambition for his English homeland was expressed in fervent prayers that "this great and warlike nation—the Britanic Empire—be found the soberest, wisest and most Christian people" until the Day of Judgment, and be adequately rewarded then! In the years following the Glorious Revolution of 1688, lesser lights linked Britannia with the liberties she had won so recently as well as the empire and sea-power she had acquired in the past. As a term, "the British Empire" began to be used when people reminded the nation of its duties as well as its greatness.[29] And as the range of British rule widened, the "fortunate few" began to take for granted that they had a right to their good fortune.

At the end of the nineteenth century, England's world hegemony and European expansion more generally were publicly justified on the ground that colonialism rendered a public service. Imperialism had a civilizing mission, but it was also a response to the impending attacks of rival powers. Only a combative attitude could cope with these dangers to national existence. The worldwide tasks imposed by national greatness provided the people of the metropolitan country with a sense of fulfilling their country's destiny.[30] The logic of this position was virtually identical with the attitude of most early industrial employers toward their workers. In both cases the service rendered justified the cult of power. The entrepreneurial and the imperial mission derived from past success, either of the individual or of the country's historical tradition. Economic and colonial advance established a purposeful relation between past, present, and future. The ever-present chance of failure justified defensive as well as offensive actions, and a combative attitude was a necessary duty under the circumstances. The resulting zealotry, good conscience, and sense of sacred obligation have divided the human community between the fortunate few and the unfortunate many, both spiritually and materially, at home as well as abroad.

Our understanding of these attitudes is not enhanced by calling them hypocritical. The imperial ideology expressed honest convictions, however misguided, for it laid claim to the advances of the scientific and industrial revolutions, and even used progressive ideals of the French Revolution to justify Europe's overseas expansion.

Adam Smith, whom later generations made the classic spokesman of laissez-faire economics, concluded his analysis with the comment that "the rulers of Great Britain have amused the people with the imagination that they possessed a great empire," when in fact most provinces of the British empire "cannot be made to contribute towards the support of the whole empire."[31] His advice was that England should divest herself of this drain on the public purse. Smith did not grasp the invidious and ethnocentric impulses underlying the economic development he did so much to advance. For the Industrial Revolution had defined the human community anew. In theory, the independent pursuit of gain by each individual would be of material benefit to all people. But, in practice, mankind became divided between the successful few and the unsuccessful many, domestically as well as internationally.

The French Revolution

By making political changes the inevitable by-product of economic transformations, Marx constructed a theoretical model out of the English industrial development and the revolution in France. In fact, the laissez-faire individualism of England and its later imperial repercussions differed substantially from the communitarian individualism of eighteenth-century France. The laissez-faire doctrine meant that the public interest would be best served by the private pursuit of gain, even if it led to a stark division between rich and poor. By contrast, communitarian individualism meant that the public interest would be best served by an education that induces in each individual the desire to identify himself with the general will of the nation. These two kinds of individualism are more easily understood if each is discussed in its own historical context. The contrast will serve as a suitable background for Rousseau's rhetorical relation to the French Revolution and its impact on a new definition of the human community: the ideal of national citizenship.

As elsewhere in Europe, individualism received a major impulse from the Reformation, which in England was initiated by Henry VIII in the 1534 Act of Supremacy. In a society with intense religious preoccupations, this act of political expediency led to a close link between secular and ecclesiastical affairs. Two consequences followed. In response to frequent changes in official religious policy, Protestant orthodoxies proliferated in sectarian fashion. Since the English sovereign had become the head of the church, treason and heresy became indistinguishable. From 1534 to 1553, Catholics were under suspicion of both, while doctrinal disputes increased among Protestants. Under Mary Tudor (1553–58), Catholicism was in ascendance while Protestants were persecuted and regarded with suspicion by the authorities. Finally, some degree of religious accommodation was achieved by the Anglican church under Elizabeth I (1558–1603), but Catholics became suspect once again while Protestant sectarianism continued. In this unsettling religious and political environment, English individualism acquired a strong doctrinal streak that resulted in the overthrow of the monarchy and the civil war half a century later.

A newly defined, national community eventually emerged from these antecedents. England's Glorious Revolution of 1688 put the country on a par with the Crown, an achievement that was followed by a widespread sense of well-being. Overseas expansion, a quickening pace of economic development, and the rising social confidence of merchants and industrial entrepreneurs went hand in hand.

Yet the social conscience of the period was superficial at best. The crowds that tried to drown their misery in drink, the debtors and vagrants who vegetated in prison, the mobs that rioted when harvests failed and prices rose, those who were press-ganged to serve on English ships, the women and children forced to work for long hours in crowded, unsanitary conditions were at odds with the self-satisfaction of the age. Deplorable conditions, as they seem to us, were tolerated, partly because there had been much national progress and partly because it was still felt to be appropriate for government to be in the hands of propertied families who enjoyed inherited prerogatives. Hence the arguments of political writers continued to be cast in personal terms, addressed to the powerful. Their criticism of vice and corruption in high places was blunted by the general acceptance of nepotism and corruption in a personalized political system.

In this setting it was easy to look at both sides of the question, as Adam Smith did in his consideration of moral sentiments or the character of virtue. He distinguished our own happiness from that of others:

> Concern for our own happiness recommends to us the virtue of prudence: concern for that of other people, the virtues of justice and beneficence, of which the one restrains us from hurting, the other prompts us to promote, that happiness.[32]

Smith ignored Calvinist theology and based his reasoning on "natural principles" of human feeling that were the fountainhead of moral qualities like prudence, propriety, and benevolence. Prudence was needed in the pursuit of gain, benevolence in our concern for others. Smith came to consider all moral conduct as the result of our capacity for self-command. He projected the image of an "impartial spectator" capable of distinguishing proper from excessive degrees of all our actions. Accordingly, he strongly objected to Bernard Mandeville's contention that conventional virtues merely covered up for a pervasive egoism, calling that argument a "licentious" confusion between self-love and genuine pride, between vanity and self-respect.[33]

Yet during the eighteenth century the argument gradually shifted away from this balanced ethical perspective. Even if the prudent pursuit of gain became a private vice it would lead to public benefits nevertheless. The pioneers of modern science had been the first to make this argument when they pitted foibles, such as the intense rivalry of their inquiries into nature, against the vanity of dogmatizing, because science was productive of works rather than idle disputations. Adam Smith, the economist, was not even inconsistent with Adam Smith, the moralist, when he argued for the mutual benefit arising from self-love. For the individual naturally pursues his own gain and would not know how to promote the public interest. Yet, "he is led by an invisible hand to promote an end which was no part of his intention" and that end is the aggregate advance of the wealth of nations. Faint though it is, this idea still echoes the old religious belief that only God can anticipate the consequences of human action. And in Smith's mind the prudent pursuit of self-love was compatible with such virtues as strict justice and proper benevolence.[34] In this respect, Jeremy Bentham carried Smith's point a step further when he denied that it made sense to speak of "the interest of the community," because every community is a "fictitious body composed of individual persons." He concluded by saying that there was only one meaning of community interest, namely "the sum of the interests of the several members who compose [the community]."[35] Utilitarianism elaborated the argument in many different ways, but always reverting to the main contention that all was for the best in human affairs, as long as individuals were left free to pursue their own interests. In this view there was no place for the "regard to the sentiments of other people."[36]

In France, the ideas of Jean-Jacques Rousseau contrasted with Smith's balanced recognition of self-love and benevolence as well as with Bentham's declaration that it is meaningless to speak of the interests of the community. This intellectual contrast and the bearing of Rousseau's ideas on the French redefinition of the community in the Revolution of 1789 will be discussed after divergence in French and English cultural ideas of individualism are treated. One way of doing so is to start with the French Reformation and then relate some of its elements to the social and political development under Louis XIV (1661–1715) and his successors.

In France, religious reform inspired by the teaching of John Calvin (1509–1564) was initiated from below, rather than from above as in England. The French government supported the Catholic church. But, as early as the 1520s, some Huguenots (French Protestants) became martyrs to their faith. French religious dissent resulted in a popular movement based on the Presbyterian principle that ecclesiastical authority resides ultimately in the people. Whole communities converted and assembled in religious synods. By 1561, over 2,000 communities were represented. A year later, a Huguenot worship was disrupted by a massacre, precipitating a civil war that lasted intermittently until 1598 when a charter of religious and political toleration (Edict of Nantes) was promulgated. This whole experience resulted in a literature of political protest, proclaiming the principle of government by consent of the governed. So, while in

England the more moderate principle of parliamentary representation eventually led to the idea of equality between Crown and country, in France the doctrine of consent was largely identified with the Huguenot minority in an overwhelmingly Catholic country. Hence, despite official toleration, the Huguenot issue continued to fester until in 1685 the Edict of Nantes was revoked and large numbers of Huguenots, including many successful merchants, fled the country.

This defeat of the religious reform movement contributed to the web of unresolved issues that eventually led to the French Revolution. Seventeenth-century France faced a great paradox. The country's demographic strength supported a dominant military role on the continent, and Paris became the cultural center of Europe. Despite the economic backwardness of France in comparison with Holland and England, the country engaged in foreign wars for almost fifty years between 1600 and 1700. The lack of productivity to sustain this enormous drain on resources could remain hidden for a time. For example, the French monarchy made great strides in its assertion of absolute power: representative bodies declined and administrative reforms abounded. Under the reign of Louis XIV, the Crown's income exceeded that of any other monarchy in Europe, while in numbers and organization the French army was the largest.

However, the methods used to achieve these results were ultimately counterproductive. Annuities payable by the Crown were abolished, new offices were created and sold, taxes on property and those exacted from the peasants were periodically increased. Privileges once sold were expropriated only to be resold, if possible at a higher price. Absolutist rule did not mean detailed local control of the whole country. It meant instead that royal officials exploited every imaginable function of government in order to exact more revenue by delegation and sale. In practice, the state consisted of a series of contracts made with

> the different units of which France was composed: provinces, cities, ecclesiastical foundations, social classes and even economic groups such as trade guilds. All these contracts left to each group its own liberties and privileges [or special obligations] and no one saw anything out of the way in their existence side by side with submission to the king.[37]

Year after year the exploitation expanded. The cost of the wars, abuses by tax collectors and the soldiery, bands of beggars and brigands, scarcity, famine, epidemics, counterfeit money, sudden panics aroused by rumors of new taxes, overweening greed and luxury among the aristocrats at Court and in the church combined to burden the populace. By 1715, when Louis XIV died, these institutions had lost their remaining legitimacy and for a moment people probably breathed a sigh of relief. Compared with these conditions, the nepotism and corruption of government in eighteenth-century England seems a mere side effect of inherited privilege. In eighteenth-century France, the brutal, dynastic exploitation of the whole country together with the ostentatious pleasures of the elite help to account for the exaltation of personal innocence and public virtue as a cornerstone of revolutionary doctrine.

A modern reading of Rousseau's posthumously published *Confessions* (1782–89) might interpret its equation of virtue, nature, and social isolation as the work of a paranoid exhibitionist, who enhanced his self-esteem by accusing others as well as society at large. The eighteenth-century reading was altogether different. Rousseau's description of his petty as well as glaring personal failings looked like candor and innocence against a background of fawning etiquette at court and the venality of officials. The condemnation of man in society looked like unvarnished truth, the glorification of nature like final redemption from a condition that was rotten to the core.

Rousseau begins with the statement that his autobiography has no precedent and will have no imitators:

> The man I shall portray will be myself. . . . I know my own heart and understand my fellow men. But I am made unlike anyone I have ever met; I will even venture to say that I am like no one in the whole world. I may be no better, but at least I am different.

In this version, the ultimate particularism of the individual is conjoined with the claim to universality, a theme that has been echoed ever since the eighteenth century. Rousseau's is a posture of utter, even haughty isolation amid professions of his shortcomings and declarations that he speaks the truth for all mankind. And so the book ends on a note of defiance:

> I have told the truth. If anyone knows anything contrary to what I have recorded, though he prove it a thousand times, his knowledge is a lie and an imposture. . . . For my part, I publicly and fearlessly declare that anyone, . . . who will examine my nature, my character, my morals, my likings, my pleasures, and my habits with his own eyes and can still believe me a dishonorable man, is a man *who deserves to be stifled.*[38]

All the virtues of innocence, candor, truth, unspoiled nature as well as moral indignation are on one side, all the vices of deviousness, deception, lies, corrupt artifice as well as rank immorality are on the other. This ethical dualism was one of the legacies Rousseau bestowed on the revolution. Once that dualism was accepted, a sincere man had no choice.[39]

Rousseau's personal stance and moral claims provided a model for the most vehement protest against the old regime. They greatly influenced the French Revolution, even though many of his specific political ideas were ignored.[40] Here, I limit myself to the aggregate effect of that revolution on the redefinition of the human community. As the subjects of the king became the citizens of a nation, popular sovereignty took the place of monarchical authority. The impact of that transformation can be illustrated by Abbé Sièyes's 1789 pamphlet *What is the Third Estate?*, which contained an early and authoritative formulation of revolutionary doctrine. Three main points are of interest here:

1. The Third Estate is everything. "The people" in the sense of the vast majority will rule the country. They will no longer be dominated by the nobility and the clergy—a mere 200,000 in a nation of 25 million.
2. It is a question of merit. "While the aristocrats talk of their honor, but pursue their self-interest, the Third Estate, (i.e., the nation) will develop its virtue; for if corporate interest is egotism, national interest is virtue." Note the equation between majority, nation, and virtue.
3. It is a question of law. A government has authority only when it is based on a constitution; it is legal only when it is based on prescribed laws. But "the nation is prior to everything. Its will is always legal, indeed it is the law itself."[41]

The revolution redefined the human community in terms of the equation between the people, the nation, virtue, and the law.

That equation rests on an identification of the people as the fountainhead of both virtue and sovereignty. When the revolutionaries referred to Rousseau's work of moral regeneration, they saw it as a model of the public regeneration accomplished by the revolution. Inspired by an emotional fusion between self-absorption and the claim to speak for all human beings, the revolutionaries thought it possible to reject custom, break with convention, and construct a new social order in harmony with nature. From an attribute of the individual, as the Scotch Moralists like Adam Smith had seen it, virtue became an attribute of a whole people. This led to a conclusion on which all revolutionary factions could agree: No one may govern unless authorized to do so by the people. Under the old regime royalists had espoused the idea that the absolute ruler has a single will. Now, Rousseau's idea that the people are one, embody virtue, and have a single will became the accepted slogan of the revolution. With the help of these verbal substitutions faction after faction in the revolutionary struggle made the indivisibility of popular sovereignty the new basic, moral, and political tenet of the country. Robespierre, Saint-Just, and others took up the slogan that only the people are good and in the same breath identified themselves with the people. At one point, Robespierre declared: "You dare to accuse me of wishing to mislead and flatter the people. How could I! I am neither the courtier, nor the moderator, nor the defender of the people; I am [the] people myself."[42] By identification with the people, Robespierre and his fellow revolutionaries became the only authentic spokespersons who sought nothing for themselves as they defended the people's virtue against all enemies. In this *emotional* fusion between the self and the people one finds the same identification between the individual and all mankind that marks the beginning sentences of Rousseau's *Confessions*.[43]

As a result of that identification, revolutionary spokesmen of the people challenged each other by "demonstrating" their own greater vigilance against the people's enemies. That process was prominent in the French Revolution, but hardly confined to it. Where it develops, the human community gets redefined in terms of who belongs to it and who does not. For example, in 1793, the Jacobins excluded from the people of France not only the royal family, monarchists, and aristocrats but also vicious men, the wealthy, actors, mercenary writers, and, last but not least, women.[44] But such a doctrinal definition of groups excluded from the human community was not the same as political implementation, and the communitarian practice was different.

A simple examination of the revolutionary slogan "liberté, egalité, fraternité" shows how France as a national community actually developed. The ideal of liberty consisted initially in attacks on the inherited privilege of king, aristocracy, and clergy. Those privileges were to give way to a constitutional order based on popular sovereignty. However, the legal definition of the right to vote on the part of the people who constituted the citizens of France was altogether different from "le peuple" as a revolutionary symbol. Sieyès, Mounier, and others advocated private property and a government of laws. Once the Jacobin radicals were defeated, it became clear that the franchise would be available only to men of twenty-five or over, meeting certain tax and residence requirements. All women, servants and economic dependents were excluded. Thus, the liberty that had been won consisted in the freedom of all property owners from governmental interference.

It was this liberty that was transformed into a synonym of equality. By restricting the definition of the people through the franchise, one also restricts the people whose equality counts. As George Herbert Mead has written:

> If one wills to possess that which is his own so that he has absolute control over it as property, he does so on the assumption that everyone else will possess his own property and exercise absolute control over it. That is, the individual wills his control over his property only in so far as he wills the same sort of control for everyone else over property.[45]

Yet while the right to property was sacrosanct, many other rights, especially those of assembly, were sacrificed in the name of national citizenship.

In practice, liberty and equality were restricted, but fraternity was extended to the whole country. Radicals as well as moderates insisted that groups of people associating for the sake of a common goal was tantamount to treason, an unacceptable challenge to popular sovereignty. Already before the revolution, the Jesuits were outlawed because they monopolized education. Then mutual-aid societies of workers were prohibited because the needy should look to the state for assistance. Women were not allowed to organize because their place was in the home. Most striking of all, the family was regarded with suspicion as an "aristocratic" preserve that interfered with the direct relation between each child and the nation-state.

This anti-associational tendency had the authority of Rousseau behind it. In *The Social Contract* we read:

> If the people came to a resolution when adequately informed and *without any communication among the Citizens* [italics mine], the general will would always result from the great number of slight differences, and the resolution would always be good. But when factions, partial associations, are formed to the detriment of the whole society, the will of each of these associations becomes general with reference to its members, and particular with reference to the State: it may then be said that there are no longer as many voters as there are men, but only as many voters as there are associations. . . . It is important, then, in order to have a clear declaration of the general will, that there should be no partial association in the State, and that each Citizen should express only his own opinion.[46]

That was written in 1762, long before French revolutionary authorities mobilized the entire population in response to war emergencies.

Rousseau had anticipated the anti-associational bias that made fraternity, or the unity of all, the highest goal of the people and the nation. The revolution was not only eager to rid itself of aristocratic and clerical cabals. It was bent on isolating the individual so that the nation would be more communal, especially in times of war. Military organization became the one institution in which the national community of all Frenchmen was realized. Bertrand Barrère, chairman of the committee charged by the Convention of 1793 with preparing appropriate legislation, justified national conscription on these grounds:

> What would you have us do? Supply a contingent from each departmental and territorial division? Let us leave the venal use of this seigneurial or federalist method to the Germanic corps, to the confederacies of Germany and to the imperial edicts. To ensure its liberty, France's contigent comprises the whole of its population, the whole of its industry, the whole of its labours and the whole of its genius.[47]

Here, equality means the universal obligation to serve the nation, on a par with the obligation to go to school, to obey the laws, and to pay taxes. The French Revolution redefined the human community as a national whole, with each individual in his or her place, honor bound to serve the "general will." The French Revolution established the first modern regime based, at least ideologically, on the governmental simulation of combat, in peace as well as war.[48]

One outcome of these revolutionary antecedents was the potential incompatibility between freedom and fraternity. Looking back upon an age of inequality, Tocqueville saw that the power of kings had been curbed by aristocrats, who went to great lengths to defend their inherited rights, their liberties in the medieval meaning of that term. That meaning of freedom was destroyed when leaders of the French Revolution proclaimed that no associations with their intermediate power, like guilds, municipalities, or mutual-aid societies, should intervene between individual citizens and the sovereign will of the nation. Such powers were regarded as conspiracies against the people, a position that left each individual unrelated to his fellow men. Self-reliant men do not want to shackle themselves to others and do not expect any assistance from them. In their isolation and impotence, they turn to the assistance of government to do for them what they cannot achieve by themselves. The result is a concentration of power in the hands of government and a consequent threat to individual freedom.[49]

The incompatibility between equality and fraternity is still more intractable. Rousseau was well aware that the will of all as individuals was not the same as the common or general will, which is always right because it is a synonym of the public good. His descriptions of the ideal political state were couched in extraordinarily seductive language, bringing out the intense longing for an immediate communion with others and imbuing that longing with an aura of moral superiority.[50] Since he and his revolutionary followers attributed the general will to the inherent virtue of the people, they had to see to it that the individual totally identified with the nation and its government. Accordingly, the leaders of the revolution were influenced by Rousseau's educational rather than his political ideas. Education would inculcate the sense of brotherhood, a belief in the national community that would reveal the pristine nature of the people.

Rousseau and the revolutionary leaders who followed in his spirit set an enormous task for themselves and their countrymen. They projected the creation of a new man, in order to overcome the incompatibility between the freedom and equality all people desire and the general will that is needed to put popular sovereignty into effect. Having rejected original sin by claiming that the people are good, they proposed to recreate human nature, to transform each individual into a part of the greater national whole from which each can receive anew his personal life and his being. As Rousseau saw it, man must be deprived of his natural strength as an individual in order to give him a communal strength that he cannot use without the help of others. The more man's individual strength is destroyed, the more durable will be his acquired strength, and the more solid and perfect will be the institution of government.[51]

To that end, Rousseau recommends public demonstrations reminding the people of their "misfortunes, their virtues, and their victories, interest[ing] their hearts, inflam[ing] them with lively emulation and attach[ing] them firmly to the fatherland." However, the most important means of creating each individual's love of country was education by the state, because the family is the institution most inimical to the nation. Hence, the public authority should expropriate the authority of the fathers. If children would then be taught to respect the laws and the general will above everything else, if they were surrounded by exemplary objects that speak to them ceaselessly of the tender mothcr [sic] who nourishes them, of the love she has for them, of the inestimable benefits they receive from her, and of the return they owe her, let us not doubt that they will learn to love one another like brothers, never to want anything but what the society wants.[52]

At this rhetorical level, equality becomes a synonym of fraternity by the common identification of all individuals with the country of their birth.

This is a tautological definition of community. All individuals will be equal, provided they submit to the "general will" of the people and thus acquire a national sense of brotherhood. At the practical level, this sense of equality means the subjection of all individuals to the nation-state while permanently dividing mankind at large into congeries of mutually exclusive countries. An equality so understood would be incompatible with the brotherhood of man. At the secular level, the French Revolution reenacted the ancient paradox of ethical dualism, that what is good for the national community of France necessarily excludes the good of all other nations. Still, within this national framework, the revolution established a constitutional order based on the rights of man and the citizen that (in the countries of Western civilization) has led to a system of state-supported entitlements. The illusion that the libertarian principles of such a constitutional order are somehow synonymous with a more or less equalitarian distribution of a nation's resources accounts for the worldwide reverberations of the French Revolution.

But particular benefits to all groups within a country, just like the larger idea of one nation and all humanity, are incompatible imperatives. Rousseau as well as Marx sought to overcome this contradiction between particularism and universalism. But Rousseau's attention was focused on the nation; Marx wanted to emancipate all mankind. Marx's commanding influence on the Bolshevik Revolution and the Marxist impact on the world at large have been based on the belief that the worldwide transformation of man and society is a meaningful goal of human action.

Communitarian Backlash: The Marxist Tradition

As we enter the final decade of the twentieth century, communism and the Soviet empire are disintegrating. The future of Eastern Europe is in doubt. Under these conditions it may seem superfluous to discuss Marx and the Bolshevik Revolution as the last redefinition of the human community in Western civilization, a phase of history that cannot be compared with the lasting influence of Christianity or science, of capitalism or the French Revolution. Renaissance science, the Industrial and the French Revolutions, while promoting different kinds of individualism, also included universalist appeals. Science and capitalism made that appeal in terms of benefits that the few bestow upon the many. The French Revolution, on the other hand, started a communitarian backlash by its appeal to the general will. Subsequently, Marx and the Bolshevik Revolution epitomized this modern definition of the human community by leading to a collectivist excess, albeit in the name of individualist ideals. That excess is a counterpart to the individualist excess that preceded it. Marx and his successors redefined the human community by claiming that all individual goals can only be achieved collectively.

Just as leaders of the French Revolution received their inspiration from Rousseau's autobiographical and educational writings, so leaders of the Bolshevik Revolution derived their inspiration from the writings of Karl Marx. Rousseau and Marx were intellectuals, out of touch with any particular class; they projected images of mankind in response to their own isolation. Rousseau believed that by reading his own heart he had found the clue to the nature of his fellow men and to a national community that would terminate man's degradation by society. And Marx believed that by making theoretical assumptions about man, he had objectively interpreted human nature and world history. Mankind as a whole would be reorganized under the aegis of the world proletariat. To speak of individualism in a Marxian context may appear paradoxical. Nevertheless, such usage may be allowed, if it enables us to see together what is usually examined separately. I have tried to show that individualism has been a root metaphor of the modern era, whether we consider Renaissance science, the Reformation or the economic and political revolutions of the last two centuries. But at each of these junctures, individualism has been combined with the ambition to speak for mankind. The same is true of Marx.

Marx and Engels's statement about the nature of man has been as easily turned in an individualist as in a collectivist direction:

> Man can be distinguished from animals by consciousness, by religion or anything else you like. They themselves begin to distinguish themselves from animals, as soon as they begin to *produce* means of subsistence, a step which is conditioned by their physical organization.[53]

Man cannot exist without food, clothing, and shelter and, according to Marx, the production of these necessities is "the first historical act." In his view, production is not only the driving force of human history. It is also the main field in which man can realize his full potential, an idea that is part of the modern Promethean tradition going back to the Renaissance. When Marx declared that "philosophers have only *interpreted* the world, the point, however, is to *change* it," he had man's highest goal in mind, the fullest possible realization of his capacities.[54]

The ideal of individual self-realization is a main theme in Marx's principal work *Das Kapital* (1867), not just a youthful notion of his early philosophical manuscripts, as some have maintained. The fragmentation and deprivation imposed by modern industry is rejected in the name of

> the fully developed individual, fit for a variety of labours, ready to face any change of production, to whom the different social functions he performs, are but so many modes of giving free scope to his own natural and acquired powers.

To illustrate the point, Marx quotes the biography of a French worker, a letter-press operator, who came to America during the Gold Rush, and who exemplifies this meaning of self-realization. The author lists the many different skills he developed in mid-nineteenth-century California, and exclaims that as a result he "feels less of a mollusk and more of a man."[55] Such personal fulfillment in a frontier society stands in stark contrast to the division of labor under capitalism that downgrades all human capacities, particularly among the working class. This contrast between the dehumanization of the masses and the realization of man's full potential underscores Marx's goal to abolish the division of labor and the class struggle in the socialist society of the future.

Marx's mature work contains only a few remarks about that future, because he rejected all detailed speculations as utopian. However, these remarks are revealing. He retained the Enlightenment ideals of his youth, that individual creativity and rationality are the basis of self-realization. Yet he was equally beholden to the communitarian backlash against individualism in the name of the proletariat. That double emphasis appeals to intellectuals, who want to be "philosopher kings." Marx projected a reorganization of society that would allow men to realize collectively what, under modern conditions of production, they cannot achieve individually.

Let us now picture to ourselves . . . a community of free individuals, carrying on their work with the means of production in common, in which the labor-power of all the different individuals is consciously applied to the combined labor-power of all.

Rousseau had rejected the idea of original sin. Now Marx rejected not only the division of labor, which gave rise to social classes, but Christianity, which appeared to him as the sentimental smoke screen of capitalist exploitation:

The life process, which is based on the process of material production, does not strip off its mystical veil until it is treated as production by freely associated men, and is consciously regulated in accordance with a settled plan. . . . [The] religious reflex of the real world can, in any case, only then finally vanish when the practical relations of everyday life offer to man none but perfectly intelligible and reasonable relations with regard to his fellowmen and to nature.[56]

Accordingly, the fulfillment of individual creativity can only be recaptured collectively, and the proletariat under capitalism is the only historical force capable of accomplishing this end. Once that goal is achieved under socialism, men can finally gain control over their fate as well as unfettered clarity in their social relations. This Manichaean view of the human condition contrasts the children of light belonging to the socialism of the future with the children of darkness belonging to human prehistory. Marx's "prehistory" extends from the beginning of class struggles and human exploitation in ancient times to the coming revolution of the proletariat. He seems to have been unaware of the early Christian origin of his view of history.

Marx thought of himself as a realist who based his theories on the hard facts of life and did not speculate about the future. In his view, the dehumanization of life under capitalism can be overcome only when the workers' mounting protest against their degradation is complemented by a theoretical understanding of the capitalist system. Marx championed a unity of theory and practice, which alone makes sense of his lifelong effort to analyze the capitalist economy. For scientific theory would give direction to the cumulative and ultimately successful struggle of the working class against their oppressors. This idea defined the human community in a novel way, and that definition inspired Lenin's revolutionary leadership and the communist regime he initiated.

According to Marx, the exploited masses are in no position to develop the intellectual tools required for the coming reorganization of society. And the theorists who develop those tools are powerless utopians (even if their theories are correct), unless they establish close links with the working-class movement. And so we get the unity of theory and practice, as the *Communist Manifesto* defines it,

> in times when the class struggle nears the decisive hour, the process of dissolution going on within the ruling class, in fact within the whole range of old society, assumes such a violent, glaring character, that a small section of the ruling class cuts itself adrift and joins the revolutionary class, the class that holds the future in its hands. Just as, therefore, at an earlier period, a section of the nobility went over to the bourgeoisie, so now a portion of the bourgeoisie goes over to the proletariat, and in particular, a portion of the bourgeois ideologists, who have raised themselves to the level of comprehending theoretically the historical movement as a whole.[57]

As we know today, this was wishful thinking. For two centuries, the history of the labor movement has demonstrated that workers are suspicious of intellectuals, however often the latter have played an important role in labor organizations. The postulate of unity between theory and practice sought to overcome the social isolation of intellectuals, as well as their marginal role in public affairs. That postulate linked them to the proletariat, supposedly a world-historical force, and thus provided them in their own eyes with the chance to reorganize society from the ground up.

Marx thought of his work as scientific, believing that his detailed economic analysis demonstrated "the natural laws of capitalist production, . . . of these tendencies working with iron necessity towards inevitable results."[58] Expressions like these reflect mid-nineteenth-century notions of science, which help to account for Marx's confidence in the coming revolution. But his historical outlook rested on philosophical rather than scientific foundations. He took as dark a view of the human condition as Rousseau, though without the latter's belief in man's capacity for virtue. Here again a Manichaean division between total good and total evil prevailed. In terms of science, technology, and productivity a complete satisfaction of human needs seemed possible. However, under capitalism the ruling classes subjected the masses to the most inhuman deprivations. Under these conditions it was unrealistic to appeal to moral sentiments, as Smith and Rousseau had done. Instead, Marx combined the emphasis on economic self-interest with the ancient, originally religious idea that the consequences of human action result not from our intentions, but from forces beyond our control. An inhuman organization of production rather than Smith's "invisible hand" or Hegel's "transcendental reason" would force the working class to overthrow the capitalist order.

> If socialist critics attribute this world-historical role to the proletariat, this is by no means . . . because they regard the proletarians as Gods. On the contrary. Since the fully formed proletariat represents, practically speaking, the complete abstraction from everything human, even from the appearance of being human, since all the living conditions of contemporary society have reached the acme of inhumanity in the living conditions of the proletariat, . . . the proletariat can and must liberate itself.[59]

Only a revolution based on these objective conditions of working-class existence will bring about the decisive change.

Just how decisive that change would be is revealed by the apocalyptic terms in which Marx envisaged the future.

> This antagonism between modern industry and science on the one hand, modern misery and dissolution on the other hand; this antagonism between the productive powers and the social relations of our epoch is a fact, palpable, overwhelming, and not to be controverted. . . . We do not mistake the shape of the shrewd spirit that continues to mark all these contradictions. We know that, to work well, the newfangled forces of society . . . only want to be mastered by newfangled men—and such are the working men.[60]

At the end of this road, society would be reorganized because men would be created anew, a belief that made atheism a basic tenet of the Marxist tradition.

Marx and Engels believed that the proletarian revolution would occur in the industrially advanced countries of Western Europe but that, with the spread of capitalism, the class struggle would become internationalized. Still, even the mounting crises of capitalism were not enough. To make conditions "ripe" for a revolution, workers must develop class consciousness and "bourgeois ideologists" must develop a scientific theory that will point the mass movement in the right direction. While the force of the revolution comes from class-conscious workers, its ideas come from intellectuals, and both will result from the class struggle nearing "the decisive hour." Built into this prognosis is an intellectual safeguard against the possibility of failure or falsification. For developments that go against the predicted tendency would be due either to conditions not having advanced sufficiently or to the false consciousness of workers and intellectuals. This "guarantee" of being right about the inevitable course of history has had a powerful attraction for Marx and his many followers. It is also directly related to the political order established in Marx's name and to the definition of the human community on which that order was based.

**

Today, as we witness the breakup of the Communist system, it is important to recall in what ways Lenin and later Stalin transformed the Marxist tradition. As the Soviet Union developed, the Promethean impulse, originally individualist and humanitarian, was redefined. In Lenin's view, the task of the Bolshevik dictatorship was to catch up with the advanced countries, culturally as well as economically. Under Stalin, the fate of one country became identified with the welfare, indeed the salvation of mankind. My focus will be on the coming crisis of capitalist society and on the relations between workers and their leaders.

Lenin (1870–1924) believed that at the end of World War I the revolutionary labor movement would gain the upper hand in the industrialized countries of the West. Like Marx and Engels before him, he scanned the events of his day for portents favorable to his expectations. But as the actual leader of a revolutionary movement in an economically backward country, he was interested in signs of impending support for the Russian Revolution from the more advanced countries. During the last years of his life, his writings present a strange mixture of emphases. They insist on the theoretical validity of Marxist theory. They continue virulent polemics against deviationists. Occasionally they strike a rather plaintive note about how difficult it is "to keep going until the socialist revolution is victorious in more developed countries."[61]

Accordingly, Lenin developed theories concerning the impending internationalization of the class struggle due to the imperialist expansion of capitalism. Following World War I, the chaotic conditions of Russia were aggravated further by Western support of internal opposition to the revolutionary government. For Lenin, that was both proof of capitalist expansionism and evidence of a temporary setback of his cause. He believed he had reason to hope for support of the Russian Revolution from abroad. Long before 1917, he had put much effort into a theory of imperialism that, in his view, proved the eventual inevitability of a worldwide revolution that would support Russia's pioneering effort.

Lenin's theory of monopoly capitalism is founded on five related propositions:

1. In the most industrialized countries the organization of production is becoming concentrated in ever fewer hands.
2. Because of increasing dependence on credit, the banks are acquiring a commanding influence over the economy (Hilferding's finance capitalism).
3. The export of goods is increasingly superseded by the export of capital, leading to growing dependence of underdeveloped countries on advanced countries.
4. Nationwide monopolies are turning into international cartels that will be followed eventually by military contests for worldwide hegemony.
5. As advanced countries expand in order to find foreign markets for their excess production they may reduce the intensity of the class struggle at home, but only at the price of intensifying it abroad.[62]

And that intensified struggle would support the Bolshevik regime. This was an update of Marx's conclusion in the *Communist Manifesto*: "Let the ruling classes tremble at a Communistic revolution. The proletarians have nothing to lose but their chains. They have a world to win. Working men of all countries, unite!"

To reach this goal, Lenin had redefined the human community on a worldwide scale. Ever since his 1902 pamphlet *What is to be Done?* he had been preoccupied with the task of strengthening the revolutionary preparedness of the labor movement. The spontaneous development of that movement could not, in his view, go beyond trade unionism and social reform. He put less emphasis than Marx on working-class protest against exploitation. Looking from a Russian perspective at the labor movements of the advanced countries, he concluded that workers everywhere could acquire political class consciousness only with the help of revolutionary cadres from outside their own ranks. Where Marx had combined the economic with the political developments of England and France, Lenin combined the reformism of workers in advanced economies with their revolutionary tendencies in backward economies. He believed that in principle only revolutionary "tribunes of the people" can transform

> every manifestation of tyranny and oppression . . . into a single picture of police violence and capitalist exploitation, [by explaining] to all and everyone the world-historical significance of the struggle for the emancipation of the proletariat.[63]

In effect, Lenin minimized Marx's concern with the workers' own reaction to capitalist exploitation.

From the beginning of his political career (1893–94), Lenin divided the proletariat into a mass of trade-unionist workers and an elite of professional revolutionaries. By 1917, if not earlier, he related that division to his theory of imperialism. In that theory the spontaneous trade unionism of the workers appeared as the natural outlook of a "labor aristocracy," which benefited from the imperialism of the economically advanced countries. During World War I, Lenin developed this idea into a world-historical theory.

In his view, the leading force of the revolution was in the hands of professional revolutionaries. He saw the increasing class struggles under capitalism mitigated by the benefits that imperialism could bestow on the working class. That did not prompt him to give up hope for a revolution in the advanced countries, for he put enormous energy into the fight against social-democratic revisionism in Western Europe. But he did not rely on that hope, even though he knew that the revolution in backward Russia needed help from abroad. In his different setting he combined theory with practice once again. The force required for the revolution would arise from the imperialist spread of capitalism, and the theory that was needed would be based on Marx's ideas as developed by a revolutionary elite.[64]

Thus, Lenin combined the theory of imperialism with the demand for disciplined cadres of professional revolutionaries. Imperialism had shifted the class struggle from the national to the international arena. Colonies and other economically dependent countries were ruthlessly exploited and thereby became the natural allies of the revolutionary proletariat. Imperialism intensified the uneven development of countries, while the internal contradictions of monopoly capitalism reinforced the tendencies toward war. Sooner or later, the "chain" of world capitalism was bound to break at one of its peripheral links. Therefore, the Marxist thesis is reversible. The revolution, rather than occurring in the most advanced countries, may be initiated instead in a backward country and thereby encourage revolutionary developments elsewhere. Lenin reasoned that Russia was the country predestined to pioneer a successful proletarian revolution. Russia was an imperialist power in its own right, but three quarters of her capital investment was in French, English, and German hands. Thus, she was a half-colonial country on the periphery of world capitalism. The workers, rather than being bribed by successful capitalism, suffered the worst exploitation. Intellectuals had the incentive to become professional revolutionaries because they too suffered from the most cruel system of oppression. According to Lenin, the revolution will occur in the country that is just industrializing and hence manifests exploitation at its worst. At the same time the country is so backward that its institutions can be overthrown most readily. Where Marx had identified himself with the proletariat in countries with capitalist economies, Lenin identified himself with Russian workers and peasants, because the revolutionary breakthrough was likely in their country and dictatorial rule could catch up with cultural and economic advances abroad. Two versions of communitarianism, two intellectual efforts to redeem all mankind from the excesses of individualism.

Lenin, who prepared the revolution but did not live to govern the country, was bound to differ from Stalin, the dictator of an established regime. Both took their inspiration from Marx, the theorist of a coming revolution. All three redefined the human community in kindred, but far from identical ways. Here I restate these similarities and differences in terms of the hypothetical unity between the practice of workers and the theories of intellectuals. For that postulated unity stands for the Communist redefinition of the human community, originally created by the economic and political revolutions of the late eighteenth century.

Marx had attributed the revolutionary potential of workers to the dehumanization to which they were subjected by capitalism. Lenin disagreed because workers benefited in successful imperialist countries and only developed a trade-union consciousness. Marx had attributed the radicalization of bourgeois ideologists to their growing awareness of the crisis of capitalism. Lenin disagreed because this crisis was abated by imperialism so that the bourgeois ideologists of the labor movement were only reform-minded social democrats. They lacked the discipline required of professional revolutionaries.

Marx's economic theory made the final crisis of capitalism appear inevitable due to the cumulative effects of such tendencies as the declining rate of profit, cyclical crises of overproduction, and increased dehumanization. Marx expected that the proletarian revolution would occur in countries of the most advanced industrialization. Lenin thought that the revolution was more likely in backward countries on the exploited periphery of capitalist advance though he recognized Russia's cultural as well as economic backwardness. Therefore, he proposed a Bolshevik dictatorship tough enough to raise his war-ravaged country to the industrial and cultural levels of the advanced countries—before attempting the establishment of socialism.[65]

Under Stalin, the Leninist position was vulgarized in the interest of defending the Soviet Union. Lenin's complicated arguments about Russia's revolution as the break of the weakest link in the imperialist system became the Stalinist revival of Russian nationalism. Lenin's distinction between trade-unionist workers and professional revolutionaries became the Stalinist distinction between the working masses and the cadres of party activists. In a sense, the slogan of "socialism in one country" tells the story. The Bolshevik leaders interpreted their revolution as a proletarian dictatorship in a backward country. Early on, even Stalin believed that the success of the new regime would depend on the support of labor movements in the more advanced countries. But when that expectation was disappointed, party ideology simply turned the sequence around, a strategy for which Lenin had provided an unwitting precedent. Because the revolution had occurred in Russia, that country had become the vanguard of all revolutions and the champion of oppressed humanity. The human community was redefined once more. Before World War II, under the leadership of the Communist International (Comintern) controlled by Moscow, all non-Russian Communist parties had to subordinate their policies to the supreme interests of the Soviet Union. After World War II, the same reasoning was used to justify Soviet expansion in Eastern Europe and Soviet support for colonial liberation movements around the world. Only Mikhail Gorbachev's reform movement in the Soviet Union since 1985 and the Eastern European liberation movements since the early 1980s have put this latest definition of the human community into question.

***

The Bolshevik Revolution and its repercussions are a part of the communitarian backlash against economic individualism and its theoretical dismissal of all concern for the public good.[66] The intellectual opposition to capitalism is hardly confined to the Marxist tradition. It has ranged from Rousseau in the eighteenth century down to the existentialism of Martin Heidegger in the twentieth. Antimodernism is all about us, but the underlying affinity among all communitarian reactions to the individualist or anarchic impulses of modernity is not self-evident. This linkage may be exemplified by the early writings of Georg Lukács.

In his essay on the theory of the novel (1916) Lukács extolled the Homeric and the medieval world as the last historical phases in which the individual had been fully integrated in the community. Since then, but especially in the modern period, man had found himself in a position of "transcendental homelessness" (*transzendentale Obdachlosigkeit*). Against the background of World War I, Lukács labeled capitalist modernity as the "age of ultimate sinfulness," borrowing a phrase of Fichte from the beginning of the nineteenth century. Lukács joined the Hungarian Communist party in 1918 because he wanted to be part of a morally intact community. In an article on the moral mission of the Party, he wrote that it "must be the first embodiment of the realm of freedom, in which for the first time the spirit of fraternity, of true solidarity, of the ability and willingness to sacrifice oneself should dominate."[67] As the Hungarian who had absorbed much German philosophy and then identified himself with communism and the Russian Revolution, Lukács embodied in his person the intellectual backlash to Western European individualism, especially as it took form since the eighteenth century.

This communitarian questioning of modern civilization from within its own Western tradition occurred in Eastern Europe, where that tradition and the capitalist economy were weakest but the idealization of community flourished. With the wisdom of hindsight one can understand that the multifaceted individualism of European civilization since the Renaissance reached its nadir on the periphery, where it was replaced by totalitarian collectivism as a principle of rule. The demise of that principle in the last decade of the twentieth century does not mean that the opposition between individual particularism and collective universalism is resolved, or that the distinctions will cease between those who belong and those who do not. It is more likely that new definitions of community will be attempted.

In this discussion I have substituted phases in the definition of community for Max Weber's thesis of increasing rationality. Judaism, Christianity, science, capitalism, the French and the Bolshevik Revolutions: each established a hierarchy of values and a system of thought. In all these cases reasoning went together with a communal and spiritual commitment: learning and piety in Judaism; piety and hierarchy in Catholicism; knowledge-seeking by the few and benefits to the many in science; profit-seeking by the successful few and increasing wealth for the whole country under capitalism; formal equality of all individuals before the law under a constitution expressing the general will in the French Revolution; and under Bolshevism the complete subordination of all to a single-party regime in the name of a secular myth of creation and redemption. Though I doubt that these junctures have been instances of cumulative rationality, each has affected our world with its efforts to make sense of our lives. I hesitate to put the Bolshevik Revolution on a par with the others because in this case ethical and political dualism together with the claim to universal validity were driven to such extremes that the end of this regime was marked by the formal repudiation of the party's monopoly and public declarations that "we do not have all the answers." An adage is making the rounds: "Workers of the world, we are sorry."

My interpretation of community in Western civilization is based on the idea of multiple rationalities, each establishing its own hierarchy of values with its principle of inclusion and exclusion. As long as we are unable to encompass mankind as a whole, I do not foresee an end to further elaborations along these lines. I have examined six junctures in the development of Western civilization that are unthinkable without the intellectual leadership of rabbis, priests, scientists, political economists, and the theorists of revolution. They echoed and elaborated popular distinctions between those who belong and those who do not, and thereby helped to form the communities in which we live. With the demise of Communist rule in Eastern Europe it appears that ethnic identity, nationalism, and efforts to create regional associations among nations will be the guiding ideas of the twenty-first century.

Notes

1. Max Weber, *The Protestant Ethic and the Spirit of Capitalism* (New York: Charles Scribner, 1958), 13.
2. In the interest of brevity, I omit considerations of other types of monotheism as well as a more detailed discussion of polytheistic beliefs.
3. See Gershom Scholem, *Über Einige Grundbegriffe des Judentums* (Frankfurt: Suhrkamp, 1970), 96–98.
4. The best introduction to Renaissance science is by E. A. Burtt, *The Metaphysical Foundations of Modern Physical Science* (New York: Doubleday, 1954).
5. My discussion is based on, and paraphrases, Hans Jonas, "The Practical Uses of Theory," *Social Research* (Summer 1959), 127ff.
6. Quoted in Burtt, *Metaphysical Foundations* , 51.

7. For fuller documentation on Galileo cf. Reinhard Bendix, *Embattled Reason*, vol. 2 (New Brunswick, NJ: Transaction Publishers, 1989), chapter 12.

8. Thomas Sprat, *History of the Royal Society*, ed. J. I. Cope and H. W. Jones (London: Routledge and Kegan Paul, 1966), 54–56.

9. Cf. Robert Nisbet, *The Quest for Community* (New York: Oxford University Press, 1953).

10. The poem is quoted in Theodore Spencer, *Shakespeare and the Nature of Man* (New York: Macmillan Co., 1955), 22.

11. Pico della Mirandola, "Oration on the Dignity of Man," in Ernst Cassirer, Paul O. Kristeller, John H. Randall, eds., *The Renaissance Philosophy of Man* (Chicago: University of Chicago Press, 1948), 228.

12. The reference is to the work of Norbert Elias, *Über den Prozess der Zivilisation*, 2 vols. (Bern: A. Francke Verlag, 1939). The work is now available in English.

13. Blaise Pascal, *Pensée*, no. 115 (New York: Modern Library, Random House, 1941), 44.

14. See Ralf Dahrendorf, *The Modern Social Conflict* (London: Weidenfeld and Nicolson, 1988), 5.

15. I shall leave to one side the large literature dealing with the common grounding of these methods in the Puritan variants of Protestantism. The best summary of the literature is Gordon Marshall's *In Search of the Spirit of Capitalism, an Essay on Max Weber's Protestant Ethic Thesis* (New York: Columbia University Press, 1982).

16. Alexis de Tocqueville, *Democracy in America*, vol. 2 (Vintage Books: New York: A.A. Knopf, 1954), 187.

17. In a phrase of Thomas Aquinas, "the good of any thing is that which belongs to the fullness of being which all things seek after and desire." Quoted in Jonas, "Practical Uses of Theory," 117.

18. See Otto Brunner, *Adeliges Landleben und Europäischer Geist* (Salzburg: Otto Müller Verlag, 1949).

19. John Stuart Mill, *Principles of Political Economy*, vol. 2 (Boston: Charles C. Little & James Brown, 1848), 319–20.

20. Tocqueville, *Democracy in America*, vol. 2, 188.

21. A modern literary portrayal of this patriarchal setting from the servant's standpoint is Kazuo Ishiguro, *The Remains of the Day* (New York: Random House, 1989).

22. Adam Smith, *The Wealth of Nations*, vol. 1 (New York: Dutton, 1964), 13.

23. Edmund Burke, "Thoughts and Details on Scarcity," in *Works*, vol. 5 (Boston: Little Brown & Co., 1869), 142.

24. H. H. Gerth and C. Wright Mills, eds., *From Max Weber* (New York: Oxford University Press, 1946), 271 and Weber, *Protestant Ethic*, 182.

25. Mill, *Principles*, vol. 2, 322–23.

26. Karl Marx and Friedrich Engels, *On Britain* (Moscow: Foreign Languages Publishing House, 1953), 491–92.

27. For details see Reinhard Bendix, *Work and Authority in Industry* (Berkeley: University of California, 1974), chapters 2 and 4.

28. Quoted without citation in K. M. Pannikar, *Asia and Western Dominance* (London: George Allen & Unwin, 1959), 26–27.

29. My discussion is based on Richard Koebner, *Empire* (New York: Grosset & Dunlop, 1965), chapter 3. The quotations are also taken from this chapter.

30. Heinz Gollwitzer, *Europe in the Age of Imperialism 1880–1914* (London: Thames & Hudson, 1969), chapter 13.

31. Adam Smith, *Wealth of Nations*, vol. 2, 429–30.

32. Herbert W. Schneider, ed., "The Theory of Moral Sentiments," in Adam Smith's *Moral and Political Philosophy* (New York: Hafner Publishing Co., 1948), 274.

33. Schneider, "Introduction," in ibid., xx–xxi.

34. Smith, *Wealth of Nations*, vol. 1, 400. This seems to me a possible solution to the so-called Adam Smith problem. See the detailed analysis by Laurence Dickey, "Historicizing the 'Adam Smith Problem': Conceptual, Historiographical and Textual Issues," *Journal of Modern History* 58 (September 1986), 579–609.

35. Jeremy Bentham, "An Introduction to the Principles of Morals and Legislation," in E. A. Burtt, ed., *The English Moral Philosophers from Bacon to Mill* (New York: Modern Library, Random House, 1939), 792. Bentham's treatise was published in 1789, the year of the French Revolution.

36. A main point in Adam Smith's *Theory of Moral Sentiments*. This emphasis is not incompatible with his economic treatise when one considers his very critical attitude toward the merchant class. See Smith, *Wealth of Nations*, vol. 1, 117, 231–32.

37. Pierre Goubert, *Louis XIV and Twenty Million Frenchmen* (New York: Random House, 1970), 52. Even religious minorities like the Huguenots were self-governing despite their second-class status, but as such they became liable for additional taxation.

38. Jean-Jacques Rousseau, *Confessions* (Baltimore: Penguin Books, 1953), 18, 605–6. My italics.

39. Cf. the essay by Jean Starobinski, "The Accuser and the Accused," *Daedalus* (Summer 1978), 41–58 for an analysis of this Manichaean approach.

40. See Bernard Martin, "Rousseau," in François Furet and Mona Ozouf, eds., *A Critical Dictionary of the French Revolution* (Cambridge: Harvard University Press, 1989), 829–43.

41. Emmanuel Joseph Sieyès, *What is the Third Estate?* (New York: Praeger, 1963), 99–105.

42. Quoted in Carol Blum, *Rousseau and the Republic of Virtue, the Language of Politics in the French Revolution* (Ithaca: Cornell University Press, 1986), 160. My discussion is indebted to this comprehensive study.

43. The point is noted in ibid., 164–65.

44. Ibid., 203.

45. George Herbert Mead, *Movements of Thought in the Nineteenth Century* (Chicago: University of Chicago Press, 1938), 17.

46. Jean-Jacques Rousseau, *The Social Contract* ed. Charles Sherover (New York: The New American Library, 1974), 45.

47. Quoted in Pierre Birnbaum, *States and Collective Action* (New York: Cambridge University Press, 1988), 61.

48. The organizational simulation of combat in peacetime is analyzed in Bendix, *Work and Authority*, 367 ff. in relation to the one-party dictatorship in East Germany. I do not subscribe to the idea of "totalitarian democracy" as developed by J. L. Talmon, but there are striking organizational and ideological analogues.

49. I have paraphrased a main idea developed by Tocqueville, *Democracy in America*, vol. 2, 187–95.

50. The point is documented in Blum, *Rousseau*, 108.

51. Quoted from Rousseau's correspondence in ibid., 111.

52. Quoted from Rousseau's correspondence in ibid., 117.

53. Karl Marx and Friedrich Engels, "The German Ideology" in Robert C. Tucker, ed., *The Marx-Engels Reader* (New York: W.W. Norton, 1972), 114. My italics. For ease

of reference I quote from this excellent collection of the major texts, unless otherwise noted.

54. Ibid., 109. The "Theses on Feuerbach" from which I quote were written in 1845, but published in 1888. Marx and Engels characterized the Theses as well as the basic precepts of "The German Ideology" (see esp. pp. 119–21) as settling accounts with their "erstwhile philosophical conscience."

55. See Karl Marx, *Capital* (New York: The Modern Library, 1936), 534 and n. 2. I quote the original, because the footnote to which I refer is omitted from Tucker's collection.

56. Tucker, *Marx-Engels Reader*, 222, 223. These passages are taken from the chapter on the "fetishism of commodities" in the first volume of Marx's *Capital*.

57. Ibid., 343.

58. Ibid., 193. From the preface to the first edition of Marx's *Capital*.

59. Ibid., 105. Italics in the original.

60. Ibid., 428. My italics.

61. V. I. Lenin, "Better Fewer, but Better," in Robert C. Tucker, ed., *The Lenin Anthology* (New York: W.W. Norton, 1975), 743.

62. V. I. Lenin, "Imperialism, The Highest Stage of Capitalism," in ibid., 204–74.

63. V. I. Lenin, "What is to be Done?" in ibid., 51.

64. Note the parallel. Marx had "used" England and France in order to construct his theory of an economic substructure giving rise to a political superstructure. Now Lenin "used" imperialism and the distinction between a trade-unionist mentality and professional revolutionaries in order to construct his theory of historical force arising from expanding capitalism and historical direction arising from a revolutionary elite.

65. For this point I am indebted to Israel Getzler for his unpublished paper "Martov's Lenin."

66. Recently, the environmental devastations under Communist regimes have been shown to be much worse than those perpetrated under capitalist auspices. A comparative analysis of the reasons for this difference would be worthwhile.

67. Georg Lukács, *Werke*, vol. 2 (Neuwied: Luchterhand, 1968), 110.

4

Relative Backwardness and Intellectual Mobilization

Nationalism is the secular faith of the modern world. Cosmopolitan ideas took second place to national appeals during the French Revolution and the rights of man became subordinate to the duties of citizenship. In Russia more comprehensive cosmopolitan ideas were advanced by the Bolshevik Revolution of 1917, appealing to a theory of existence affecting all human history. Yet in the final decade of the twentieth century these cosmopolitan ideas are on the wane. In their place a popular protest with strong ethnic and nationalist overtones has undermined the Communist parties of Eastern Europe. This resurgence is not confined to Eastern Europe: there are ethnonationalist movements in Palestine and Ireland, in Spain and France, as well as in the Americas. We witness the culmination of a nationalist faith, which since the sixteenth century has fused nearly everywhere with the idea of government by popular mandate. Even dictatorial regimes practicing the most outrageous suppression still proclaim the popular legitimation of their rule. Just before his execution in 1989, the Rumanian dictator Nicholea Ceascescu rejected a hastily assembled military tribunal on the ground that he was solely responsible to "the working class"; yet he had been responsible for subduing by the most brutal police methods a population of 24 million people for a quarter of a century.

Nationalist movements, including this latest upsurge in Eastern Europe, have been greatly facilitated by intellectual mobilization, the growth of a reading public and of an educated secular elite dependent on learned occupations. Recognition of this mobilization need not detract from the familiar causes of economic development such as urbanization and the commercialization of land, labor, and capital. But there are movements since the sixteenth century such as the Reformation, and

85

agitation for religious autonomy, freedom, equality, and fraternity, which do not have a simple basis in the division of labor or in class interest. Nationalism is particularly noteworthy for its protean reaction to the international position of one's native country, whether it is a superpower or a "new state" searching for its identity. Ideas travel fast. In many parts of the world, people have become aware of their backwardness in comparison with some more advanced countries. Once they do, the search is on for ways to overcome backwardness and acquire a respected place among the nations.

In the twentieth century, few countries have been exempt from this condition, or they have been countries like England, France, or the United States, which possess a sense of civilizational mission, bolstered by a feeling of cultural superiority. Even after losing an empire, the English historian Eric Hobsbawm could say that the trouble with the English is that "we have no confusion as to who we are: the English are English, and anybody who isn't, isn't."[1]

Bureaucracy means the administration of public resources in accordance with established rules; and rules mean that the people to whom they apply are grouped by abstract categories in the interest of equity and efficiency. Such categories cannot take account of most matters of concern to individuals and groups. The result is that administrators disregard many differences among people in order to do their work, and groups of individuals organize in order to protest against that disregard of their interests. Ethnic mobilization is one form of that widespread, antibureaucratic tendency.

Usually, nationalist movements have a territorial base and aim at political independence. Anthony Smith distinguishes between ethnocentric and polycentric nationalism. In the first, power and value inhere in a cultural group with an exclusive relation to the transcendent powers so that all other groups are not truly human (barbarians, aliens, etc.). In the second, power and value inhere in many nations, and one's own country seeks to have, or acquire, its rightful identity and place among them. Nationalism in this polycentric sense is an "ideological movement for the attainment and maintenance of self-government and independence on behalf of a group, some of whose members conceive it to constitute an actual or potential 'nation' like others."[2]

The literature on nationalism is large and on the whole marked by efforts to define and analyze the attributes shared by people who believe themselves members of the same nation and who strive for political autonomy. But even comprehensive discussions do not exhaust the diversities of language, culture, and ethnicity existing among people who belong to a country and are treated as citizens of the same nation. Once again, social scientists consider a general term like "nation" indispensable, but are unable to define it clearly. As Max Weber put it,

> If the concept of "nation" can in any way be defined unambiguously, it certainly cannot be stated in terms of empirical qualities common to those who count as members of the nation. . . . The concept undoubtedly means that it is proper to expect from certain groups a specific sentiment of solidarity in the face of other groups. Yet, there is no agreement on how these groups should be delimited or about what concerted action should result from such solidarity.[3]

Despite these difficulties, it is useful to agree on a rudimentary meaning of the term, which may be put under three headings:

1. Common attributes. The expectation of solidarity in the face of other groups marks the nation as a type of community characterized by territorial boundaries, a common language, and an "education lasting for centuries" (Tocqueville). These shared attributes are reinforced in modern times by the rights and duties of citizenship. Such common attributes go together with a sense of belonging to the same nation. That feeling of solidarity can wax or wane as the divisions among the people, or the importance attributed to them, increase or decrease. It is a common observation that national solidarity rises quickly when people feel that their country is threatened, but becomes a matter of course and is reserved for ceremonial occasions when that threat subsides.
2. Myths. These constitutive beliefs of a nation are a secular faith, because nations "always loom out of an immemorial past and glide into a limitless future," thus simulating eternity.[4] Nationalism transforms creation myths into a people's mythic historical past and ideas of immortality into their mythic historical future.
3. Institutions. Nations in the modern sense depend upon a political structure that developed very gradually out of the representative institutions of medieval Europe. Government based on a mandate of the people made national citizens out of the subjects of a ruler. In this sense modern nations originated in the French Revolution, even though their antecedents can be traced to the distant past. Turning points like the French Revolution are noteworthy for their worldwide repercussions. The ideal of a popular mandate has spread, quite apart from the conditions that gave rise to it in eighteenth-century France, so that aspirations to nationhood have developed where none of the European institutional traditions have existed.

Intellectual mobilization has been an essential ingredient in the diffusion of the national idea. Mobilization is a precondition of the modern nation. It is also important for the "demonstration effects" from advanced to follower societies. The effect has been a division among nationalists between modernizers and nativists in one country after another.

Intellectual Mobilization

Since the sixteenth century, the world has been periodically revolutionized, if by that term we understand the thoroughgoing transformation of societies due to technical and economic changes, wars, political interventions, and the overthrow of "old regimes." In his *Novum Organum* (1620), Francis Bacon noted that printing, gunpowder, and the magnet had "changed the whole face and state of things throughout the world."[5] Guns mounted on ships were the technical means by which explorers and conquerors initiated the era of European expansion overseas.[6] The lifetimes of the explorers Columbus (1445-1506), da Gama (1469?-1524), and Magellan (1480-1521) overlapped with those of Luther (1483-1546) and Copernicus (1473-1543) so that there is a broad concurrence between exploration, overseas expansion, and the transformation of the prevailing religious and scientific worldview. All of this had been preceded by the invention of printing, the first Gutenberg Bible appearing sometime before 1455. The number of educated people increased, as did the number of those whose livelihood depended upon teaching or some other occupation dependent on the written word. The new facility of printing also explains why overseas exploration, the Reformation, and the early development of science resulted in a burgeoning literature of travelogues, religious pamphlets, as well as scientific and political tracts.[7] The term "intellectual mobilization" refers to this whole process of a more rapid reproduction and diffusion of ideas and the related increase in the number of readers and writers.

Facilitated by the invention of printing, old learned occupations turned secular, new professions based on learning developed, governments became bureaucratic, and secular education rose in social esteem and functional importance.[8] Furthermore, the Reformation gave an impetus to literacy by encouraging middle as well as lower strata of the population to read the Bible, thereby breaching the clerical monopoly of interpreting sacred texts, and promoting writing as a profession, albeit unintentionally. Before these developments, people had been confined to religious observances and popular amusements; now many of them became consumers of secular culture as well. This emergence of a culture-consuming public is the background for the intellectual leadership of an active minority composed of lawyers, teachers, ministers, writers, amateur scholars, and others. The development of such cultural elites in England and France illustrates analogous changes in many parts of the world.

In late sixteenth-century England, three groups developed that coalesced in opposition to the rule of Charles I (1625–1649). The first group consisted of Puritan divines, led by men who had been persecuted under the reign of Mary Tudor (1553–1558). After Elizabeth I came to the throne (1558), these men wanted to divest the Anglican church of its Catholic residues in doctrine and ritual. They wanted to do so from within the church through reform of the Church service, by establishing the presbyterian principle of Church organization, and through widespread lecturing.[9] The second group consisted of common lawyers, members of a conservative profession, many of whom had a guildlike interest in the common law courts as against the prerogative courts of the king.[10] The third group consisted of prominent landed gentry in Parliament, men of great standing in the realm who sponsored the Puritan clergy through their control of church benefices and employed common lawyers in their many legal disputes. These aristocratic representatives of "the country" were often legally trained and many of them were Puritans as well.[11] The ties of family, sociability, and interest that linked these three groups have been the subject of much controversy. It seems to be generally agreed that these men of faith, vested interest, and high social standing were originally prompted by the English Reformation to define the position and aspirations of their country in conscious opposition to the Spanish world empire, which was in alliance with the papal attack on the English heresy.[12]

One can put the development of eighteenth-century France in analogous terms. Louis XIV died in 1715, leaving a country that was culturally and politically preeminent in the world, but also exhausted from the decades of war leading to that position.[13] In the wake of Louis XIV's reign, opposition to the *ancien regime* and ultimately to the monarchy also showed a strong convergence of religious beliefs, vested interests, and high social standing. The *philosophes*, under the inspiration of Newton and Locke, formulated their doctrine of natural rights in opposition to the church and the nobility. The famous *Encyclopédie*, beginning its publication in 1751, linked a burgeoning natural science, which had found widespread acclaim, with the principles of reason and natural law applied to man and society. Soon, these ideas were taken up by others whose social position gave great weight to their opinions. One group consisted of the *parlementaires,* a *noblesse de robe* serving on the sovereign courts of France, primarily in a judicial capacity. These *parlementaires,* especially those of Paris, had the duty to register governmental edicts without which no royal decree was legally valid. When they refused to do so, as they often did during the eighteenth century, they used the language of the *philosophes* to justify their actions. Another group consisted of the high nobility of France, congregating not only at the court in Versailles, but in the salons and masonic lodges of Paris, where they mingled freely with the luminaries of French culture. The language of the *philosophes,* the *parlementaires,* and the nobility was suffused with ideas derived from English parliamentary institutions and from the struggle for independence of the American colonies. In this way, the opinions of the educated elite that led up to the French Revolution were mobilized by invidious comparisons between the freedoms achieved or fought for in England and America and the vested interests and abrogation of rights characteristic of the *ancien regime.*

The French Revolution and the populist revolutions that followed must be distinguished from the English revolutions of 1640 and 1688. In England, revolutionary thought was limited by the religious and legal contexts in which the old justifications of authority had been questioned. English theory and practice remained compatible with oligarchic rule, though on the new basis of the "king-in-parliament." Royal prerogative was combined with a representative body of oligarchs, whose privileges included their claim to speak for the country. By contrast, French revolutionary thought went beyond such limitations, because it attacked the monarchy as well as the aristocracy, and in their place made the will of the people and the nation the foundation of all authority. In France as well as in England the movement toward revolution was spearheaded by men of standing in the established society of their day. Unlike earlier aristocracies, they had been educated and hence had been affected by intellectual mobilization. This pioneering position of France and England was the culmination of what had made Western civilization distinctive over many centuries; and the location of this breakthrough is directly related to the shifting center of economic development from the Mediterranean to the Atlantic.

This recital of familiar facts describes the breakthrough to the modern world that originated in Western Europe. I take this to be a fact that does not arise from a Eurocentric perspective, or imply a claim of cultural superiority. The Western European origin of the developments I have sketched is rather the basis for the uneven developments of countries outside that Western European perimeter ever since the sixteenth century. Those uneven developments have been accompanied by intellectual movements that sought to mobilize the people in order to combat their country's position of relative backwardness. Of course, uneven developments have occurred throughout history as a byproduct of innovation and conflict.

The breakthrough resulted in an outward thrust through overseas explorations and eventual colonization. Very old societies have lain on the periphery of that thrust, whether one considers countries on other continents or those that lie to the east within Europe itself. Of course, these societies had important cultural and institutional developments of their own. But none of them possessed the vigorous, indigenous developments that had led to the breakthrough in Western Europe, such as representative institutions, an economically and politically active aristocracy and bourgeoisie, or an educated elite pioneering in science and administration. On the periphery of "the West," these old societies became arenas of intellectual mobilization, in which officials, teachers, literary people, and others coalesced into loosely associated groups of their own. There is a correlation between economic backwardness and this kind of intellectual mobilization, which the German folklorist Wilhelm Riehl already described in the 1840s. Riehl characterized the motley group of educated people without status in their society as an "intellectual proletariat" (*Proletarier der Geistesarbeit*):

> Intellectual work shoots up like weeds, because economic enterprise does not provide it with sufficiently extensive opportunities for growth, and this growth in turn cannot come to fruition, because every surplus of energy is dissipated in an endless foliage of books.[14]

Riehl's attention was focused on Germany in the mid-nineteenth century. He only failed to see that intellectual mobilization applies more generally as an attribute of follower societies developing a national identity. In this respect, pioneering countries like England and France were the exception, because their political, economic, and intellectual mobilization occurred more or less simultaneously, and with the participation of leading groups in society. Outside these pioneering countries with their sense of an imperial mission, intellectual mobilization comprises educated people, often of low social status, who are sensitive to developments beyond their country's frontier as well as anxious to find a more viable mode of social organization for their native land.

Demonstration Effects

Social change as ever-recurring phenomenon should be distinguished from revolutions. The latter occur only when a social order is dramatically transformed and reconstituted, whether this is initiated from below as in France and Russia or from above as in Japan's Meiji Restoration. These and other revolutionary transformations of modern history were brought to a head by intellectual mobilization, even though they were caused by cumulative antecedents in all aspects of society. That mobilization began with the invention of printing in the fifteenth century and has been accelerating through new forms of communication ever since. Communication and intellectual mobilization cannot remain indigenous developments. More often than not, educated people take their cues from developments abroad, usually combining imitations of those developments with resistance against their repercussions. As a result, each revolution or restoration of modern history since the sixteenth century has influenced the next.

In the sixteenth and seventeenth centuries, England underwent the great upheaval of the Henrician Reformation (1534, 1536), the civil war and revolution of 1640–1660, and the "Glorious Revolution" of 1688. Each of these turning points had important indigenous antecedents, but at least the first two also responded to developments abroad. The English Reformation followed Luther's earlier challenge to the Catholic church (1517) and the civil war followed a long development of representative institutions on the continent as well as in England. One might even speculate that the balance achieved between Crown and country in the revolution of 1688 owed not a little to the paradoxical reinforcement by the Norman conquest (1066) of tendencies toward representation, first formalized by the Magna Carta of 1215.

Many other developments of pioneering countries like England or France, or follower societies like Germany and Japan, show such demonstration effects. The English "Industrial Revolution" of the eighteenth century was facilitated by long-run technical and scientific developments that had preceded it on the Continent. The French Revolution was stimulated by developments in England and America. The whole German enlightenment of the eighteenth century as well as the Prussian institutional reforms (1807-1814) were greatly influenced by earlier developments in France. The unification of Germany under Bismarck (1870-1871), occurring as it did after more than a millennium of political separatism, was in part a by-product of colonial rivalries among the European powers. The Meiji restoration of Japan in 1868 was a response to the opening of her harbors, which the U.S. Navy under Commander Perry forced upon the country in 1853-54. Finally, the Bolshevik Revolution of 1917 was preceded by an intellectual mobilization under the tsars that went back to the Decembrist revolt of 1825 by Russian army officers and intellectuals who had been inspired by Western European constitutional ideas. A century earlier, Peter the Great (1689-1725) had been inspired by the technical and economic innovations of Holland and England.

In whatever form these influences from abroad appeared, none of them could take hold without intellectual mobilization. The revolutions or restorations I have listed, as well as the many others that have occurred since the sixteenth century, were collective responses to conditions inside and outside the society, and with repercussions beyond the frontiers of the country in which they occurred. After each transformation, the world had changed in keeping with the saying of Heraclitus that you cannot step into the same river twice. Personal rulers are always at risk, but once the English king Charles I had been executed in 1649, the monarchical institution was in jeopardy. After parliamentary rule was stabilized in England, the idea of parliamentary government was launched abroad. Once industrialization had been initiated, other economies became more backward by comparison, both technically and in the minds of the people. Once the French Revolution had proclaimed the idea of legal equality before a worldwide audience, inequality became a burden too heavy to bear.[15]

Inequality as an accepted condition of life prevailed until well into the nineteenth century. Therefore, the breakup of the old patriarchal order cannot be understood solely in terms of its final phase. Masters ruled over their servants in the household as the king ruled over his subjects throughout his realm. In Tocqueville's view, the "whole course of society" since the eleventh century had been marked by an increasing equality of condition. Wars dispersed and diminished noble estates. The clergy acquired power and opened its ranks to all classes. Commoners obtained high positions at court, enriched themselves through commerce, and acquired title by purchase. Every improvement in trade and manufacture, every acquisition of property, and every discovery in the arts created "new elements of equality," as did the great historical events of this long period.

> The Crusades and the English wars decimated the nobles and divided their possessions; the municipal corporations introduced democratic liberty into the bosom of feudal monarchy; the invention of firearms equalized the vassal and the noble on the field of battle; the art of printing opened the same resources to the minds of all classes; the post brought knowledge alike to the door of the cottage and to the gate of the palace; and protestantism proclaimed that all men are equally able to find the road to heaven. The discovery of America opened a thousand new paths to fortune and led obscure adventurers to wealth and power.[16]

Little would be gained by trying to "complete" this list of changes. Tocqueville was right in emphasizing the very gradual spread of ideas and practices whose equalitarian effects are discernable only in retrospect. However, he did not examine the processes of communication and intellectual mobilization, by which such ideas spread from country to country.

Advances in one part of the world have provided impulses for change in others. Sixteenth-century England was still comparatively slow in the commercialization of labor and capital, but the country witnessed a flourishing trade, the rapid commercialization of land, and a high degree of intellectual mobilization. The awakening of national awareness and self-confidence mixed with apprehension was due in good part to English perceptions of Spanish, French, and papal intentions. Spain dominated the western Mediterranean and encircled the globe, France dominated Europe, and the pope controlled an international church with hierarchical connections in all the relevant countries. The Spanish empire, the French kingdom and the Catholic church were the "reference societies" to which England's intellectual leaders and her educated public responded emotionally and politically.

The results of those responses may be termed "demonstration effects," which were effective long before the modern development of communications.[17] Henri Pirenne has shown that in the eleventh century the merchant and craft guilds of a few cities used force to win recognition of an independent jurisdiction from their feudal overlords. A good many other rulers "took the hint" and negotiated settlements with their own towns before armed conflict broke out.[18] But while demonstration effects of one society on another are probably universal, change through intellectual mobilization has certainly accelerated in the modern period. Germany is a prototype of an early follower-society. As a reaction to French antecedents, German rulers of the eighteenth and nineteenth centuries, in their efforts to maintain their inherited authority, proposed to do for "their" people by a revolution from above what the French people had done at high cost by and for themselves.[19] German classical literature can be understood as a development of successive and creative responses to cultural stimuli emanating from France, often as a conscious effort to form a distinctively German cultural profile.

While France provided major cultural and political stimuli, England pioneered the development of a modern economy. Since modern industrialization began in England, other countries followed the English model when they began to develop their own industry. However, they wished to follow the latest English development to which they could gain access, not the English practices of the 1760s with which England's own industrialization had begun. Countries were, therefore, less and less able or willing to repeat the developments of the more advanced country.[20] Demonstration effects themselves prevent countries from repeating earlier developments elsewhere, thus hindering the cultural and institutional convergence of industrial societies postulated by theories of economic determinism.

In the twentieth century, the Russian Revolution and the Soviet regime became the reference society for China after 1949 and for countries like Cuba and Vietnam, whose Communist development cannot be explained by postwar Russian occupation as in Eastern Europe. Russia's overthrow of an autocratic regime in an economically backward country, the collectivization of agriculture and the forced pace of large-scale industrialization were achieved at enormous cost, and by methods that entailed long-run liabilities. The Chinese reacted against this Russian model under Mao Tse-Tung by accepting a slower rate of economic growth and by emphasizing the peasantry, by conducting reeducation campaigns, and by placing importance on subjective commitment as a major cause of change. These two models differ in many other respects as did their demonstration effects beyond their frontiers.

Coping with Backwardness

In comparison with an advanced society or societies, the educated minority or intelligentsia of a country sees its native land as backward. This is a troubled perception, for it identifies strength if not goodness with alien forces and sees weakness if not evil in the land of one's birth. In response to this setting, ideas are typically used to locate and mobilize forces capable of effecting change and of redressing this injury to national and personal pride. As viewed from the perspective of backwardness, the strength of the advanced country is certainly formidable, but it is weakened by spiritual decay; "therefore" that advance is spurious because it should not, and will not, endure. At the same time, and despite the weakness of one's native land, its spiritual riches and the untapped sources of the people's strength will prevail in the end. Accordingly, the dominance of the advanced country carries within it the seeds of its own destruction, while the people of the backward country possess unused capacities that portend a bright future. In this set of interlocking beliefs, the advanced country is ultimately weak because its people are evil, while the backward country is ultimately strong because its people are good.

When sensitive and articulate men and women suffer from the weakness and deprivation that is all around them, they will leave no avenue untried to better the fortunes of their country and its people. When practical measures to do so are unavailable or insufficient, free play is given to ideas. The result is a kaleidoscope of national aspirations linked to a world history of uneven developments and increasing inequalities. Secular prophecy has been an important factor in nationalist efforts to achieve the social and economic development of backward countries by routes other than those already traversed by a pioneering society.

Karl Marx stated that "the country that is more developed industrially only shows, to the less developed, the image of its own future," and Alexander Herzen wrote even more optimistically that "human development is a form of chronological unfairness, since late-comers are able to profit by the labors of their predecessors without paying the same price."[21] Such progressive views of the mid-nineteenth century failed to consider the unprecedented problems facing each "modernizing" country, the human suffering that development exacts, and the uncertainty of the outcome. Even the advanced countries that had been building their political institutions over the centuries still had to cope with the liabilities incurred by industrialization and the whole process of modernization, even where these proved to be successful. Near the end of the twentieth century, there are poignant reminders of these liabilities in the repercussions of slavery for American race relations, or of the troubled political and religious history of Ireland for English civilization. If that is the case in two advanced countries, one can get a measure of the enormous problems facing the "new states," which have more models to choose from than before but which for the most part lack institutional structures and cultural preconditions that can facilitate economic advance and political restructuring.

Riehl's characterization of the discrepancy between economic backwardness and intellectual mobilization applies not only to Germany and other countries during the nineteenth century. The same discrepancy applies to most countries of the Third World today. Educated people react strongly, even frantically, to the extreme backwardness of their country in comparison with advanced countries.

Examples and techniques taken from abroad are, or can be, actual assets to the economic development of a country, but they are also a reminder of its comparative backwardness. Such images are both a challenge to be emulated and a threat to national identity. What appears desirable from the standpoint of material progress often appears dangerous to national self-respect and independence. The revolution in communications since the fifteenth century has been accompanied by ever-new confrontations with this cruel dilemma, and the rise of nationalism has been the response nearly everywhere.

Theoretical Implications

Why has nationalism become the secular faith of the modern world? So far I have summarized major historical trends leading to intellectual mobilization and the demonstration effects of advanced economic and political developments. One can approach the same question from a more theoretical perspective by contrasting class-formation and nation-building. Both are important, but modern history since the French Revolution seems to give the edge to the latter. Why? To answer this question one can contrast class and nation as two definitions of the human community. Both are appeals to solidarity that can be related to the human life cycle.

Children are affected by class primarily through their dependence on the economic status of their parents. Marx saw this dependence as exploitation of children by their parents in response to oppression by the capitalist class. Yet we have learned that the economic and emotional exploitation of children occurs at all levels of society, not only among working-class families and not only as a result of oppression. By contrast, an emphasis on the nation would give greater weight to the child's socialization, the acquisition of cultural and linguistic skills as major elements in identity formation.

Much the same argument applies to adolescence. The capacity for idealistic commitment is at its height prior to full entry into the labor force. That helps to account for the prominence of students in liberation movements of every kind. Adolescence is the most important phase of identity formation, and national allegiance satisfies the underlying need more readily than class interest.

Marx gave special attention to marriage and the family because he sensed that family interests were antagonistic to class consciousness, just as Rousseau thought them antagonistic to the general will of the nation. Perhaps it is as simple as the contrast between selfishness and altruism. The *Communist Manifesto* declares that under capitalism family relations among the bourgeoisie are mere money relations, while among workers exploitation leads to the practical absence of the family and to prostitution. Much the same argument is applied to the nation. Nationalism is a bourgeois prejudice that serves the interests of capital, while the workers have no country. Both conditions will be eradicated through the internationalization of capitalism and the class struggle, which will lead to the eventual abolition of classes along with the abolition of nations.[22]

There is much truth in the idea that economic individualism militates against family cohesion. But while modern families often disintegrate, nationalism continues to thrive. Why? Tocqueville's answer was that the erosion of families and the viability of national governments go together. He starts from the secular rise of equality and individualism, which leads each person to advance his own ventures independently. As long as things go well, one has no need of assistance and each thrives on his own isolation. When things go badly, one cannot appeal to the assistance of others who are likewise engaged in isolated ventures even if they are members of one's own family. Accordingly, enterprising individuals appeal to the government for assistance that they can no longer expect from their fellow men.[23] In this way, the whole growth of the welfare state is not just the result of the class struggle, but of the multifarious pressures that individuals and groups isolated from one another bring to bear on government for services and assistance. Dependence on government underscores the importance of the nation.

Aging shows the ambiguity of interest as an explanatory factor. Marx's conception of class somehow takes it for granted that material interest retains the same meaning throughout the life cycle. This is false for personal as well as economic reasons. As we grow older, we become increasingly dependent on our previous investments of time and effort because the skills we acquired in the past become more difficult to change. Vested interests of this kind are a main reason for the welfare state. Only the national government can make up for the cumulative liabilities of aging, which consist in part in preserving the economic value of skills acquired over a lifetime. For these several reasons "nation" rather than "class" has proved to be the more important explanation of human behavior in the modern world.

Current Concerns

The contemporary world has made us familiar with the tension between progress and national identity. Each country must cope socially and politically with the disruptive impact of ideas and industrial practices taken from abroad. Its ability or inability to do so is conditioned to a considerable extent by its own history. The advanced countries of today have had their own periods of underdevelopment and of responding to the "advanced world" of their day. They had to grapple for centuries with internal divisions and the problems of political integration and still struggle (as all countries must) with the unresolved legacies of their histories. Terms in the singular like "state" or "nation" play down or ignore these persistent divisions, but their political unity remains a proximate achievement, even when it is not in doubt.

More recently, new states have emerged from very old societies that look back upon centuries of experience with a mixture of languages, religious beliefs, and economic systems. This is the base from which they must master the impact of the "advanced world." Only by understanding the peculiarities of each affected civilization can one assess how different countries will cope or will fail to cope with the ideas and institutions of the industrially and politically influential countries. In the new states of the "Third World," the predominance of civil ties over the affinities of language, religion, and ethnicity is a recent and precarious development. Fifty-one countries founded the United Nations in 1945; by 1988, 108 additional countries had become sovereign. Most new states have had to establish their governments on a new basis and define "the people" as the ultimate source of authority. In this setting, nationalist appeals are heard frequently.

However, nationalism, while a nearly universal phenomenon in modern history, is not a force that easily unifies countries. In fact, once countries have to come to terms with challenges from abroad, their intellectual mobilization is frequently a period of intellectual polarization as well. Typically, modernizers are opposed by nativists. In eighteenth- and nineteenth-century Japan, advocates of Dutch learning wanted to complement their native heritage with Western knowledge, while advocates of national learning wanted to derive all guidance from the Japanese tradition. In seventeenth-century Russia, the Nikonian reformers battled the Old Believers over the introduction of foreign ideas into the Orthodox church, while in the nineteenth century Westernizers and Slavophiles argued over the best way of preserving and enhancing "Mother Russia." A Westernizer like Alexander Herzen commented on his "affinity" with the Slavophiles: "Like Janus, or the two-headed eagle, we looked in opposite directions, but one heart beats in our breasts."[24] In the early twentieth century, some Chinese intellectuals used the Western model of "Mr. Science" and "Mr. Democracy" as their guide, while neo-Confucian scholars sought to elaborate their own ancient tradition.

Intellectuals attempt to cope with the dilemma of adopting an advanced model and invite its attendant corruptions, or falling back upon native tradition and risk its inappropriateness to the world of power and progress. Both parties share the concern with their native country; the heated debates and uneasy compromises between them are the foundation of modern nationalism. Educated people want their country recognized and respected in the world, and to this end even the modernizers reconstruct its history in an effort to resacralize authority in the name of the people. Appeals to civic loyalty and national brotherhood abound, while divisive communal attachments are excoriated because birth in a common homeland makes all people members of one nation sharing equally in its past glories. The desire to be recognized and respected in the world also calls for the development of a modern economy and government, and that focuses attention upon the advanced country of one's choice.

Still, at the end of the twentieth century we must add a new pattern of coping with the problem of backwardness: the decolonization movements in Eastern Europe, including the Soviet Union. These are also old societies struggling to become new states, but they are a case apart insofar as they were politically independent before they were occupied by tsarist Russia or the Soviet Union. The *Communist Manifesto* of 1848 began with the sentence: "A specter is haunting Europe—the specter of Communism." Now looking back from the last decade of the twentieth century, we have to say that two specters have haunted Europe: the specter of Communism and the specter of Germany. Though the specter of Communism is receding, a reunified Germany makes many wonder whether the country will come to haunt us once again.

An earlier version of this chapter was published in Reinhard Bendix, *Force, Fate and Freedom* (Berkeley: University of California Press, 1984), chapter 6. The present text contains substantial revisions.

Notes

1. Quoted in Jane Kramer, "Letter from Europe," *The New Yorker* (14 January 1991), 60.
2. Anthony Smith, *Theories of Nationalism* (London: Gerald Buckworth, 1977), 171. See also pp. 158–60. The second edition of 1983 has appeared under the American imprint of Holmes & Meier with an important new preface surveying the more recent literature.
3. Max Weber, *Economy and Society*, vol. 2, trans. and ed. Guenther Roth and Claus Wittich (New York: The Bedminster Press, 1968), 922.
4. Benedict Anderson, *Imagined Communities* (New York: Verso Press, 1981), 19.
5. Francis Bacon, "Novum Organum," in E. A. Burtt, *The English Philosophers from Bacon to Mill* (New York: The Modern Library, 1939), 85.
6. Carlo Cipolla, *Guns and Sails in the Early Phase of European Expansion, 1400–1700* (London: Collins, 1965).
7. Elizabeth Eisenstein, *The Printing Press as an Agent of Change* (New York: Cambridge University Press, 1979).
8. A. M. Carr-Saunders and P. A. Wilson, *The Professions* (London: Frank Cass, 1964).
9. Michael Walzer, *The Revolution of the Saints* (New York: Atheneum, 1970).
10. W. R. Prest, *The Inns of Court under Elizabeth and the Early Stuarts* (London: Longmans, 1972).
11. P. Zagorin, *The Court and the Country, The Beginning of the English Revolution* (New York: Atheneum, 1971).

12. G. Wiener, "The Beleaguered Isle, a Study of Elizabethan and Early Stuart Anti-Catholicism," *Past and Present*, no. 51 (May 1971), 27-62.
13. Pierre Goubert, *Louis XIV and Twenty Million Frenchmen* (New York: Random House, 1970).
14. Wilhelm Riehl, *Die bürgerliche Gesellschaft* (Stuttgart: Cotta, 1930), 312-13.
15. Reinhard Bendix, "Tradition and Modernity Reconsidered," in *Embattled Reason*, vol. 1 (New Brunswick, NJ: Transaction Publishers 1988), chapter 12.
16. Alexis de Tocqueville, *Democracy in America*, vol. 1 (New York: A.A.Knopf, 1948), 5.
17. The term "reference society" is modeled after Robert Merton's concept of "reference group" and "demonstration effect" is familiar from economic theory.
18. Henri Pirenne, *Medieval Cities* (New York: Doubleday, 1956), 121-37.
19. Klaus Epstein, *The Genesis of German Conservatism* (Princeton, NJ: Princeton University Press, 1966), 391.
20. Alexander Gerschenkron, *Economic Backwardness in Historical Perspective* (New York: Praeger, 1965).
21. Karl Marx, preface to the first edition of *Capital* in Robert C. Tucker, ed., *The Marx-Engels Reader* (New York: W. W. Norton, 1972), 193. Herzen's statement is quoted in Avrahm Yarmolinsky, *Road to Revolution* (New York: Macmillan, 1962), 73.
22. Karl Marx and Friedrich Engels, *The Communist Manifesto* in Tucker, ed., *Marx-Engels Reader*, 338-39, 349-50.
23. Tocqueville, *Democracy in America*, vol. 2, 311-12.
24. Quoted in Yarmolinsky, *Road to Revolution*, 73.

5

The Case of Germany

Eighteenth-century Germany was a backward society compared with France and England. Each of her 260 sovereign territories had a princely court bent on following the model of Versailles. French was spoken at court and in aristocratic circles, while German was considered a lower-class dialect. Economic development was hampered by a multitude of weights and measures, customs dues, and currencies. Trade on the great rivers was slowed as a result, and unlike England, there were few canals. The German territorites were backward in comparison with English science and technology else the German craftsmen would not have traveled so frequently to England to acquire the latest technical expertise. Germany was politically backward as well. Her estate assemblies were much less significant than the English Parliament, and German princely rule appeared petty and imitative in comparison with the absolute monarchy of France. In political theory, German writers took their cue from Montesquieu and Rousseau. By instituting a constitutional order of popular sovereignty, the French Revolution provided educated Germans with a world historical model that dominated their thought. The question is how Germany reacted to this palpable backwardness in view of the tenacious peculiarities of the country, which were the "consequence of an education that ha[d] lasted for centuries" (Tocqueville).

It is important to guard against the fallacy of retrospective determinism. The German historical development, like any other, is *not* the outcome of an inevitable cumulation of causes. In the past the future was as uncertain as it is today, although in retrospect one is always tempted to bypass possible developments because of the weight of what has happened. The role of alternative possibilities must always be kept in mind, even if attention is focused elsewhere. Put differently, we should be on guard against the idea that events that occurred were unavoidable. Hence, we should think of history in terms of the assets and liabilities of our situation, allowing for the role played by chance and alternative possibilities.[1] By dealing with the peculiarities of the German tradition, I bypass events that would allow for a consideration of alternative developments.

To provide the setting, a historical reminder is in order. The territorial and political divisions of eighteenth-century Germany had a millenial prehistory in the Holy Roman Empire of the German nation. The formal abolition of that empire occurred in 1806 under the impact of Napoleon's conquest of Europe. Then, in 1820, the Allied powers that had defeated Napoleon at Waterloo (1815) established a new German Federation of some thirty-nine sovereign territories. A half century later, following the Franco-Prussian war of 1870–71, Germany was unified for the first time in a thousand years. This political unity lasted for seventy-four years. During this period Germany helped to initiate World War I, established one of the worst tyrannies of human history, and then caused World War II. At the end of World War II, the Yalta agreement of 1945 stipulated the division between East and West Germany. In 1989, the withdrawal of Soviet power from Eastern Europe nullified that postwar settlement and in 1990 led to the second unification of the country.

Within this historical setting, German culture has been marked by a contradiction. Goethe (1749–1832) wrote that an individual's personality is the greatest happiness of humankind. Yet during his lifetime, the ancient Greek community with its language and culture was considered worthy of emulation as humanity's highest achievement, an emulation in which German scholars played a leading role on behalf of their country. In a uniquely German way, personality was considered the result of a cultivation (*Bildung*) that paralleled the natural spirit (*Geist*) of the people (*Volk*) as embodied in their language. This consonance between person and community was a cultural and unpolitical version of Rousseau's educational and political idea of the general will.[2] Many familiar attributes of Germany such as emphasis on learning, bureaucracy, work ethic, nationalism, and others have been associated with these ideas. They are the constitutive elements of the German concept of community.

There is a distinctively German idea of a nation of culture with a cultural mission. These ideas were caught up in the national liberation movement against Napoleonic rule. In the process, humanist education merged the idealization of Ancient Greece and of the German people, a blend of communalism and personal identity. The special fate of the educated elite in the failed revolution of 1848, the political unification of 1871, and its further developments in the Wilhelmine and post-Wilhelmine period were very important in this process. While in its own eyes this elite (or *Bildungsbürgertum*) represented the best of the country, opposition to the Wilhelmine establishment flourished as well. It consisted in both a manifold artistic reaction to its stultifying effects and the frontline experience of soldiers in World War I, which was rationalized as another reaction to that stultification. The outbreak of the war was greeted with initial enthusiasm in many countries. Germany was probably unique in having important groups use the symbol of a wartime comradeship at arms, common soldiers under the leadership of an ideal officer, as a political model for the reorganization of society in times of peace. My aim is to characterize an educational tradition that has left liabilities down to the present.[3]

A Nation of Culture

Eighteenth-century Germany was a case of relative backwardness and intellectual mobilization. Under these conditions, the German definition of community was not at first concerned with national identity, although that concern was brought to the fore following the French Revolution and Napoleon's sweep of Europe. The division of the country into many principalities, imperial cities, and bishoprics discouraged any notion that "Germany" was one country rather than many. Each territory was under the patriarchal rule of a prince, a patrician elite, or a bishop, so that the dominant idea of community was the hierarchical relation between a ruler and his subjects.

It is useful to start with Germany's most famous man of letters, Johann Wolfgang Goethe. Like all his contemporaries, he was acutely aware of German dependence upon the countries to the West. He fashioned a unique creative synthesis out of that experience that provided a model for future generations. Goethe did not admire the French Revolution because the terror repelled him and any future benefits were still unknown. He was also troubled by the revolutionary agitation in Germany, which appeared to him artificial in contrast to France, where such agitation had resulted from a "great necessity." In his view, revolutions occur because governments fail to be alert to necessary changes until it is too late and radical change is forced upon them from below. Govern-ments, he thought, must adapt to the constant change in human affairs, and become arbitrary when they support what is bad and outdated. Yet change is beneficial only if it accords with what "comes naturally" to a country, so that the imposition of foreign innovations will fail if they run counter to a country's tradition. Goethe believed that revolutions like those of Christ and Luther were beneficial because they undid what was untrue, unjust, and deficient.[4]

Goethe was not nearly so detached in his own field of endeavor. He felt that artists in Germany were impoverished in their isolation and experienced very little response from their own people. Men of talent lived apart from each other so that personal contacts and intellectual stimulation were rare. Compare that with a city like Paris where the best minds of a large realm were in daily communication, sought to excel one another, where all the riches of nature and art were on display, and where every bridge and plaza was replete with historical associations.

> We Germans are outdated. For about a century, our cultivation has improved, to be sure. But it may take several more centuries before a higher culture and spirit becomes rooted among our people. Only then will they be able, like the Greeks, to admire beauty or become enthusiastic about a pretty song, and one can then say of them, that it has been a long time since they were barbarians.[5]

There was no "Paris" on Goethe's German horizon and he was opposed to national unification.

He had a list of the changes he wanted to see: good roads and the development of the railroads, a common currency, a common standard of weights and measures, no customs or passport controls among the principalities, and no invidious distinctions among them as if they were foreign territories. In Goethe's view, an admirable culture pervaded the country. Though the people remained unresponsive, Germany had some twenty universities, over a hundred public libraries, over seventy theaters and even more musical organizations, a large number of art collections and naturalist exhibits, Gymnasia and technical schools in abundance, and a school in every village. Goethe wrote a veritable paean to the beauty of the small community:

> Every prince has seen to it that such good and beautiful things are nearby. . . . It is not only the several principalities . . . which sponsor and cultivate [that development] . . . Frankfurt, Bremen, Hamburg, Lübeck [and other cities] are great and brilliant, their effects on the prosperity of Germany is hard to calculate. I have reason to doubt

that they would remain what they are, if they lost their own sovereignty and were incorporated as provincial towns in some larger German Reich.[6]

True, these conversations reflect the serenity of an old man who had served his prince in an important office with distinction, and who spoke "for the establishment." But let us look at a trajectory of his work, in order to see how he came to terms in the provincial setting he described in old age with the conflicting imperatives of the individual and the community.

In his youth, his hymn to Prometheus projected the image of a half-divine creator who forms human beings by himself in defiance of the gods. And just like their Promethean creator, these beings "suffer, cry, savor and enjoy" in total independence from the higher powers. In his middle years, Goethe wrote *Hermann und Dorothea*, a poetic celebration of the quiet home of good people who watch the upheavals caused by the nearby armies of the French Revolution. The heroes of this epic are moved by pity and fear, conscious of their community as a safe haven still distant from the terrors of great events. Looking back upon it, he said that everything in *Hermann und Dorothea* was "reasonable, bourgeois, without great passion or poetic imagination." These qualities have an affinity with the retreat to the hearth and home of the Lutheran pastor (*Pfarrhaus*), scanty but emotionally rewarding in its inwardness, which was a main theme of German literature throughout the nineteenth century. Then in old age, Goethe concluded the second part of *Faust* with an image that united the celebration of Promethean striving with the hero's final immersion into the human community. At last, the Faustian creator and supreme individualist, having faced danger throughout a life spent in active endeavor, now stands surrounded by the throng of humankind and shares his freedom with the freedom of the multitude.[7] Though it refers to "the people," this lofty vision is deeply antipolitical. Despite his own extensive experience as a distinguished public servant in Saxony-Weimar, Goethe would not have a writer[8] "meddle" in public affairs. In his view, the poet should rather be like "an eagle which soars with untrammeled view across the lands, utterly indifferent whether the rabbit on which he pounces is running in Prussia or Saxony."[9]

Accordingly, Goethe's work encompasses the cultural problems arising for his contemporaries from Germany's backwardness in comparison with France and England. German teachers and writers had to come to terms with what was presented to them as the cultural, political, and

material progress occurring beyond their frontiers, and did so through
intellectual mobilization.[10] The German fascination with the French
Enlightenment was followed by abhorrence at the terror of the revolution,
consternation at the revolutionary wars, and revulsion mixed with awe
at Napoleon's conquest of Europe. Prussia's military defeat and the
French occupation of German territory complicated this reaction. In
response to this welter of experience, none of the German-educated
public could match Goethe's serenity. One need only contrast his dispassion with the excitation of Friedrich Hölderlin (1770-1843). In a famous
couplet of 1796 Goethe and Schiller pointed out that German hopes to
build a nation were futile, that instead Germans should aim at the
cultivation (*Bildung*) of their human qualities.[11] By contrast, here is
Friedrich Hölderlin's formulation of the same idea, written in 1799:

> It is a harsh statement and yet I say it, because it is the truth: I cannot think of a people
> more torn apart than the Germans. You see artisans but not men, thinkers but not men,
> masters and servants, youths and established people but not men. Is it not like a
> battlefield where hands and arms and all limbs lie about dismembered, while the
> spilled lifeblood melts into the sand?[12]

Among leading German writers allowance must be made for this grating
sense of provincial inferiority. Another example that expresses the same
sentiment midway between Goethe's serenity and Hölderlin's passion
was Johann Gottfried Herder (1744-1803) who wrote a poem in 1789
that called upon Germans to wake up and unite. In the East they bordered
on a Russia that had developed with the aid of German teachers; in the
West they faced the power and thriving culture of France. "Is your name
to waft away? Are your fathers, your own heart, your language not
worthy above all else?"[13]

The idea of a nation of indigenous culture as an alternative to national
dependence on foreign models of politics, literature, or science can be
considered a compensatory response. The classicist J. J. Winckelmann
(1717-68) and the poet Friedrich Georg Klopstock (1724-1803) exemplify the combative reaction of the day, and may be taken as representative of the communalism and individualism that has marked German
culture ever since.

Winckelmann's national and cultural objectives were explicit: "The
only way for us to become great and possibly even inimitable is to imitate
the Ancients . . . particularly the Greeks, [whose works of art embody] a
noble simplicity and quiet greatness." However contradictory, the state-

ment projects an ideal image of ancient Greece as a nation of culture, and this image had a major impact on German education in the nineteenth century. The ideal had several components:

1. The cultural development of ancient Greece is both original and autonomous, hence it follows its own laws (*Eigengesetzlichkeit*) and in the process totally transforms foreign influences.
2. By virtue of its internal unity Greek culture expresses the holistic character of its people (*Volkscharakter*) in all its political, spiritual, and artistic achievements.
3. The idealism and self-expression of ancient Greece finds its consummation in art.
4. Accordingly, ancient Greek culture, though it manifests the character of one people, embodies at the same time the loftiest totality of which humanity is capable and hence the principal object of humanistic studies.[14]

Not surprisingly, Winckelmann had a low opinion of the French and English writers who rejected his idealization of antiquity. His aim was to create works in German so unprecedented that they would show foreigners what Germans were capable of achieving. Winckelmann's defensive-aggressive posture is transparent. He uses the ideal community of the inimitable ancients as a way of achieving German cultural autonomy (if not superiority) in opposition to French and English culture. Until near the end of the nineteenth century, that posture influenced generations of the German-educated elite (*Bildungsbürgertum*), a theme to which I return below.

The personal side of this idealization comes into view when one considers the work of Klopstock. In his poetry, Klopstock cultivated a language far removed from everyday experience, full of enthusiasm, exaltation, passion, and inward feeling. Prose is appropriate for reasoning and mundane matters, following a regular syntax. But poetry follows a logic of its own, corresponding to the incomparable position and autonomy with which the poet, by the singularity of his language, expresses his intense excitation. In *Dichtung und Wahrheit*, Goethe praises Klopstock for having initiated a period in which poetic genius becomes aware of itself, consciously creates the conditions under which he can work and thereby lays the foundations of its own independent dignity. He concludes his eloquent description of Klopstock's *Messiah* by stating, "The dignity of the [poetic] theme increased in the poet the feeling of his own personality."[15] That comment underscores the embattled position of German writers in the eighteenth century. In the face of aristocratic disdain and despite Germany's relative backwardness in science, politics, and economic development, they were striving to establish their own autonomy as well as a communal ideal with which they could identify.

In this setting, Goethe as the poet laureate of the *Kulturnation* became emblematic for the whole country. His view of the human condition encompassed Promethean, domestic, and communal themes while espousing detachment from public affairs.[16] To subsequent generations he was not only a great artist and philosopher. He became a cultural hero and symbol, which educated people used to reinforce a humanistic tradition modeled on ancient Greece and education as the foundation of the educated elite or *Bildungsbürgertum*. The ideal of that education was the general cultivation of an individual's capacities (*allgemeine Menschenbildung*).[17] There are other ways of characterizing Germany as a follower society with her special blend of communalism and individualism. There is little dispute that the ideal of *Bildung* is one of Germany's distinguishing characteristics.

A Cultural Mission

The German humanists of the eighteenth century, Wilhelm von Humboldt (1767–1835) foremost among them, advanced an educational ideal that challenged contemporary education. In the prevailing estate society it was customary to prepare children for their prospective station in life and their submission to the established order. Rights were recognized only as part of a family inheritance, and were typically confined to the upper strata of society. However, by the late eighteenth century, enlightened opinion was sensitized to impending change, whether these consisted of an emerging industrial society in England or of human rights broadcast by the French Revolution. The ideal of an education aiming at the fullest but disciplined development of the individual's personality was a challenge in all three contexts. Attention to every human being subverted the idea of immutable inequalities in an estate society. A general education modeled on an idealization of classical Greece was at odds with a training adapted to an increasing division of labor. Although the ideal of *Bildung* was greatly indebted to Rousseau's educational program, it proved to be inimical to any political conception of human rights. For all these reasons educational reform set German culture apart and, in the minds of its advocates, tended to provide the country and its people with a superior national identity.

According to Humboldt, reform was aimed at the nation as a whole. Its goal was the development of human capacities: memory training, mental acuity, firm judgment, formal abilities, as well as the refinement of moral sentiments. These qualities are "equally necessary for all social ranks." In Humboldt's view, once character and independence are achieved, they could be combined with "the skill and knowledge indispensable for each occupation."[18] The *Bildung* of man in his entirety, *Menschheitsbildung*, is prior to the education of the citizen (*Bürger*) and to all specialized training. The introduction of either civic or occupational subjects into the schools was seen as an affront to humanity. Humboldt believed that youths educated in this humanistic sense (*Gebildete*) will create a better social and political order. That goal can be best achieved by learning classical Greek.

> If the learning of Greek, solely as a language, is the great and well-understood aim, not the inconvenient means to some distant gainful pursuit, and if that aim is a national one, which is as dear to the prince as it is to the lowest of his future subjects, then [it follows that] the learning of the Greek language is necessary for our entire people without regard to birth, status, or future destination—distinctions which a true education of youth should never take into account.[19]

This identification of a nation of culture (*Kulturnation*) with ancient Greece derived its force from Humboldt's conviction that the Greeks in the multifaceted and harmonious development of their faculties came closest to the "idea of the purely human," "the character of MAN as such." Or, as Friedrich Schlegel (1772–1829) put it, the Greeks are "the strongest, purest, most definite, simplest, and most complete image of general human nature."[20]

These celebrations of ancient Greece combined a total immersion of the individual in the community, a total individualism based on the full development of human faculties, and the identification of ancient Greece as the consummate development of mankind. This heady mixture had equally heady connotations. Language is the soul of the nation, embodying its image of the world. Humboldt believed that, if properly conducted, language teaching by itself develops all the intellectual, emotional, and moral faculties of the individual student. Since ancient Greek is unique in expressing the highest human achievements, it is eminently suited to form the character of a modern nation. As principal of a Gymnasium in Nürnberg (1809), G. F. W. Hegel (1770–1831) expressed the goal of German classical education by saying that the riches of the ancients can only be acquired by learning their language in the original because this would cultivate patriotism, moral integrity, and a many-sided excellence.[21]

Under the guise of that inspiration, hypocrisy and vulgarization set in all too soon. Consider Hegel's declaration that

> the final purpose of education is liberation and the struggle for a higher liberation still. . . . In the individual subject, this liberation is the hard struggle against pure subjectivity of demeanor, against the immediacy of desire, against the empty subjectivity of feeling and the caprice of inclination. The disfavor showered on education is due in part to its being this hard struggle; but it is through this educational struggle that the subjective will itself attains objectivity within, an objectivity in which alone [the will] is for its part capable and worthy of being the actuality of the Idea.[22]

Hegel believed that this educational ideal remains ethically valid even if the people as individuals or the state as an institution prove incapable of the desired "objectivity" and "liberality."

***

Ideals can have unforeseen consequences that run counter to our best intentions, and during the nineteenth century the ideal of *Bildung* had such consequences for the German definition of community. Classical learning was quite controversial. In the Napoleonic period Germany was in the grip of a national liberation movement that put a premium on the teaching of German and of German history. To the Holy Alliance that followed the defeat of Napoleon, teaching of the classics was politically suspect because it encouraged students to identify with the ideals of freedom and the overthrow of tyrants. Christian spokesmen saw a rival to religious education in the classical ideal of personal development. Men of affairs opposed the teaching of dead languages which, as they saw it, had little practical value. Therefore, humanistic learning was under attack, because the cosmopolitan intent of classical education was not widely shared. The spokesmen of humanistic learning had answers to all these objections, but they were put on the defensive. What then accounted for the continued prominence of classical education in secondary schools?

Evidence for such prominence is provided by the tripartite German educational system: the *Gymnasium* in which Greek and Latin are required, the *Realgymnasium* in which only Latin is required, and the

Oberrealschule in which only modern languages are required. Evidence on enrollments is available for the second half of the nineteenth century, the student population of Prussia increasing from 68,406 in 1864 to 232,692 in 1911. During this period *Gymnasium* enrollment was 69 percent in 1864, over 50 percent until 1901, and fell to only 46 percent by 1911. Enrollment in the *Realgymnasium* ranged from 24 percent in 1864 to 21 percent in 1911. By combining the two sets of figures in 1864, 93 percent of the students in Prussia learned at least one classical language and 67 percent were still doing so in 1911. Students who studied modern languages exclusively (in the *Oberrealschulen*) remained below 10 percent until 1901 but rose to 17.5 percent by 1911.[23] Classical education remained prominent until well into the twentieth century.

One reason lay in the educational requirements of the Prussian civil service. This provided institutional support for a school system in which classical learning played the major role.[24] Prussian reforms of the early nineteenth century were the work of enlightened monarchs and their public servants. Prior to the French Revolution, there had been efforts to make absolutist rule more efficient and more independent of estate representation. After the revolution, that efficiency was put at the service of combating the agitation for human rights and a constitutional monarchy. Officials were given lifetime tenure, pension rights, and regular promotion in salary and rank based on judgments of performance. Inevitably, at the highest level, preferment depended on wealth and social rank as well as higher education. The social incentives for a public career were powerful below that level. Not only judges and clergymen, but many public officials even in the lower ranks wore uniforms; merit badges were awarded; legal privilege reduced prison sentences and military service obligations for many officials, depending on their education. Titles determined all forms of address on the basis of rank and at the apex the king would bestow an aristocratic title in exceptional cases. Public employment was regulated under public law, which linked these privileges to the obligation of "faithful service" (*besonderes Treueverhältnis*). Consequently, all state employees were marked off from the public at large by a whole system of conspicuous distinctions.

In the course of the nineteenth century these principles of public administration were extended to the postal system, the railroads, trade inspection, and other fields of public service like municipal administration. In this way, workers as well as salaried employees were co-opted into a system of invidious distinctions in the service of a patriarchal state. This implied at each level entrance examinations, privileges, and the obligation of "faithful service" to the monarch. The privilege and prestige of public employment was, therefore, extended far down the social scale, a condition that in Germany as a whole affected nearly 1.5 million people by the beginning of the twentieth century.

At the middle and upper levels, conditions of entry into the bureaucracy linked public employment with higher education. Entry depended upon successful graduation (*Abitur*) from an institution of higher education, a legal requirement first introduced in 1788 and elaborated subsequently with the introduction of classical learning into the schools. Since entry into the universities also depended upon the *Abitur*, classical education soon became a necessary qualification for all higher positions in the professions and the civil service. This special position of the civil service has lasted down to the present and has imparted a special prestige both to the educational requirements needed for public service and to the legal system protecting it. Some of that prestige also affected the position of public employees at lower levels, although their educational requirements, privileges, and duties were, of course, more modest.

The triad of officialdom, classical education, and public law (*Staatsrecht*) was the source of pride, inspiring invidious comparisons with "the West." A nationalist historian like Treitschke contrasted French and English administration with the "most holy legal concepts of the Germans." The *Grenzboten*, a conservative journal, denounced England in 1881 by a series of synonyms for nepotism, which together with the chase after material gain was called "the ugliest hypocrisy." In a more sober vein, the economist Gustav Schmoller declared that because the country was governed by an estate of professional officials of marked integrity, the preconditions of a parliamentary regime did not exist.[25] When, in 1911, the historian Otto Hintze supplemented this judgment by declaring that one only had a choice between the increased strength of the Social Democrats and an extension of the civil service, he referred to the fact that Germany was distinguished by its bureaucracy as a main buttress of its political order.[26] As a result, the German word for civil service, *Beamtentum*, is not a translatable term. Its use implies the cultural distinction of high-ranking officials, whose disinterested discharge of their public duties put them at a level above the selfish multitude. Imitations of that model tended to affect the behavior of lower-ranking officials, primarily because people near the bottom of the social scale aspired to that lower rank.

What then happened to the meaning of *Bildung*, as classical education developed during the nineteenth century in the institutional context I have sketched? Through their effect on education, the German classics and their cosmopolitan idealization of ancient Greece helped to shape German nationalism, however unwittingly and paradoxically.

A Creeping Cultural Crisis

A spiritual link was said to exist between ancient Greece and modern Germany. The German language itself made the country into a nation of culture, much as classical Greek had done for the "ancients." A cult of classical German literature developed on this basis and a partial listing of its themes includes:

1. In art and philosophy, the Germans are the teachers of mankind.
2. German cultural achievements are superior.
3. The term *Geist* is a mark of that superiority, for it connotes "absolute spirit" in contrast to the world of material goods; it also connotes human intelligence, which in conjunction with feeling can mediate between gross matter and the highest faculties of mind.
4. The disadvantages of backwardness were turned on their head. German poets and thinkers could achieve a universality denied to other people, just because they imitated so many foreign models, especially those of France and England.
5. Accordingly, German spokesmen possessed a sense of mission expressed in the idea of a nation of culture.[27]

To be sure, Germans are hardly unique in proclaiming the superiority of their national community over others. It is rather the content of their claim that makes it remarkable, leading to what Fritz Stern has called "the unpolitical German."[28]

Classical education had idealized ancient Greece, because this ideal combined the individual's total immersion in the community with the fullest development of individual personality and the superiority of a nation of culture. A peculiarly German way of claiming greatness developed in the context of this idealization, which began with Johann Gottfried von Herder's theory of language as the fountainhead of *Geist* or spirit. Stripped of its metaphysical trappings, the idea is simple. Mankind is divided into many people with their different languages. Anyone who has tried to translate one language into another can confirm that each language has its own way of articulating even the most commonplace experience. Herder saw the plenitude of God's creation in this linguistic diversity, with each people contributing their own legitimate share to the common education of mankind. This was a generous and enlightened conception of the diversities we find among men, an idea worthy of our best feelings to this day. Herder was far removed from the nationalist twist given to his emphasis on language by Johann Gottlieb Fichte (1762–1814), giving weight to Thomas Nipperdey's judgment that the Napoleonic experience marked the beginning of modern Germany.[29]

According to Fichte, German was the original language (*Ursprache*), which by its primeval quality has the capacity and mission to rejuvenate mankind. Language refers to what a whole people have in common and to the idea that the educated elite (with language as its special province) can speak of and for the people (*das Volk*). Germany has the distinction of originating a cult of language as distinguished from the cultivation of language. In this view, German is the embodiment of the folk whose God-given value waits to be discovered. The scholarly elite is able to do so because their *Bildung* reflects the image of God.

Fichte's *Reden an die deutsche Nation* (1807–8) shows how this linguistic nationalism was reconciled with the idealization of ancient Greece. The German treatment of classical antiquity was contrasted with that of foreigners. Germans pointed the way to the future by plumbing the depth of the ancients, whereas foreigners cast flowers upon the great pathways (*Heerbahnen*) of antiquity and "weave a dainty garment over them" (*mit Blumen bestreuen und ein zierliches Gewand weben*).[30] In plain language, profundity versus superficiality distinguishes Germans from foreigners. In the midst of the wars of liberation against Napoleon, the idea of a "cultural nation" based on classical learning was merged with Germany's national-cultural mission in the world at large.

In the eighteenth century, the idealization of ancient Greece had served as a counter to the cultural and material advances of France and England. In the context of the struggle against Napoleon, Fichte emphasized the parallel superiority of Germany and ancient Greece. He put national against cosmopolitan principles, interpreting revolutionary ideals like humanity, liberality, and the general will as evidence of lassitude and conduct lacking in dignity. In the same spirit, teachers increasingly treated classical learning as a means of reinforcing the belief in a national mission, which, in turn, buttressed the importance of classical learning.

Fichte put a metaphysics of language at the center of his thought. German was to him the primordial expression of national essence just as classical Greek had been. French and English were by contrast merely derivative. Napoleon's victory over Prussia was evidence of the country's moral degradation. Hence, Germany needed a moral renewal that would result from an education modeled upon German language and thought. In this way Germany would be to the modern world what Greece had been to the ancient.

***

The reciprocal reinforcement between national renewal and classical learning became increasingly tenuous as Germany underwent a very rapid industrialization and critiques of humanistic education mounted in the late nineteenth century. However, the prestige of classical learning remained more or less intact until the 1890s. Consider two turning points of nineteenth-century German history. Following the defeat of Napoleon, the Holy Alliance (1815) established the German Confederation (consisting of thirty-nine sovereign territories) in place of the Holy Roman Empire of the German nation. At the end of the Franco-Prussian war (1870-71), the German Confederation was united into one state under Prussian leadership. Classical learning played different roles under these two political dispensations.

The governing principle of the German Confederation was to uphold the authority of each legitimate ruler as opposed to the liberal ideas that had come to the forefront in the struggle against Napoleon. In an effort to suppress all liberal agitation, the Karlsbad edicts of 1819 established censorship of publications, prohibited dueling fraternities, dismissed politically suspect teachers, and controlled the universities. Under these conditions classical learning was politically suspect, because many teachers advocated national unification and hence criticized the particularism of the status quo. Professionals were prominent in the revolution of 1848, and when that popular drive for constitutionalism failed, teachers became even more suspect. Accordingly, classical learning added new luster to its earlier symbolic value with respect to Germany's cultural mission in opposition to English materialism and French superficiality. For after 1848, that learning provided an outlet for the liberal and national ideas that had been officially suppressed.

Then the military victory in the Franco-Prussian war (1870–71) led to a political unification that altered the setting of education once again. The rise of national self-confidence was palpable, leading to invocations of divine providence that had punished France for her arrogance and blindness while according victory to Germany as "the silent and misunderstood power" that now stepped to the center of the stage to fulfill her cultural mission.[31] This military and cultural chauvinism was further strengthened by rapid industrialization and the legal institutionalization of the new monarchy. The unified *Reich* was recognized as the guarantor of national reconciliation. In this altered setting, the high moral ground of classical learning resumed its compensatory prestige, paradoxical as this may sound.

One example must suffice. Rudolf Lehmann was a prominent pedagogue of the period, who advocated an educational synthesis of Goethe with Bismarck. Like many of his contemporaries, his purpose was to combine the ideals of learning, here symbolized by Goethe who was steeped in the classics, with the national, political achievement symbolized by Bismarck. Personal identity should be developed through *Bildung*, yet the individual's greatest personal fulfillment was to be found in his identification with the national community.[32] Teachers put their humanistic learning at the service of the new state. In their view, military victory and national unity were evidence of Germany's cultural mission.[33] The monarchy that had accomplished this had thereby resolved all problems of personal identity. That accomplishment appeared to be threatened only by the Social Democrats with their theoretical Marxism and by exacerbated differences between Protestants and Catholics.

Yet the paradox of German unification was that it failed to bring enduring satisfaction even to those who greeted it with elation and whose strutting bravado probably hid underlying doubts. Superficially one can attribute that reaction to the great depression, which followed the victory over France, and to the crass materialism and corruption, which provided the period with a special epithet: "the age of the founders" (*Gründerzeit*). Other dislocations in the next thirty years (from 1871–1910) went much deeper, undermining the moral fiber of German society by an all-pervasive hypocrisy. In their efforts to cope with these dislocations, Germany's dominant classes were caught in their own prejudices.

The East-Elbian landowners (*Junker*) buttressed their declining economic fortunes by doing what they most despised: engaging in commercial transactions and intermarrying with rich Jewish families. Then they "recouped" their self-regard by exaggerating the aristocratic pretensions that had always served their social and political dominance. At the same time, many successful entrepreneurs of the period became preoccupied with converting their economic success into the legal claims of aristocratic privilege. A good many purchased entailed estates so that the emperor would be personally obliged to bestow an aristocratic title upon the new owners.[34] More commonly, entrepreneurs and other prominent members of the bourgeoisie reveled in the plethora of titles that distinguished them from the "common herd."

Humanistic learning became hypocritical when it was used to justify the cultural mission of Wilhelmine Germany. In the 1890s, curricular debates brought to a head the frequently voiced skepticism about the classics. Germany partly replaced ancient Greece and Rome by pushing her own history back to the defeat of the Roman legions (9 A.D.) by local Germanic tribes under the leadership of Arminius, in whose honor a great monument was erected. As the emperor pointed out in 1890, the goal was to educate young Germans, not young Greeks and Romans, to teach national communalism (*Volkstum*) rather than cosmopolitanism. Meanwhile, the leading strata of the country consisted of people whose very conduct belied the pretentious claims of Germany's cultural mission.

The commanding influence of Otto von Bismarck (1815–1898), Prussia's prime minister since 1861 and Reichschancellor since 1871 also markedly influenced the German sense of community. In foreign policy, no one has ever questioned his stature as a statesman. Internally, he pursued a policy of defending the monarchy, strengthening the army and opposing parliamentary "interference" with autocratic government. His politically skillful ruthlessness took on a petty character, which increased with the years and had a nearly stifling effect upon a population whose social leaders had little experience in opposing so formidable a figure. As Gordon Craig has summarized it:

> Bismarck's success in the constitutional conflict of the 1860's had a permanent effect upon his parliamentary practice. Whenever the monarchical-conservative principle was threatened, . . . he tended to revert to . . . violent posturing, the identification of political opposition with lack of patriotism and subversion, the ruthless employment of calumny and harassment against individuals and parties labelled *Reichsfeinde*, the menacing references to worse things to come, the attempt to go over the heads of the *Reichstag* and to appeal to the German people in campaigns in which the issues were over-simplified and distorted.[35]

Elements of this "syndrome" frequently occur in politics. But Bismarck employed these methods in such "masterly" fashion that he left his opponents politically emasculated.

Finally, the legal prohibition of the Social Democratic party (1878–1890) was one of many efforts in the 1870s and 1880s to exclude groups from the German community. The government followed this prohibition by a policy of systematically harassing individuals and groups. Despite these efforts, the party retained two-thirds of the votes compared with the previous election. In 1890, when the prohibition was lifted, the Social Democrats proved to be the strongest party with 20 percent of the votes. The damage was done. Symbolically, the prohibition ostracized the "working class" from the national community. This effect was heightened by the social insurance legislation beginning in 1881, which reinforced Bismarck's message that the state would do for the workers what they could not do for themselves. This strategy followed the invidious, six-year campaign against Catholics and Polish immigrants (1872–78) as well as the officially tolerated anti-Semitic campaign that Court Chaplain Adolf Stoecker combined with his virulent agitation against socialism. It seems appropriate to speak of the "social pollution" of public life in Wilhelmine Germany, a corruption of Germany's self-definition as a national community with a cultural mission.

The work of two leading critics of the Wilhelmine establishment, Friedrich Nietzsche (1833–1900) and Ferdinand Toennies (1855–1936), is readily understood against this background. Selected, central aspects of their writings facilitate our understanding of the cultural crisis that turned Germany into a specter of the twentieth century.

Friedrich Nietzsche began his attack with *The Birth of Tragedy* (1872) and continued it with a series of penetrating and deeply disturbing essays until he succumbed to insanity in 1888. He exposed the hypocrisy that turned military victory and material success into tokens of cultural superiority more effectively than anyone else.[36] He hardly bothered with the businessmen and politicians whose greed and venality he took for granted. Educated philistines (*Bildungsphilister*) were his special target, because they laid claim to a false superiority and thereby garbed their vested interest in learning with a false cultural aura. Nietzsche was also deeply disturbing because he turned his critique of the German status quo into a searing indictment of modern civilization as a whole. He excoriated scientific rationality, for which Socrates served him as a convenient symbol. The truths that scholars can attain, are not the highest value, yet scholars treat "knowledge for its own sake" as a fetish that cannot be questioned.[37] By extolling "life" Nietzsche polemicized against the kind of knowledge-seeking that turns means into ends. He juxtaposed the heroic image of the superhuman (*Übermensch*) with the shoddy aspects of philistinism, especially that of classicists and other scholars who presume that their work can stem the tide of cultural degradation. Nietzsche deified the Promethean impulse of individual creativity, beginning with the ancient Dionysian cult and extending to the glorification of art and life at the expense of reason. He did throughout his life what Goethe had only done in his youth. That glorification proved to be as corrupting an idea as "truth for its own sake." This does not detract from Nietzsche's moral insight. Rather, the very extremity of his position provides a clue to the materialism, arrogance and self-satisfied lack of taste that pervaded Wilhelmine Germany.[38]

Ferdinand Toennies, Nietzsche's junior by a generation and the second critic to be considered, published his main scholarly work, *Gemeinschaft und Gesellschaft*, in 1887. This was an analytical work, written in an archaic style and very different in content from Nietzsche's aphoristic and psychologically probing dissection of late nineteenth-century civilization. Though the book had little impact at the time, it had gone through six editions by 1926. Before and after the First World War, *Gemeinschaft* (community, polity) became a handy cultural and political slogan, used by many people who knew nothing about Toennies's book. Toennies had been impressed by Nietzsche and was equally critical of Wilhelmine Germany and modern civilization. His emphasis on community was based on a critical reading of Hobbes and Marx, not on an idealization of art and life. Hobbes' state of nature pictured human beings engaged in a continuous struggle for power, prompted by their instinct for self-preservation. Political order would arise only if each individual gave up his natural freedom and submitted to a sovereign, who could then provide security for life and property. From this model Toennies took the idea that an ordered community can arise only from an act of will, but he rejected Hobbes' individualism. In turn, Marx had treated that individualism as a generic attribute of the capitalist system, arising from the ownership of private property. Yet he did not attribute the order of the capitalist system to individual decisions: "individuals are dealt with only insofar as they are the personifications of economic categories, embodiments of particular class-relations and class-interests."[39] Although Toennies accepted Marx's indictment of a capitalist society that atrophied the individual, he rejected this collectivist disregard of human agency. Toennies was intent on retaining both community and personal identity; he sought to achieve this synthesis by contrasting capitalist society and its Hobbesian "war of all against all" with the medieval communities of the past and an ideal socialist community in the future. Harry Liebersohn described Toennies's work this way:

> *Gemeinschaft und Gesellschaft* contained a tremendous challenge to liberal society's assumption about the naturalness of possessive individualism and confronted it with a contrary image of man's natural will to a life in common.[40]

For Toennies, modern society, and capitalism in particular, depend upon human decision making (*Kürwille*), or man's arbitrary will. Community, on the other hand, depends on essential will (*Wesenswille*), meaning something like human caring or neighborliness or affinity going back to the family. The German word for arbitrary will goes back to the medieval bestowal of knighthood and is curiously archaic when applied to modern life. Essential will is a neologism that idealizes literal or metaphoric kinship and is intended to convey the sense of being at one with people whose feelings of affinity one shares. Where Nietzsche's outlook had provided a late nineteenth-century impetus to the cult of personality, Toennies's provided a comparable impetus to the cult of community. Like the classical writers before them, Germans of the late nineteenth century tried to cope with the moral dilemmas of their society by emphasizing personality and community, as if the Promethean and the communal impulses were completely reconcilable, particularly at their most extreme.

Communal and Personal Redemption?

Countries that are latecomers to the economic and political development pioneered by England and France have to cope with the experience of relative backwardness. Germany was among the first of these "follower societies" and Helmuth Plessner was among the first to call attention to this phenomenon with his seminal analysis of a "belated" nation (*Die Verspätete Nation*). As he noted, Germany lacked a tradition-forming constellation such as Elizabethan England with its combination of high culture and successful expansion overseas, or seventeenth-century France which was regarded as the cultural and political center of European civilization. In the age of early modern humanism a national mythology had developed from these foundations. Other countries in Europe and around the world lacked a comparable modern authentication, although many looked back upon more ancient antecedents. In the German territories, the religious controversies leading to the Thirty Years War (1618–1648) helped to destroy the ancient symbol of the Holy Roman Empire of the German nation although the shadowy idea of empire (*Reich*) lived on in the midst of the territorial particularism that had superseded the medieval world.[41]

When political unification actually occurred at the end of the Franco-Prussian war, it was greeted with satisfaction and high expectations. Shortly after 1871, David Friedrich Strauss wrote that Germans should put their faith in the miracles achieved during the war:

> During the last years we have taken an active part and each of us has cooperated in his own way in the great national war and the establishment of the German state, and we find ourselves inwardly exalted by the unexpected and glorious turn in the fortunes of our much tried nation.[42]

Many Germans shared this sentiment, especially among the educated elite who now put their talents at the service of the national community. I shall discuss this reaction of the *Bildungsbürgertum* in terms of social reform and colonial expansion.[43]

Before the great depression of 1873, many people recognized that unification had not solved any of the social problems brought about by the rapid pace of industrialization. The *Verein für Sozialpolitik* (Association for Social Policy) was founded in October 1873, its membership consisting of representatives of trade associations, communities, and research institutes, factory owners and higher civil servants, free professionals and business executives, and university professors. Most members had a higher education, but the economists among them played the decisive role. They made up one-sixth of the membership, one-fourth of the participants at the annual meeting, and two-thirds of the executive committee that made all the organizational and thematic decisions.[44]

There was little intellectual coherence in the association. Its statutes did not even contain a commitment to social reform with which the *Verein* was obviously concerned. Despite the differences of opinion among them, the members were quite appropriately nicknamed *Katheder-*

sozialisten or "lectern socialists." They shared the view that the state was obliged to intervene in social affairs in order to reduce class conflict. The state was an embodiment of reason and as such had moral responsibilities. According to this patriarchal view, all workers were dependent subjects so that every sign of independence, let alone opposition by the Social Democratic party, was interpreted as an affront to the monarch and justified the suspicion of treason.[45] These sentiments were shared by the educated elite, who identified with the monarchy and the political unification it had achieved. In this respect, Bismarck's domestic political strategy paid off.

This discrimination against "socialist agitators" fit in with the self-conception of the educated elite that regarded itself as the representative of the national community, though it was unable to play a political role that would have corresponded to that claim. In 1887, even Toennies, who had socialist leanings, referred to the "republic of learning" as the true representative of public opinion. Friedrich Paulsen referred to the German universities as the "public conscience" charged with assessing good and evil in politics. Hans Delbrück distinguished between an elected and a natural representation of the people, the latter consisting of all professionals with academic training who stood for the people as a whole.[46] Gustav Schmoller spoke of the "priesthood" of science, which together with the highest officials expressed public opinion and upheld the general welfare of the nation. In his opening remarks to a meeting of the *Verein für Sozialpolitik* (1899) Schmoller declared,

> We do not fight for our income, we do not fight for our property, we do not fight for our personal economic interests . . . we can view [matters] without partisanship; we are less committed to particular formulas of party-doctrines than those with whom we interact.[47]

These formulations betray the widely shared feeling that politics was incompatible with *Bildung*, an idealization of personal identity that had been developed a hundred years earlier. But by the end of the nineteenth century *Bildung* involved the claim that the educated elite spoke for the national community. Under the officially sponsored patriarchalism that claim now included the cultural ostracism of the working class, providing "educated" support for Bismarck's prohibition of the Social Democratic party. Thus, the *Bildungsbürgertum*, still basing its prestige on classical learning, now implied that in line with the dominant Wilhelmine society, it had a special warrant of speaking for the whole national community in the field of social policy.

The same cannot be said of colonial policy, and international relations generally, fields in which public opinion articulated by the educated elite tended to put pressure on the government. In the two decades before World War I, Germany's development accelerated. Between 1890 and 1914, the national budget rose from 8 million to 108 million marks. Between 1878 and 1910, the railroad network, owned and operated by Prussia, increased from 5,000 to 37,000 kilometers. Various educational reforms were initiated to prepare the bureaucracy for its rapidly increasing tasks. Requirements of legal and practical training increased at the expense of classical education, but still the latter remained predominant. In other words, Germany's economic power rose, while the educated elite remained wedded to the humanist tradition. What Nietzsche had said in the 1870s about educated philistines, who mistook military victory for cultural achievement, became even more true after 1890 when economic growth coincided with colonial expansion.

The communal and personal strivings of the educated elite found new means of expression as evidenced in the membership figures of several associations. The German Colonial Association (*Deutsche Kolonialgesellschaft*), which was founded in 1887, had a membership of about 18,000 persons in 1893, of whom 30 percent belonged to the educated elite. The German Navy Association (*Deutscher Flottenverein*), founded in 1898, had 1 million members in 1906. Again the educated elite participated prominently, though the military-industrial-bureaucratic complex predominated. The Pan-German Association (*Alldeutscher Verband*) was founded in 1891 and by 1901 had a membership of 20,000, of whom one-half belonged to the *Bildungsbürgertum*. Finally, there were 5,000 veterans associations with a combined membership of 400,000 in 1889, which rose to almost 20,000 associations with over 1,600,000 members by 1898.[48] Even in this case many propagandists and organizers probably belonged to the educated elite, although most members were recruited more broadly.

These figures suggest a high degree of national and imperial enthusiasm among the people, with the educated elite playing a leading role. German colonialism began only in the late 1880s, following centuries of English and French expansion. The imperialist ideologies were given additional impetus by the doctrines of social Darwinism in the later nineteenth century.[49] The imperial enthusiasm of the *Bildungsbürgertum* combined communalism and personal identity once again, though it was barred from a political participation commensurate with its self-image. The associations I have mentioned shared a number of themes. Foremost among them was the danger to the state arising from the growth of the Social Democratic party. National unity was the indispensable condition of foreign policy, and of colonial expansion in particular. Increasing productivity and population called for overseas outlets. The sense of inferiority compared with the British empire intensified these sentiments. Economic expansion was construed as the result of a culture that expressed the German national spirit.[50]

Three rather different versions of compensating (or overcompensating) for an experience of weakness on the part of the *Bildungsbürgertum* have been examined. The first was brought on in the eighteenth century by comparisons with France and England. The second was a response to Prussia's defeat by Napoleon and the effort to liberate the country from the Napoleonic yoke. And the third was an attempt to come to terms with the discrepancies between exhilaration, frustration, and overweening pride. Exhilaration followed the political unification of 1871. Frustration was due to Bismarck's success in emasculating his liberal opposition.[51] Overweening pride consisted in the belief that *Bildung* as such entitles the educated to a role of leadership, which combines nationalism and individualism, or communal identification with a sense of personal fulfillment.[52] When one considers Bismarck's reluctance in promoting German colonial policy, one wonders whether he yielded for domestic policy reasons in this case to an agitation largely promoted by the *Bildungsbürgertum* and certain economic interests.[53]

Some Reactions to Disillusion

A great deal of discontent developed despite the euphoria of political unification. The establishment of the Reich in 1871 was followed by the great depression of 1873 and by a mounting cultural crisis that growing prosperity did not abate. Disillusion at the development of the country went well beyond academic and literary circles. Large numbers of people from all strata, including the educated elite, rallied to the cause of the Left, the Social Democratic party. On the other hand, sections of the *Bildungsbürgertum*, which were part of the Wilhelmine establishment turned to the Right, reacted with special moral indignation at the role of money in society and the institution of the stock exchange. Such critiques from the Left and the Right have accompanied the development of capitalism everywhere. In Germany the critique from the Right became especially vindictive and conspicuous, because the denunciation of money transactions as a Jewish conspiracy against the public was closely associated with the imperial court.[54] Neither German unification nor rapid economic development seem to have given much lasting satisfaction. Nietzsche's *Bildungsphilister*, the educated elite, could not come to terms with the economic attributes of a modern society, even as they profited from them. Inside the establishment this aching discontent found expression in the rise of political anti-Semitism, a defensive-aggressive reaction of well-to-do people feeling threatened by the new market forces that brought them into competition with England.

This aching discontent also found expression in three nonpolitical critiques that questioned the very foundations of society and pertained directly to the ideal of a nation of culture. The early youth movement, the cultural protest in the arts, and the postwar idealization of soldiers at the front (*Frontkämpfer*) bring into focus the reactions to disillusion that became widespread among the youth of the middle class. I think of these developments as further symptoms of that "tenacious peculiarity," which has marked German culture since the eighteenth century even though elements of that peculiarity can be found elsewhere. Still, the cults of community and personality have coalesced with fateful consequences only in Germany.

The youth movements, the artistic outrage at Wilhelmine narrow-mindedness, and the idealization of soldiers at the front had an underlying affinity. These were the spirited efforts of young people trying to break out of the stifling cultural limits that the Wilhelmine establishment had imposed on a capitalist economy. They were various efforts to be at one with the *Volk* and with nature, to protect one's personal identity against the mindless preoccupation with money and material possessions, and to find new ways of how to conduct one's life. They were the attempts by German youths to redefine the human community in their own terms.

The German youth movement began around 1900 and represented a break with the prevailing life-style of middle class families. Its "ideological" protest consisted in a declaration of autonomy:

> This youth has its own will . . . without the need for orders, proposals, or interpreta-
> tions. Youth wants to live on its *own responsibility*, wants to have its own identity.
> *To be or have* in the fulfilled, condensed sense of the word: living its own, inner *truth*,
> eradicating all mere semblance.[55]

Unlike the imperial enthusiasm of the parents, which remained bound up with Germany's international relations, the youth movement and artistic forms of protest were domestic affairs. The stance of the movement is symbolized by the Hohe Meissner meeting of 1913, which was called to commemorate the national liberation movement against Napoleon as distinct from the official celebration of the Franco-Prussian war.

The opposition to the older generation was rooted in the petty, tired, and anxious atmosphere of everyday life. Parents did not enjoy themselves. Work did not satisfy them. They seemed to be crippled by their adamant adherence to "the rules"; yet they vilified people who broke with conventional constraints. The prospect of following in their footsteps was disheartening and school attendance brought no relief. These and related feelings found primary expression in the new life-style of the youth movement.

> To wash oneself at the well in the morning, to thank the peasant for his hospitality,
> to follow paths through the fields, to choose the brook for the lunch break, to build a
> fire-place and guard it against the wind, to follow wild animals and find one's way
> again, in the evening to ask at a farm for a hayloft and perhaps share a meal with the
> farmhands, to stay overnight under the trees against the wind, or, if one had it, to pitch
> a tent in the right place.[56]

All this taught youths to do what was needed, to explore nature, themselves and each other, to ask important questions, to plan but also to innovate on the spot.

In this description one can sense the spirit of *Gemeinschaft*, which the youth movement cultivated. Pennants, utensils, and ornaments, sagas told and customs observed, songs and games taken from the "folk tradition," dances and sporting contests, and quiet or spirited conversation around the camp fire were the elements of an alternative life-style. What seems to have prevailed on the whole was a camaraderie, a willingness to be close to each other without stepping on toes, a respect for differences together with an exuberance that was compatible with self-restraint. At first the movement was all male, but when girls were added these attitudes proved helpful in fostering an affective and exploratory but quite disciplined relation between the sexes.

Of course, there were quarrels and transgressions aplenty. Personalities clashed especially among the leaders, who were often older and more ideological. Inevitably, Eros showed its many sides as well, although modern candor probably makes us underestimate the self-imposed limits of this protest against the establishment. Finally, the relations between the band and its leader ranged from a friendly but routine to a genuinely charismatic style. In either case problems of leadership were resolved more or less easily, because the decisions involved were hardly momentous and the "subculture of hiking" was benign. Indeed, the emphasis on *Gemeinschaft* on this small and personal scale helped to foster a positive ideal of leadership.

The arts in their extremism contrasted sharply with this relatively calm setting. The arts challenged the dominant Wilhelmine definition of the human community with a definition of their own. Some extreme expressions of the father-son conflict are striking and perhaps symptomatic. A play entitled "The Son" (1914) by Walter Hasenclever (1890–1940) tells the story of a young man brutally treated by his father, who dies of heart failure as the son is about to shoot him. Another play, "The Parricide" (1920) by Arnold Bronnen, tells of a father-son relationship in the milieu of a petty official. Brutal beatings by the father alternate with scenes of sentimental reconciliation, culminating in an orgiastic murder of the father and incest between mother and son. One is reminded of Franz Kafka's "Letter to the Father" (1919) and of the psychiatrist Otto Gross, who at thirty-six (1913) was forcibly committed to a psychiatric institution by his father, a well-known Viennese expert on criminal law. Similar themes, if less extreme, appear in the writings of Max Brod, Georg Kaiser, Ernst Toller, Jacob Wassermann, Franz Werfel, and others.[57]

The combined cult of community and personality, which characterized the establishment's definition of the national community also characterized these protests against it. Whereas the youth movement extolled *Gemeinschaft*, the arts explored the possibilities of individual expression in all directions, including the most extreme. Both claimed to be an enhancement of life, expressing the individual's immersion into a variously conceived life process. Stefan George called a volume of his poetry "Tapestry of Life" (*Teppich des Lebens*), Thomas Mann characterizes the novel of Aschenbach in "Death in Venice" a novelistic tapestry, Musil writes of Rilke's poetry that it sees things connected as in a tapestry, Wagner's music is called a tapestry of sound, and so on. This idea of immersion into life was a common philosophical theme. Dilthey, Nietzsche, Bergson and Simmel tended to treat life as a primordial metaphysical given in the same way in which Fichte had treated the German language.[58] An increasing interest in the exotic, such as African sculpture or Buddhism, showed a similar tendency. As one art critic put it in reviewing a Japanese art exhibition, there is a strong sense that all things are interconnected, "that primordial feeling of the world, according to which the blossom, an animal, a mountain, a cloud and a beloved are all transformations of the same essence."[59] If one adds to this Nietzsche's ingenious polemic against academic history on behalf of "life," loose dress and sandals as against the "uptight" fashions of the day, the life reform movement, sexual experimentation, nudism and communal living in rural areas, dietary reforms and health fads, as well as many more individual experiments in alternative life-styles, one gets a picture of the scene that Franz Werfel addressed:

> Eucharistic and Thomistic,
> But at the same time Marxistic,
> Theosophic, communistic,
> Gothic-smalltown-cathedral-building-mystic,
> Activistic, arch-Buddhistic,
> Excessively-eastern taoistic,
> Seeking salvation from the contemporary
> predicament in African plastic,
> Language and barricades up-ending,
> God and the foxtrot trendily blending.
> Add to this the current billing,
> Paederasty is in, if you are willing.
> The menu of our souls, mate,
> Here you have it, early or late.[60]

Artistically, expressionism may well be the culmination of all this experimental groping. Its basic approach to painting and literature was the idea that "one must change the world at all costs."[61] Nature had been the dominant artistic motif of the nineteenth century, whether one thinks of realism in literature or sculpture, impressionism in painting, or Leopold von Ranke's programmatic statement that history deals with the past "as it really was." Now, expressionism in its many guises was an artistic and anarchist outcry "against all that," an individualist reaction to what everybody who was anybody called "reality." Expressionism rejected that dominant "reality" and replaced it with a utopian worldview, with the individual at the center of creation; it did not brood over problems of freedom, government, community, or anything else, but, with a single stroke, terminated all problems by creative action.[62]

German irrationalism was reinforced by an invidious international comparison, contrasting the country's self-definition once again with "Western rationalism," in its American and also its radical, Bolshevik form. Hermann Hesse's statement in *Steppenwolf* (1927) is symptomatic:

> It is not a good thing when a man overstrains his reason and tries to reduce to rational order things that are not susceptible of rational treatment. Then there arise ideals such as those of the Americans and the Bolsheviks. Both are extraordinarily rational, and both lead to a frightful oppression and impoverishment of life. . . . The likeness of man, once a high ideal, is in process of becoming a machine-made article. It is for madmen like us perhaps, to ennoble it again.[63]

Still, the radical animus behind all this desperate exuberance and extremism was peculiar to Germany and it came to a head already before the war.[64]

To a degree, this "retrospective determinism" cannot be helped because of the affinity underlying the themes I have traced. One can recognize Herder's or Goethe's ideas of community in the endeavors of the youth movement, just as there is some family resemblance between the romantic individualism of the classical period and the Promethean impulses of expressionism. But this is true only to a degree. It was not only the tragic experience of World War I, which after all was shared by many countries, but the cancerous, cultic buildup of efforts at grafting community onto the model of society in times of peace. In conclusion, I turn to this fusion between a communitarian and an individualist extremism, which was a possible but hardly an inevitable outgrowth of the German tradition.

Reactions to World War I had much in common among people in the participating countries. An incomplete listing would include an initial euphoria at the sudden break with tiresome routines and the cumulative discontents of the day, a nationalist scapegoating of the enemy country, appeals to national solidarity in the face of wartime disaster, a philosophical search for meaning in this catastrophe, and the increasing alienation between frontline soldiers and the civil society back home.[65] One can attempt to find distinguishing features of a specifically German aspect in these reactions. There is evidence, for example, of the prominent role that the German *Bildungsbürgertum* played in wartime propaganda in reaction to the jeopardy in which its claims to cultural leadership had been placed. One can further explore the efforts to interpret the war not just in chauvinist terms, but with popular philosophical justifications of Germany's worldwide mission as a *Kulturnation*.[66] But it was the experience of soldiers in battle, which would be used as the ideal model of a society at peace.

This retrospective idealization was the work of the political Right during the Weimar Republic. It was opposed at the Center and on the Left, even by people who had supported the war at the beginning but had become appalled by the realities of modern mechanized warfare. Even so, the rightist ideology had a strong appeal that cannot be understood by dismissing it as a crazed cult of violence. The war proved to be an unmitigated disaster, but for many Germans it was impossible to conclude that it had been a terrible mistake to have fought in vain for four years. It was evidently easier, and even exhilarating for some, to establish a positive link between wartime experience at the front and the traditions I have traced. What the youth movement and expressionist art had done separately was what war, as a model of the social order, did by combining the ideal of *Gemeinschaft* with the ideal of personal fulfillment.[67]

This idealization was synonymous with the demonization of the enemy, foreign and domestic. That again was not unique to Germany. More unusual was the degree to which the denunciation of foes went together with an idealization of a wartime experience that provided a model because it embodied the most cherished values of the nation. One can distinguish phases of that idealization.

First came the generalization of the initial euphoria. As one philosopher declared in 1929:

> The true German state can only be created by the true German *Gemeinschaft*, which consists in an enduring fusion of souls, such as we experienced all too briefly and temporarily during the first period of the war. We must look upon that experience ... as the Divine differential of a new German history.[68]

This community of the trenches not only heightened the "fusion of souls" among soldiers at the front, it also created an unbridgeable cleavage between that fusion and the society at home. After the war, combat veterans as a group (*Frontkämpfer*) stood against the "defeatist elements" who had opposed the war; they did not believe in a German victory and in war, as well as peace, continued in their petty, cutthroat dealings. This was in striking contrast to the communal experience at the front (*Fronterlebnis*).

Next came the invocation of communal feelings in the trenches. Camaraderie is too weak an expression; "all for one and one for all" with its exclusion of all selfishness comes closer. Still more to the point is the idea that all members of the group share in the great destiny of the people so that each individual "feels himself to be the instrument of that destiny."[69] Again, this community of the trenches excluded all those who were not a part of it, all civilians who remained at home.

Then also, individualism became transformed. Officers in their leadership role became a part of the community, provided they proved able to electrify their soldiers and spur them on. The shared experience at the front represented a unity that bridged all differences of class and interest, of rank and ability, depending solely on the efficiency and dependability of each man in his place. That way, soldiers are transformed into new men,

> who—through their experience at the front—break through to new values and the belief in a new order of things. That close circle of comrades, in which this germ of the New is alive, encompasses the whole personality and redirects it towards the Whole.[70]

Each officer and soldier merges with the whole and thereby realizes his highest potential as an individual personality. Germany's cultural tradition, at its best a creative tension between communalism and personal identity, finally disappeared in this collectivization of the individual. The spirit of struggle, sacrifice, selflessness, and nationalism were the new watchwords.

The demand "Germany should be governed by soldiers from the front" was frequently repeated and was not confined to the extreme Right. It is found, for example, in a book of love letters that appeared in the early 1930s and reached a wide circulation. These letters portray a love relationship between a man who is a retired British entomologist, and a woman who is a professor of political economy at the Berlin *Hochschule für Politik*. In this emotional context, the belief is voiced that only the tested men of virtue at the front are capable of saving the culture of a continent, whereas all those who have not been there are marked solely by the corruption and divisiveness that have brought misfortune upon us all. The letters contain expressions of deep affection for highly placed officials of the Weimar Republic, who are decorated soldiers from World

War I. Deeply frustrated by conflicts of interest and the dogmatism of opinions, they yearn for patriotic policies solely concerned with the great questions of national destiny. The clever talk of intellectuals sends them into a rage. Meanwhile the masses are open-minded as never before where great communal values are concerned, and are prepared, however inertly, for the concentrated attack needed to rescue our civilization. They are ready for the saving push, for the word of command, for the nod of the führer. The letters speak of men and women in all countries, moved by the emotions of soldiers at the front (*seelisches Frontkämpfertum*), and at the same time of the doom that has settled over Europe. European culture is not believed viable enough to bring together all those who have partaken of that emotion. Yet, only they are capable of bringing about the salvation of the continent.[71]

Such views are closely related to the doctrines of Carl Schmitt, Ernst Jünger, and Ernst Forsthoff. By reducing politics to relations between friends and enemies, Schmitt gave a learned interpretation of the Manichaean distinction between the light that can only come out of the *Gemeinschaft* of soldiers, and the darkness that is endemic to all civilian contention. Speaking in the name of those soldiers, Ernst Jünger declared more simply that "we are not citizens but the sons of wars and civil wars"; only if everything ordinary is swept away, will it be revealed how much "nature, elementary force, genuine ferocity, capacity for creating with blood and seed" is buried within us. And Ernst Forsthoff stated in 1931 that all nonpolitical spheres would be swept away, now that war experience had entered the spiritual life of the nation and had mobilized the people as a whole.[72]

***

A demonization of the enemy occurs in all countries, whether in times of war or as the result of a fundamentalist outlook. Liberation from bourgeois materialism and, among believers, from godlessness has been the common denominator.[73] In Germany, this warlike posture was transferred to all political opponents at home and in peacetime.

At the highest intellectual level, Thomas Mann articulated Germany's wartime cultural mission in 1919:

> I confess myself deeply convinced that the German people will never be able to love political democracy for the simple reason that we cannot love politics itself. The much

maligned authoritarian state (*Obrigkeitsstaat*) is and will remain the type of state, which is appropriate to the German people and meets their desires . . . *Geist* [that untranslatable word again] is *not* politics. . . . The difference between *Geist* and politics contains within it the difference of culture and civilization, of soul and society, of freedom and the franchise, of art and literature. The German way of life (*Deutschtum*) is culture, soul, freedom and art and not civilization, society, franchise, literature.[74]

This state of feeling, Mann continued, is an only reluctantly admitted but essential characteristic of German culture, which is inaccessible to the intellect and "therefore without aggression."

The German linguistic historian Dietz Bering has demonstrated this fact by examining the curse words that the Right as well as the Left in Weimar Germany attached to the term "intellectual." In the view of the Right, intellectuals are abstract and without instinct, overeducated, Jewish, destructive, sick and rootless, metropolitan, un-German, the enemy pure and simple. In the view of the Left, intellectuals are apparatchiks, without discipline, individualistic, stuck-up because of their education, theoretical and without instinct, garrulous, sick, opportunistic, vacillating, without beliefs, always negative, and alien.[75] Since intellectuals were the articulate spokesmen for every conceivable political grouping, the effect of these pejoratives carried over to the people whose interests and opinions they represented.

Where every civilian opponent is demonized as the enemy who must be eradicated root and branch, the proponents must represent themselves as the incarnation of the good. In this way we return, however unwittingly, to Fichte's claim that German is the primeval language that is deeply rooted in times out of mind, and that is to be distinguished from all other languages because they are derivative. The root of this claim is not language as such, but any attribute like name, ethnic origin, common history and suffering, which all genuine members of the *Volk* can be said to share, in stark contrast to those who do not. Perhaps language has pride of place in this intellectual strategy. For the "enemy inside the gate" speaks it too, and must therefore be distinguished as sharply as possible from the speakers who claim for themselves a monopoly of virtue.[76] Nazi Germany has the doubtful distinction of having carried this age-old division of the human community to new extremes.

Notes

1. See the systematic analysis of this position by Alexander Demandt, *Ungeschehene Geschichte* (Göttingen: Vandenhoeck & Ruprecht, 1986), passim. For an application of this approach to the German case see Helga Grebing, Doris von der Brelie-Lewin, and Hans-Joachim Fanzen, *Der "deutsche Sonderweg" in Europa, 1806–1945, Eine Kritik* (Stuttgart: W. Kohlhammer, 1986).
2. This German syndrome is examined in Adolf Löwe, *The Price of Liberty* (London: The Hogarth Press, 1937), who pointed to the positive role of social conformity in England and contrasted this with the German emphasis on individual personality.
3. These ramifications of German cultural history have been discussed frequently. They are here examined in the context of Germany as a follower society. Important suggestions in this direction are contained in Hajo Holborn, "Der deutsche Idealismus in sozialgeschichtlicher Beleuchtung," in Hans-Ulrich Wehler, *Moderne deutsche Sozialgeschichte* (Köln: Kiepenheuer & Witsch, 1966), esp. 88–93.
4. Fritz Bergemann, ed., *Eckermann, Gespräche mit Goethe*, vol. 2 (Frankfurt: Suhrkamp [Insel Taschenbuch], 1981), 508–11.
5. Ibid., 586–87.
6. Ibid., 653–55.
7. See Jochen Schmidt, *Die Geschichte des Genie-Gedankens in der deutschen Literatur, Philosophie und Politik* (Darmstadt: Wissenschaftliche Buchgesellschaft, 1988), 261–69; Bergemann, ed., *Eckermann, Gespräche*, vol. 1, 130, 210; and Johann Wolfgang Goethe, *Faust*, vol. 2, verses 11570–86.
8. "Writer" (*Schriftsteller*) came to have a derogatory implication in German. The proper word was "poet" (*Dichter*), suggesting a higher inspiration than the people who wrote for a living.
9. Bergemann, ed., *Eckermann, Gespräche*, vol. 1, 475–76.
10. For a discussion of that mobilization see Reinhard Bendix, *Kings or People* (Berkeley: University of California Press, 1978), chapter 11.
11. Zur Nation euch zu bilden, ihr hoffet es, Deutsche, vergebens; Bildet, Ihr könnt es, dafür freier zu Menschen euch aus! Your hope to develop as a nation, you Germans, is futile. Instead, do what you can [accomplish], cultivate yourselves as human beings.
12. Quoted in Hans-Georg Hass, ed., *Sturm und Drang*, vol. 2 (München: C.H. Beck'sche Verlagsbuchhandlung, 1966), 1545.
13. Quoted in Hans-Ulrich Wehler, *Deutsche Gesellschaftsgeschichte, 1700–1815*, vol. 1 (München: Verlag C.H. Beck, 1987), 515.
14. This sketch is indebted to Conrad Wiedemann, "Germanistik als Nationalphilologie?" in Heinz Schilling and Conrad Wiedemann, eds., *Wes Geistes Wissenschaften?* (Giessen: Ferber'sche Verlagsbuchhandlung, 1989), 29–30 and Joachim Wohlleben, "Beobachtungen über eine Nichtbegegnung: Welcker und Goethe," in William Calder III, Adolf Köhnken, Wolfgang Kullmann and Günther Pflug, *Friedrich Gottlieb Welcker*, Hermes Einzelschriften no. 49, (Stuttgart: F. Steiner, 1988), 18. Winckelmann's statement is quoted in Wohlleben.
15. Johann Wolfgang Goethe, *Dichtung und Wahrheit*, vol. 2 (Frankfurt: Insel Verlag, 1975), 444.
16. In eighteenth-century Germany that detachment is easy to understand. All public affairs were in the hands of territorial rulers, whose instructions were carried out by highly placed officials who thought of themselves as personal servants of the prince.

Public affairs were an aspect of patriarchal rule, in which private associations existed only by the grace of the prince. In that setting there was no contradiction between Goethe's own role as the servant of his prince and his emphasis on the detachment of poetry from affairs of state.

17. I have translated *Bildung* as cultivation or self-cultivation, but I will use the German term because of its far-reaching implications. *Bilden* means "to create" and medieval mysticism explored the belief that man was "created in the image of God." Though by the eighteenth century that belief had become attenuated, it was still vivid, as in Wilhelm von Humboldt's statement in a letter: "I feel that I am driven towards a unity. I think it trite to call that unity God, because [to say so] externalizes the idea unnecessarily. That unity is mankind, and mankind is nothing other than myself." Quoted in Michael Naumann, "Bildung und Gehorsam," in Klaus Vondung, ed., *Das Wilhelminische Bildungsbürgertum* (Göttingen: Vandenhoeck & Ruprecht, 1976), 35–37. The last sentence echoes Rousseau's *Confessions*.

18. Quoted in Margret Kraul, "Bildung und Bürgerlichkeit," in Jürgen Kocka, ed., *Bürgertum im 19. Jahrhundert*, vol. 3 (München: Deutscher Taschenbuch Verlag, 1988), 46–48. My italics.

19. Quoted from Franz Passow, a contemporary of Humboldt, in Manfred Landfester, *Humanismus und Gesellschaft im 19. Jahrhundert* (Darmstadt: Wissenschaftliche Buchgesellschaft, 1988), 34 n.9.

20. Quoted in ibid., 36 and n.16.

21. See the panegyric statement quoted in ibid., 41 n.34.

22. T. M. Knox, ed., *Hegel's Philosophy of Right* (London: Oxford University Press, 1965), 125–26. My quotation omits Hegel's characteristic phrasing which distinguishes ethical actions in their immediate, natural form and in their intellectually reflected form. In his view only the latter is worthy of education at its best. Note the underlying similarity of Hegel's position with Adam Smith's emphasis on self-command in his *Theory of Moral Sentiments*.

23. These figures are presented in Bernd Wunder, *Geschichte der Bürokratie in Deutschland* (Frankfurt: Suhrkamp, 1986), 77. Unless indicated otherwise, the following discussion of educational requirements and civil service careers is based on this study.

24. That is at least one main reason. There are others like the cultural prestige of Wilhelm von Humboldt's educational reforms and the increasing role of associations of philologists and teachers. My references are to Prussia; conditions varied in different parts of Germany.

25. Quoted in John C. G. Röhl, "Beamtenpolitik im Wilhelminischen Deutschland," in Michael Stürmer, ed., *Das kaiserliche Deutschland* (Düsseldorf: Droste Verlag, 1970), 288.

26. Quoted in Wunder, *Geschichte*, 83.

27. For documentation see Aira Kemiläinen, "Auffassungen über die Sendung des Deutschen Volkes," *Annales Academiae Scientiarum Fennicae*, vol. 101 (Helsinki-Wiesbaden, 1956).

28. Fritz Stern, *The Failure of Illiberalism* (Chicago: University of Chicago Press, 1975), 4–25.

29. Thomas Nipperdey, *Deutsche Geschichte 1800–1866* (München: C.H. Beck, 1983), 11ff.

30. See J. G. Fichte, *Reden an die deutsche Nation* (Leipzig: Felix Meiner, 1943), 88 and passim.

31. This and related declarations are quoted in Gordon Craig, *Germany, 1866–1945* (New York: Oxford University Press, 1978), 34–37.
32. See Reinhard Bendix, *From Berlin to Berkeley*, (New Brunswick, NJ: Transaction Publishers, 1986), 49. Lehmann was a teacher of my father and the brother-in-law of Franz Boas, the American anthropologist.
33. For ample documentation on this point cf. Landfester, *Humanismus*, 132–64.
34. These points were noted already in the writings of Thorstein Veblen and Max Weber. Among perceptive modern analyses of this complex situation cf. Hans Rosenberg, "Die Pseudodemokratisierung der Rittergutsbesitzerklasse," in *Probleme der Deutschen Sozialgeschichte* (Frankfurt: Suhrkamp, 1969), 7–49; Stern, *Failure of Illiberalism*, 26–57; and Martin Doerry, *Übergangsmenschen, Die Mentalität der Wilhelminer und die Krise des Kaiserreichs*, 2 vols. (Weinheim: Juventa Verlag, 1986).
35. Craig, *Germany*, 143. A telling description of the long-run effects of these methods is contained in Max Weber, "Bismarck's Legacy," in *Economy and Society*, vol. 3 trans. and ed. by Guenther Roth and Claus Wittich (New York: The Bedminster Press, 1968), 1385–92.
36. For an early example of this critique see the first of four essays entitled "Thoughts out of Season" (*Unzeitgemässe Betrachtungen*), in Friedrich Nietzsche, *Werke*, vol. 1, ed. Karl Schlechta (Darmstadt: Wissenschaftliche Buchgesellschaft, 1982), 137–49. Nietzsche's *David Strauss, der Bekenner und der Schriftsteller* was published in 1873.
37. Nietzsche did not refer to Marx in his writings, but his argument about knowledge as a "fetish" is strikingly similar to Marx's argument about the "fetishism of commodities."
38. I sidestep a further discussion of Nietzsche, because his Promethean position isolated him, though generations of readers have found his writings to be a mesmerizing expression of their discontents.
39. From the preface to the first edition of Karl Marx's *Capital* in Robert Tucker, ed., *The Marx-Engels Reader* (New York: W. W. Norton, 1972), 194.
40. Harry Liebersohn, *Fate and Utopia in German Sociology, 1870–1923* (Cambridge: The MIT Press, 1988), 28.
41. See Helmuth Plessner, "Analyse des deutschen Selbstbewusstseins," in *Gesammelte Schriften*, vol. 6 (Frankfurt: Suhrkamp, 1982), 253–60.
42. Quoted in Craig, *Germany*, 181–82.
43. The literal translation of "educated bourgeoisie" is inadequate, but there is no good alternative. The special connotations of *Bildungsbürgertum* have to do with the prestige and rank consciousness of all people who completed their secondary education and attended a university, including not only university professors, but teachers, clergymen, doctors, judges, officials, artists, technicians, and businessmen. My term "educated elite" should be understood with these qualifications in mind.
44. Dieter Lindenlaub, "Richtungskämpfe im Verein für Sozialpolitik," *Vierteljahresschrift für Sozial- und Wirtschaftsgeschichte*, Beiheft 52 (Wiesbaden: Franz Steiner Verlag, 1967), 6–7.
45. The phrase "journeymen without fatherland" (*vaterlandslose Gesellen*) was so widely used as an epithet that the fear of being branded by it still plays a role in German politics more than a century later. *Gesellen* is better translated as "riff-raff."
46. For further documentation see Rüdiger vom Bruch, *Weltpolitik als Kulturmission* (Paderborn: Ferdinand Schöningh, 1982), 50ff.

47. Quoted in Lindenlaub, "Richtungskämpfe," 26–27. In the original the last phrase is grammatically incomplete; my translation gives the sense of Schmoller's statement.

48. These figures are taken from Peter Hampe, "Sozioökonomische und psychische Hintergründe der bildungsbürgerlichen Imperialismusbegeisterung," in Klaus Vondung, ed., *Das Wilhelminische Bildungsbürgertum* (Göttingen: Vandenhoeck & Ruprecht, 1976), 68–70 and from Röhl, "Beamtenpolitik," 289.

49. For the German variant of Western imperialist ideology see Fritz Bolle, "Darwinismus und Zeitgeist," *Zeitschrift für Religions- und Geistesgeschichte* 14 (1962), 143–78.

50. For fuller documentation see Peter Hampe, "Die ökonomische Imperialismustheorie," *Münchener Studien zur Politik* 24 (München: C.H. Beck, 1976), 265ff and vom Bruch, *Weltpolitik*, passim.

51. Still the most telling analysis of the effects of Bismarck's policies on the German middle class is contained in Max Weber, "Parliament and Government in a Reconstructed Germany," in *Economy and Society*, vol. 3, trans. and ed. Guenther Roth and Claus Wittich (New York: Bedminster Press, 1968), 1385–92.

52. I am not aware of a study that focuses attention on the socially invidious use of titles and prestige based on higher education.

53. Hartmut Pogge von Strandmann, "Germany's Colonial Expansion under Bismarck," *Past and Present*, no. 42 (February 1969), 140–59.

54. See Paul Massing, *Rehearsal for Destruction* (New York: Harper, 1949) for the details. Max Weber's essay on the stock exchange, "Die Börse" in *Gesammelte Aufsätze zur Soziologie und Sozialpolitik* (Tübingen: Mohr, 1924), 256–322, was explicitly written to refute partisan misconceptions of this institution. The essay was first published in 1894.

55. From the programmatic declaration of the *Freideutsche Jugend* at the Hohe Meissner (1913) in Werner Kindt, ed., *Die Wandervogelzeit* (Düsseldorf: Eugen Diederichs Verlag, 1968), 492.

56. My account and this quotation are taken from Hans Bohnenkamp, "Jugendbewegung als Kulturkritik," in Walter Rüegg, ed., *Kulturkritik und Jugendkult* (Frankfurt: Vittorio Klostermann, 1974), 27 and passim.

57. See Corona Hepp, *Avantgarde* (München: Deutscher Taschenbuch Verlag, 1987), 143–47. Cf. also the case study by Emanuel Hurwitz, *Otto Gross, Paradies-Sucher zwischen Freud und Jung* (Frankfurt: Suhrkamp, 1979), passim.

58. Georg Simmel expressed many facets of this common belief. Cf. David Frisby, *Sociological Impressionism* (London: Heinemann, 1981), 132–64.

59. Statement by Hermann Bahr quoted in Wolf-Dietrich Rasch, "Die Reichweite des Jugendstils," in Rüegg, ed., *Kulturkritik*, 131.

60. Quoted in Hepp, *Avantgarde*, 147–48. I have completed the partial translation in Craig, *Germany*, 771.

61. Statement by Walter Hasenclever quoted in Hepp, *Avantgarde*, 94.

62. I have modified an early characterization of expressionism (1920) by Friedrich Markus Huebner quoted in Hepp, *Avantgarde*, 93.

63. This statement by Hesse's protagonist in *Steppenwolf* is quoted in Craig, *Germany*, 482–83.

64. For a masterly summary of this complex phenomenon cf. the analysis by Gordon Craig in ibid., 479ff.

65. Comparative material on these points is contained in Klaus Vondung, ed., *Kriegserlebnis, Der erste Weltkrieg in der literarischen Gestaltung und sym-*

bolischen Deutung der Nationen (Göttingen: Vandenhoeck & Ruprecht, 1980), passim.

66. These perspectives are explored in Klaus Vondung, "Deutsche Apokalypse 1914," in Vondung, ed., *Das Wilhelminische Bildungsbürgertum*, 153-71 and Hermann Lübbe, *Politische Philosophie in Deutschland* (München: Deutscher Taschenbuch Verlag, 1974), 171ff.

67. My discussion is indebted to Kurt Sontheimer, *Antidemokratisches Denken in der Weimarer Republik* (München: Deutscher Taschenbuch Verlag, 1978), chapter 5.

68. Quoted from Hermann Schwarz, "Deutsches Wesen und deutsche Weltanschauung," in Sontheimer, *Antidemokratisches*, 97.

69. From a statement of Franz Schauwecker quoted in ibid., 99.

70. This paraphrase by Sontheimer, *Antidemokratisches*, 99 is based on the rightist literature of the 1920s; it is oddly similar to Karl Marx's statement.

71. M. B. Kennicott, ed., *Das Herz ist wach, Briefe einer Liebe* (Tübingen: R. Wunderlich, 1955), 65-68, 83-85, 188. The presumptive editor of this eloquently German book, which appeared under an English pseudonym, was Gertrud Hamer von Sanden (1881-1940), a longtime companion of Gertrud Bäumer, the well-known leader of the German feminist movement. Guenther Roth has examined these materials in his introduction to Marianne Weber's biography of *Max Weber* (New Brunswick, NJ: Transaction Publishers, 1988), passim.

72. Sontheimer, *Antidemokratisches*, 81-82, 104, 107. Forsthoff was a student of Carl Schmitt, the political theorist. Ernst Jünger's work consists of a linguistically captivating celebration of war.

73. Modris Eksteins, *Rites of Spring* (New York: Doubleday, 1989), 90-94.

74. Thomas Mann, "Betrachtungen eines Unpolitischen," in *Werke, Das Essayistische Werk*, vol. 1 (Frankfurt: Fischer Bücherei, 1968), 23. The following sentence of my text paraphrases a statement on p. 24. In later life, Mann finessed these statements. See John Seery, *Political Returns* (Boulder: Westview Press, 1990), chapter 5.

75. Dietz Bering, *Die Intellektuellen, Geschichte eines Schimpfwortes* (Stuttgart: Klett-Cotta, 1978), passim.

76. For two probing analyses of this linguistic strategy, dealing prominently with the philosophy of Martin Heidegger, cf. Theodor W. Adorno, *Jargon der Eigentlichkeit* (Frankfurt: Suhrkamp, 1964) and Robert Minder, "Heidegger und Hebel oder die Sprache von Messkirch," in *Dichter in der Gesellschaft* (Frankfurt: Suhrkamp, 1972), 234-94.

Part III
Political

6

Politics and the Legitimation of Power

Distinctions between those who belong to a community and those who do not, lead to different types of ethical dualism. As we have seen, each type is associated with its own universalist appeal. A community constituted in this manner still has to order its internal and external affairs. It is convenient to separate the social distinctions examined so far from this political arena, although the two are obviously linked in many ways.

For work in political theory to proceed constructively, it is necessary to arrive at shared understandings of what we mean by the terms we use. Experience shows that the meaning of terms changes over time. Therefore, we must develop as much common terminological ground as possible in order to formulate our contemporary problems as lucidly as we can. In addition, the case study of Germany is continued in order to examine the utility of such conceptual clarifications before attempting to proceed further. In a discussion of changing definitions of community it is appropriate to place a country at center stage where the efforts at self-definition have probably been more articulate and consequential, more unsettled and unsettling, than anywhere else.

Politics or Fate and Freedom

Modern social science developed when the idea of man the maker gained ascendance over speculations about transcendent cosmological forces. Key words such as God, sin, grace, and salvation declined while terms like nature, natural law, first cause, and reason were upgraded.[1] This change did not alter the belief, derived from the Old Testament, that the future of the human community will be different from the present.[2] But will it be better or worse? Human communities are confronted with scarcity and have always had to struggle with the politics of distributing limited goods among conflicting interests. Marx was right in saying that religion sought to compensate people for the miseries they suffered. He was wrong in assuming that technical advances would abolish suffering. Progress has created new forms of suffering by awakening more needs than can be satisfied, and in the meantime many have dispensed with the consolations of religion.[3] This grating excess of aspirations goes back to the Renaissance conception of man as the maker of his destiny.

The Promethean belief in man's unlimited potential was never untroubled, however. Reflections on the politics of the human community and its art of the possible insisted on the limits of human power. Machiavelli (1469–1527), a contemporary of Pico della Mirandola, at times agreed with those who thought worldly events "so governed by fortune and by God, that men cannot by their prudence change them." But he would not let it go at that: "Nevertheless, that our free will may not be altogether extinguished, I think it may be true that fortune is the ruler of half our actions, but that she allows the other half or thereabouts to be governed by us."[4] We really do not know, Machiavelli seems to be saying, but in politics we can act only if we believe we can make a difference.

Two centuries later, Montesquieu (1689–1755) made this belief explicit. In a comment written in 1722 or 1723, he wrote,

> It is useless to attack politics directly by showing to which extent it runs counter to morality, reason and justice. This kind of discourse convinces everybody and affects nobody. There will be politics as long as there are passions not subjugated by laws.... The majority of events occurs in such a singular manner or depends upon such imperceptible and far removed causes that one can hardly foresee them.[5]

In his major work, published in 1748, Montesquieu took a position that in its own terms came to the same conclusion as Machiavelli. Men have laws of their own making but they are also subject to laws they never made. They are not like vegetables that invariably conform to natural laws because they have neither understanding nor sense. Accordingly,

> the intelligent world is far from being as well governed as the physical. For though the former has also its laws, which of their own nature are invariable, it does not conform to them so exactly as the physical world.[6]

Machiavelli might have characterized this as a balance between "fortuna" and "virtù," but in more contemporary terms, we would see it as a balance between fate and freedom, or between constraint and reason.

This balance was undone by the eighteenth- and nineteenth-century belief in science. Confidence in human power superseded balance, nourished by a century-long glorification of Newton and by the general adulation of scientists, as in Fontenelle's funeral orations.[7] One can see how the balance became unraveled in the ambivalence of Karl Marx. In *The Eighteenth Brumaire of Louis Bonaparte* (1853) he seemed to retain the older tradition when he wrote that "men make their own history, but they do not make it . . . under circumstances of their own choosing, but under circumstances directly found, given and transmitted from the past." However, by 1867, in his preface to *Capital,* man the maker gives pride of place to science and predictability. Likening his own economic theory to the compelling attributes of physics, Marx writes this conclusion to his work:

> Intrinsically, it is not a question of the higher or lower degree of development of the social antagonisms that result from the natural laws of capitalist production. It is a question of these laws themselves, of these tendencies working with iron necessity towards inevitable results.[8]

Freedom, reason, virtù seem to have given way to science and predictability, but in fact, throughout his life, Marx wanted to have it both ways. He wanted to know accurately and dispassionately, but he also asserted that the knowledge gained was bound to play a constructive role in human affairs. In effect, he eliminated uncertainty from the quest for knowledge.

In this respect, he was heir to a philosophical scientism that gave little or no weight to fate or fortune, to the laws which men have not, and cannot, make. In France, philosophers like Cabanis, Helvétius, and de Tracy developed a "science of ideas," founded upon the study of sensation, in an effort to lay a foundation for basic educational reforms. Their work became widely influential through the writings of Henri de Saint-Simon (1760–1825). These writers made physiology the basic discipline of the human sciences. Saint-Simon wanted to introduce physiology into public education because he believed that as a result all the uncertainties of our lives could be eliminated:

> Morals will become a positive science. The physiologist is the only scientist who is in a position to demonstrate that in every case the path of virtue is at the same time the road to happiness. The moralist who is not a physiologist can only demonstrate the reward of virtue in another world, because he cannot treat questions of morality with enough precision. . . . Politics will become a positive science. When those who cultivate this important branch of human knowledge will have learned physiology

during the course of their education, they will no longer consider the problems which they have to solve as anything but questions of hygiene.[9]

In other words, increased knowledge means a diminution of uncertainty. If we make physiology a requirement of public education, we thereby turn problems of morals and politics into daily routines. What becomes routine is no longer problematic.

Modern social scientists have not followed this "scientistic" tradition without qualifications, but they are beholden to it. They acknowledge uncertainty, but then maintain that their work is confined to a study of conditions of human action similar to Machiavelli's fortuna, Montesquieu's immutable laws, and Marx's organization of production. In the 1930s, Harold Lasswell wrote a widely recognized text on politics that may be taken as representative. He focused attention on the "working attitude of practicing politicians . . . , [who], caught up in the immediate, lose sight of the remote." There is no point in becoming "precise about the trivial"; we should study the immediate experience of politicians, but that is not science. The scholarly task is to attend to the remote, which politicians tend to ignore.

> One skill of the politician is calculating probable changes in influence and the influential. . . . The study of politics is the *study* of influence and the influential. The *science* of politics states conditions; the *philosophy* of politics justifies preferences. This book, restricted to political analysis, declares no preferences. It states conditions.[10]

In other words, the science of politics should confine itself to what can be known with precision, namely the remote conditions of immediate action. Hence, preferences are left to political philosophers, and the calculation of probable changes of influence and the influential to practicing politicians. One senses that a division of labor is intended: politicians and political philosophers deal with uncertainty while political scientists deal only with objects of precise knowledge. But with such a division it becomes difficult to know how to relate the precise knowledge of conditions either to political preferences or to the calculations needed for practical politics.[11]

These predicaments make it advisable to step back from the ideal of precision implied by the term "political science." After all, what would be the use of confining the analysis of politics to what can be known with certainty, if uncertainty is endemic in political decision making and the calculation of influence? It seems more productive to reintroduce uncertainty into the analysis of politics, and thereby return to the early modern view of the human condition. I propose to do so by examining the legitimation of power.

Authority or the Legitimation of Power

In modern history, the term legitimacy has been associated with the wars of the Holy Alliance of European powers against Napoleon, ending in 1815. The purpose was to uphold princely or royal claims to authority against all challenges on behalf of popular sovereignty. The idea of legitimation is much older, of course, going back to Aristotle's familiar distinction between different types of government and their corresponding forms of corruption.

As long as the dynastic principle prevailed, communities were defined by the common subjection of the people to their ruler. The legitimacy of this political order was established by the undisputed right of hereditary succession.[12] Nevertheless, the people immediately affected, as well as historians interpreting the record, regularly distinguish between strong and weak rulers, which suggests that royal authority is a dynamic concept. Even a weak monarch enjoys a sanctified legitimacy and may appear indispensable. But weakness in a ruler is also a reason for recurring struggles over succession, whereas a strong one is not only formally legitimate but can win additional legitimation through his personality and decisive action.

By contrast, a modern state's monopoly of power involves a complex of institutions functioning impersonally and acquiring acceptance by the public through the real or imagined service they render. That is, governments acquire their legitimation through an intermittent but frequent "plebiscite" of public opinion that is experienced more continually than it is expressed. Where a consensus of all participants exists, say when a policeman controls traffic in accordance with well-understood rules, one finds instances of such impersonal and everyday functioning. In that case one does not think of politics at all. But where consensus falls short of general agreement, politics enters in and becomes more personal. And whenever groups lose out in a struggle over particular issues, they will be tempted to question the legitimacy of governmental operations.

A suitable starting-point for considering these matters is Denis Diderot's article on political authority in the first volume of the

Encyclopédie ou Dictionnaire raisonné des sciences, des arts et des métiers (1751). The article begins with the statement that no man possesses a natural right to give commands to another. Authority exists "naturally" only where the father exercises legitimate power over his children, who must bend to his will. But the father possesses that authority only as long as his children cannot care for themselves. When we consider societies (rather than families), we find power to be of two kinds. Either an individual seizes power by violence, or he exercises it by consent of the governed. In the latter case we may speak of an "implicit contract" that the governed have made with the individual exercising authority. According to Diderot, the father's natural right to command, the forceful seizure of power, and a hypothetical contract are the three conceptual modes of exercising power.[13]

This threefold division is still serviceable. A right to command can arise from sheer force of personality. Power seized and exercised by force alone is usurpation and may last only as long as force prevails. However, such power can become legitimate if its actions acquire some agreement by the governed, regardless of how difficult it is to distinguish real from manipulated consent. In any case, Diderot separated power based on repression from authority based on consent. Authority, or legitimate power, serves the people of a society and that service cannot be rendered in the absence of law and order.[14] Nevertheless, political order is a means to an end, not a value in its own right. Authority justifies its mandate by rendering services to the community of the governed.

To do so, power must be limited if it is to be legitimate. As Diderot put it, man must not subject himself entirely to another man, for he possesses in God an omnipotent master to whom he is subject with his entire being. Even though during the eighteenth century the key word became *natural law* rather than God, the idea of a transcendent legitimation remained in place. Terms like God and nature came to be used interchangeably. Diderot declared that God allows man's obedience to authority because subordination is needed if society is to be maintained in the general interest. He was quick to add that obedience is justified only in relation to the sensible requirements of each situation, not blindly and without reservations. In this sense one speaks of the "contract" on which political authority rests. Legitimate rulers acquire their authority over people by their consent, however implicit it may be and however difficult it is to ascertain its viability. Even majority votes or public opinion polls remain momentary indications of public sentiment, and they leave room for minority dissent which can become the majority view. Genuine and enduring consent is typically won over in action, a contradiction in terms that accounts for the fragility of democratic rule. Accordingly, authority retains its mandate only as long as its services give "sufficient satisfaction," a condition that is usually discernable only in retrospect. Once authority becomes self-serving and manipulates opinion to simulate consent, it loses its justification.

The idea of a contract as the presupposition of authority has been clarified empirically since the eighteenth century, especially in the work of Max Weber. Recourse to his definitions will facilitate the leap to the twentieth century. Weber's types of authority (or legitimate domination in his terms) formulate basic assumptions of trust between rulers and ruled. Such assumptions are aspects of an implicit reciprocity of expectations on which people depend. This reciprocity is suggested by Weber's term *Herrschaftsverband*, which combines domination with association. Every political order depends on the threat of force over a territory, but it also depends upon the compliance of the governed, which makes force unnecessary.[15] Ideally, those in authority are sparing in their use of force in the interest of remaining responsive to public demands. Ideally, the governed comply with commands more or less conventionally on the assumption that the authorities will "serve the public interest sufficiently" and should, therefore, be allowed to proceed.

Trust rests on a reciprocity of expectations. In personal relations trust exists because an implicit quid pro quo protects us against unexpected developments; we give the other person the benefit of the doubt. Trust also exists between people and institutions, when the latter are judged to function reliably. Since we depend on such judgments every day, it should be possible to conceptualize this relationship, vague as it is.

A bank functions because its depositors believe that they can withdraw money from their accounts at any time during office hours. At the same time, the bank must invest the bulk of the money entrusted to it if it is to meet its expenses and show a profit. A contractually defined banking system depends upon a reciprocity between the implicit trust of depositors and the honesty and business acumen of the bank's managers. The legitimation of the banking system depends, therefore, on the frequent reconfirmation of mutual expectations between the parties to the transaction.

The reciprocal expectations on which we base our trust are a many-sided phenomenon. Friendship is the most personal form of such reciprocity, a purchase based on fixed prices is the most impersonal, and bargaining or haggling lies somewhere in between. Although the banking analogy makes clear what is to be understood by the confirmation of mutual expectations, one must keep the limitations of this model in mind, as with any analogy. The owner of a bank account as well as the bank's managers can base their expectations on the legal protection of their respective interests. Also, both parties are only concerned with one object of exchange, money, however complicated that might be in detail. By contrast, the relations between citizens and the state are concerned with many more, and much less clearly definable, "exchange objects." Moreover, these objects are for the most part not protected by law; they involve relations much closer to haggling than to either friendship or trading goods at fixed prices. Yet despite these qualifications of the banking analogy, its use seems to make sense in interpreting the authority relations, contract, and trust in a secular political context.

Max Weber's concepts of "domination" are based entirely on behavioral criteria unlike Diderot's idea of an authority subject to God and limited in its extent for that reason. Weber also thinks of limited authority but in his case that limitation depends on the interaction between rulers and ruled. The reference to God is not excluded thereby, but it plays a role only insofar as the actors are explicitly or implicitly concerned with it. In this way, the conception of God is transformed from a moral-religious imperative to an empirical question of the ideas that affect our lives.

Weber defines authority as the probability "that a command with a given specific content will be obeyed by a given group of persons." Every authoritative order claims legitimacy for itself, but its success in doing so depends "on the *belief* of those concerned in the existence of a *legitimate order*."[16] Thus, legitimacy exists only insofar as people believe in it. This question-begging formulation is not empty, however. Trust or the reciprocity of mutually reinforcing expectations exists only insofar as beliefs sustain it for whatever reason. As the banking analogy makes clear, such beliefs must be solidly based on experience if a run on the bank is to be avoided. Weber's familiar distinction between a traditional, legal, or charismatic legitimation of authority operates with a similar idea of reciprocity. At the core of each type there is uncertainty between rulers and ruled that must be assuaged if power is to be legitimate and trust is to endure.

Authority is traditional if "legitimacy is claimed for it, and believed in, by virtue of the sanctity of age-old rules and powers."[17] The phrase "age-old rules" refers to two, partly opposed principles of action, not to any one set of commands. Tradition means attachment to the specific content of ancient practice, but it also entitles the ruler to exercise his "arbitrary will." How does a ruler combine the commands sanctified by old usage with his claim that he has the right of arbitrary command? His insistence on having his own way always runs the risk of violating traditional precepts. Rulers may command at will, but they violate tradition at their peril. The governed must obey, but they may protest if tradition is disregarded for too long. Though these limits are indeterminate, one can speak of a quasi-contractual exchange as long as the reciprocal claims of rulers and ruled achieve some balance.

The rule of law is Weber's second type of authority. Such rule prevails wherever rulers and ruled act in "compliance with formally correct enactments, which have been made in the accustomed manner."[18] Enactments may come about through agreement between the interested parties or through imposition. Essential for the legitimacy of the rule of law is the belief in that legitimacy. That circular reasoning is the basis of compliance with enacted rules, however much it may be reinforced by fear and convention. The instructions of an American judge to the jurors before a trial are a case in point because they exemplify the beliefs that sustain the rule of law. He tells them that following the presentation of the evidence, the cross-examination, and the arguments of the lawyers, he will explain to the jury those parts of the law that are relevant to the dispute. Among these may be legal enactments, which one or another of the jurors considers unjust, perhaps even one that he or she has already opposed in public. Can each of the jurors declare that even in that case he will comply with the instructions of the judge because that is the presently valid law? Any juror who declares that under these circumstances he would be unable to apply the law will be excused from serving on the jury. For opposition to a law belongs to the political arena and it cannot be part of the legal system, nor does it have a place in the jury deliberations that follow the presentation of the dispute. Yet this formal exclusion of political interests and ideas from the legal proceedings cannot prevent their substantive impact upon lawyers, judges, and jurors, or on the law itself. The inscription "In God we trust" on our money and standards, as vague as *"voluntary* action," *"good* faith," or *"unfair* competition," shows that ideas of equity, derived from the "natural law" tradition, play a role in the legal system. Accordingly, legal authority also depends upon a quasi-contractual quid pro quo, an ever-shifting balance between procedural requirements and substantive ideas of justice.

Charismatic authority differs in kind from the other two because it involves an "extraordinary" mandate to rule. In the New Testament (2 Cor. 12:7–10), the Apostle Paul beseeches the Lord to relieve him of his mission, to which the Lord answers, "My grace is sufficient for thee: for my strength is made perfect in weakness." Accordingly, Paul glories in his "infirmities, in reproaches, in necessities, in persecutions, in distresses for Christ's sake," for these ensure that he is not "exalted above measure." Weber transferred this religious idea to the secular context by suggesting that charismatic leaders feel compelled to undertake their political mission, as Paul felt compelled by God's command. And like Christian believers, the governed believe in the "supernatural, superhuman, or at least specifically exceptional powers or qualities" of the charismatic leader.[19] In these terms, the followers have the duty to recognize the "higher" mandate of charismatic authority, while the leader regards any resistance in the ranks as disobedience toward God, a spiritual crime in extreme cases punishable by death.

Even in a secular context, the ruler or leader experiences his extraordinary power as a mission, endowing him with special gifts that entitle him to total obedience. In turn, the followers are prompted by their hopes and fears to recognize those charismatic gifts, from which they expect to benefit if their belief is firm enough. However, these beliefs are under constant pressure, a quasi-contractual quid pro quo between the ruler's claims and his followers' duty. The ruler must be successful, though he regards demands for proof of his claims as treason; and the ruled search for signs that their belief is justified, though the lack of trust expressed in a hope for miracles may jeopardize their benefits. Charismatic authority comes into question when success eludes the leader for too long, and that result is hastened when the followers clamor for "miracles." The quid pro quo then consists in the willingness of ruler and ruled not to claim too much, though neither side knows what is "too much." For charismatic authority is jeopardized as well when the ruler hesitates in his claims, or the followers falter in their belief. For these reasons, charismatic authority is the most unstable relationship among Weber's three types of domination.

***

This discussion of Diderot and Weber highlights the idea that political authority is based on a more or less unstable exchange relationship. Every exercise of authority is the focus of contention among competing interests. After all, even a father's authority over his children involves claims and counterclaims that limit each other. A good father's legitimate demands of obedience will be moderated by his care for the child and by reining in his own temper. And the child, in keeping with its drive to survive and grow, makes demands on the parents while gradually learning to control unruly impulses. This mixture of extroversion and self-restraint is charged with emotion. Demands for obedience can be tyrannical, tempers explosive, self-assertion can turn into aggression or basic distrust, and demands for affection or reassurance can become insatiable or addictive. A good father-child relationship is possible only where each person involved draws back from the excesses of his own inclination.

The same considerations apply to authority relations. For political interchanges, like personal ones, are always evidence of "asocial sociability," which Kant defined as "the propensity of men to enter into society, which propensity is, however, linked to a constant mutual resistance which threatens to dissolve the society."[20] How are we to think of conditions under which the legitimation of power weakens and the exchange relations underlying authority are eroded, or destroyed altogether? Here it must suffice to juxtapose legitimate with illegitimate power in the national community, or the reciprocity of expectations with the breakdown of this implicit exchange-relationship between rulers and ruled in the twentieth century.

Illegitimacy

Start with the banking analogy once again. The mutual expectations of banks and owners of bank accounts are supported by governmental controls—as long as everything runs smoothly. The crisis of the American savings and loan industry during the 1980s makes clear what happens when these controls are abolished or weakened in the name of free enterprise while the public insurance of private accounts is retained. Where private investors are lured into a feeling of security, the way is opened for risky investments and huge profits by unscrupulous managers. Because of public insurance, a major collapse of the system can perhaps be avoided, but only at the expense of the taxpayer. One can compare this situation with the inflation of the early Weimar Republic, which grew to catastrophic proportions because the government sought to cope with the rising public debt by increasing the money supply. The social unrest of the early 1920s was a widespread answer to the resulting loss of legitimation by the government.

These and related instances suggest that every system of laws can be curtailed, or even undermined, by illegal activities or by unwise policies. Such facts alone do not invalidate legitimate authority. On the contrary, by curbing illegalities or by correcting policies that have proved counterproductive, authority vindicates its reason for being.[21] When illegal actions become organized, they can acquire so much illegitimate power that they threaten the existing authority structure. Familiar examples are the crime syndicates in the United States and Italy, the drug cartel in Columbia, or the rise of crime and barter in the Soviet Union. Such illegal organizations cannot be eradicated altogether. The critical question is whether in the end they come to replace, and hence destroy, the existing system of authority and the mutual expectations on which it rests.

The corruption or delegitimation of power has been a main theme of political theory since ancient times. The totalitarian regimes of the twentieth century have developed new ways of destroying the exchange relationship underlying governmental authority. In East Berlin, on the occasion of the workers' unsuccessful uprising for higher wages in 1953, that destruction was summed up by Bertolt Brecht in a biting epigram. Party officials had declared

> that the people had forfeited the trust of the government and could regain it only through redoubled effort. Would it then not really be simpler for the government to dissolve the people and elect another one?

This epigram can be used to interpret the illegitimacy of one-party regimes in theoretical terms.[22]

Communist governments claim that the party is the only legitimate mouthpiece of the working class. That claim goes back to the theory of historical materialism with its sole access to the scientific understanding of the "history of class struggles." The theory was reflected in Lenin's distinction between professional revolutionaries "who have raised themselves to the level of comprehending theoretically the historical movement as a whole" and the working class with its trade-unionist preoccupations. Lenin's distinction was based on the Marxian thesis of a "portion of the bourgeois ideologists . . . , a small section of the ruling class, which cuts itself adrift and goes over to the proletariat, the class which holds the future in its hands."[23] From here it is only a small step to the monopolistic claim of the Communist party. What have been the organizational consequences of this claim that have undermined the legitimation of the communist power structure?

A succinct answer must start from the monopolistic power of the party. Power means "the probability that one actor within a social relationship will be in a position to carry out his own will despite resistance."[24] In the present case this means that the politburo at the top of the party hierarchy is free to decide whatever it wishes, while all responsibility for the outcome is relegated to subordinate persons and agencies. Walter Ulbricht, the leader of the East German Socialist Unity party from 1945 to 1971, formulated the application of this principle with commendable clarity. "Even some experienced colleagues and faithful comrades," he said, "disregard the laws of social development and do not understand that *what was correct yesterday is already outdated and incorrect today.*" By a statement of this kind the party elite claims for itself the possibility of changing its instructions from one day to the next without being held accountable, since each decision is based on the only true knowledge of those "laws." Therefore, all responsibility is borne by subordinate officials, who were reminded by Ulbricht that "the word *impossible* is to be banned once and for all from the vocabulary of the German language."[25] This linguistic *tour de force* means that the politburo attributes every deviation from its mandatory plan as a transgression of subordinates. By eradicating the word "impossible" the party puts pressure on the whole population, for every explanation why something is impossible becomes an excuse. This suspicion that more could have been achieved if only the people had tried harder is institutionalized by a double hierarchy of government.

The Communist one-party system lacks legitimation because it destroys the possibility of regular reciprocity between rulers and ruled. The monopolized truth of the politburo and the total suspicion, to which the people are subjected, create a Manichaean worldview, not only ideologically but also organizationally. Party functionaries are assigned to every social activity and they are under a double mandate. In the case of industrial relations, the functionaries must support the orders of the factory director with all the means of agitation and supervision at their disposal. On the other hand, they must publicly expose and correct through their contact with the masses all the mistakes of management. All this occurs while that management is subject to the plans issued by the relevant ministries whereas the cadres of functionaries are controlled by the higher echelons of the party. In this way a Kafkaesque guarantee of party infallibility is created, for higher party authorities can change the party line depending on the dictates of the moment and thereby put either the management or the work force under suspicion. That way one can explain the typical fluctuations of the party line, for a simultaneous pressure on management and the work force would deprive the party hierarchy of its freedom to maneuver at will.

This ideal type of Communist one-party rule is compatible with different strategies of the party leadership in its response to changing contingencies. Even a monopolization of decision making at the top is hardly the same as total control of a society. One-party rule deliberately insulates itself against all uncensored information about public reactions from below. It operates in a self-created social vacuum: by making party membership and its benefits a reward for loyal service, the party guarantees that it will only hear the orthodoxies it has propounded itself. The *nomenklatura* is the massive organizational equivalent of the sycophants doing the bidding of a personal ruler.

Before the wall between East and West Germany was built in 1961, some 3 million people (of 19 million) had fled from East to West. There was talk of a "hemorrhage." After the wall, certain reforms and the elaboration of the social security system helped to settle the relation between the party and the population for a time. These changes were introduced to buttress the party's monopoly of decision making and provide the population with benefits to compensate for submission to the constraints imposed from above. Perhaps the regime obtained some minimal legitimation by these moves, a kind of popular resignation in which the "withdrawal of efficiency" (Veblen) takes the place of consent. This accommodation between rulers and ruled did not diminish either the party's claim to infallibility or the manipulation of suspicion to implement party controls. The collapse of the DDR regime in 1989 has taught us that such strategies were not enough to undo the illegitimacy of communist rule that had existed for decades.

The illegitimacy of any regime like the legitimation of power always remains proximate. After all, the party members who benefit from a communist regime believe in its legitimacy, or at least pretend to do so, even if the rest of the people think otherwise. In East Germany before November 1989, the Socialist Unity party had some 2.3 million members in a work force of 8.8 million. Many if not most members joined to obtain the benefits only party membership could provide. They probably mouthed party slogans to remain in good standing, whatever their private reservations. And beliefs professed under duress are not to be dismissed for that reason, for they affect both the person and the public arena. Beliefs and self-interest are not easily distinguished. Opportunism of all kinds can still help to sustain a political order, even while it blurs the distinction between legitimacy and illegitimacy. We can only know in retrospect whether the proximate degree to which beliefs play a role was sufficient to maintain a given regime.

The reason for this uncertainty lies in the ambivalence of the beliefs themselves and of the proximate way in which people are swayed by them. Beliefs arise from tradition, custom, and a sense of justice, as well as from the mixture of fear and hope with which the ruled respond to the exercise of power.[26] When we think of the reciprocity of expectations between rulers and ruled, we refer implicitly to this unstable amalgam of feelings and ideas. These uncertainties are an essential ingredient of what practicing politicians have to deal with: it will not do to eliminate what politics is about in the name of science and predictability. The members of a community distinguish themselves from those who do not belong, but relations among "the natives" are an arena of struggle and uncertainty.

Notes

1. Carl Becker, *The Heavenly City of the Eighteenth Century Philosophers* (New Haven: Yale University Press, 1932), 47.
2. Karl Löwith has traced this idea of Western civilization from modern times to its biblical roots in *Meaning in History* (Chicago: University of Chicago Press, 1949).
3. Oddly, Marx himself knew that "the satisfaction of the first need . . . leads to new needs." See Robert C. Tucker, ed., *The Marx-Engels Reader* (New York: W.W.

Norton, 1972), 120. Marx never related the infinity of possible needs to his strictures on religion.

4. Niccolo Machiavelli, *The Prince and the Discourses* (New York: The Modern Library, 1940), 91.

5. Quoted from Montesquieu's "De la Politique" in the introduction by Franz Neumann to his edition of Baron de Montesquieu, *The Spirit of the Laws* (New York: Hafner Publishing Company, 1949), xxxiii.

6. Montesquieu, *The Spirit of the Laws*, 2–3.

7. For documentation cf. Reinhard Bendix, *Embattled Reason*, vol. 2 (New Brunswick, NJ: Transaction Publishers, 1989), chapter 13.

8. The two passages are reprinted in Tucker, ed., *Marx-Engels Reader*, 192–93, 437.

9. Quoted in Frank Manuel, *The New World of Henri Saint-Simon* (Cambridge: Harvard University Press, 1956), 135. For a critical discussion of this "scientistic" tradition cf. F. A. Hayek, *The Counter-revolution of Science* (Glencoe, IL: The Free Press, 1952). A sustained analysis of how to restore the tradition of balance in economics is contained in Adolf Lowe, *On Economic Knowledge, Towards a Science of Political Economics* (New York: Harper & Row, 1965).

10. Harold Lasswell, *Politics: Who Gets What, When, and How* (New York: Peter Smith, 1950[1936]), v, 3.

11. There is a saying that a politician needs a scientific advisor the way a drunk needs a lamppost, for support not for illumination.

12. The principle is still in evidence in the British monarchy, even though royalty is now identified with its ceremonial functions and, on certain occasions, with the influence of its moral suasion. Kings and queens no longer rule, but still represent important symbols of popular allegiance.

13. Stephen J. Gendzier, ed., *Denis Diderot, The Encyclopedia, Selections* (New York: Harper & Row, 1987), 185–88.

14. It has become fashionable to decry such order in the name of participatory democracy, because government, it is said, merely serves the interest of the powerful. But mass demonstrations are not always right and the police is not always wrong. In the light of such prolonged civil wars as those in Lebanon, Ethiopia, or Sri Lanka, I regard principled opposition to authority as superficial and inhumane. Cf. the critical discussion of participatory democracy in John Bendix, *Brauchtum und Politik: Die Landsgemeinde in Appenzell Ausserrhoden* (Herisau: Schläpfer Verlag, 1993).

15. Max Weber, *Economy and Society*, vol. 1, trans. and ed. Guenther Roth and Claus Wittich (New York: The Bedminster Press, 1968), 54–56. Weber was careful to emphasize that a political order depends on force being employed only as a means of last resort, and on popular consent consisting in good part of conventional compliance. This implicit reciprocity is a main reason why the mandate to rule due to "sufficient satisfaction" can be assessed only in retrospect.

16. Ibid., 31, 53. Weber uses "domination" or *Herrschaft* as his principal term, but in English "authority" is more readily understood. Force or power are sociologically amorphous terms in the sense that they occur in all human relationships and require further specification. Events in the Soviet Union have demonstrated the crucial importance of the belief in the existence of a legitimate order. For where that belief declines or disappears, no concentration of power at the top and no amount of regulation can ensure compliance.

17. Ibid., 226.

18. Ibid., 37.

19. Ibid., 241.

20. Immanuel Kant, "Idea for a Universal History with Cosmopolitan Intent" (1784), in Carl J. Friedrich, ed., *The Philosophy of Kant* (New York: The Modern Library, 1949), 120.
21. This fact has led to the speculation that a certain rate of crime is "normal" and needed so that social controls can reinforce and validate the existing norms of society. Cf. Emile Durkheim, *The Rules of Sociological Method* (Chicago: University of Chicago Press, 1938), 64ff. However, the distinction between acceptable and intolerable levels of illegality is impossible to specify, except perhaps retroactively.
22. See my earlier study of industrial relations in East Germany in Reinhard Bendix, *Work and Authority in Industry* (Berkeley: University of California Press, 1974), chapter 6. I note the points at which events have superseded this study, originally published in 1956.
23. Karl Marx and Friedrich Engels, *The Communist Manifesto* (1848) reprinted in Tucker, ed., *Marx-Engels Reader*, 343. The phrasing of this paragraph uses the manifesto's wording in order to characterize the Leninist position.
24. Weber, *Economy and Society*, 53.
25. Cited in Bendix, *Work and Authority*, 384, 386.
26. My formulation is related to the analysis of Max Weber, *Economy and Society*, 31–38. To characterize compliant behavior Weber speaks not only of interests of the most diverse kind, but of adherence to tradition mixed with notions of legality. He did not anticipate one-party regimes in which the opportunism of the beneficiaries takes the place of all other motivations and thereby distinguishes them from the rest of the population. But where so many "toe the line" to advance their careers, people in turn come to distinguish between party members who are decent despite their affiliation, and party members who cannot be trusted at all.

7

Modern States and Civil Societies in Comparative Perspective

In modern politics, membership in the human community is defined by the state rather than the ruler and the church. Citizenship distinguishes those who belong from those who do not, in the United States as well as in Burkina Faso. At the same time, each citizen belongs to other communities as well. They are less comprehensive than the state but also closer to everyday experience. People live in families, form friendships, work in enterprises, belong to social clubs, join associations representing their interests, and so on. They engage in thousands of activities that bring them into close and more or less enduring contact with one another. These forms of sociability allow people to join in common endeavors and express common concerns. Civil society is a convenient term for the aggregate of associations and activities constituting more or less organized communities, but without public authority.

Concepts Past and Present

In the social sciences, state and civil society have reemerged only recently. The circumstances vary. A conference organized by the Social Science Research Council, entitled "Bringing the State Back In," suggested that in the United States the behavioral sciences had given the state little attention. On the other hand, "civil society" reemerged in a political context: the Eastern European liberation movements of the 1980s against Communist one-party dictatorships.[1] However, the historical mutability of meanings is not the same as achieving conceptual clarification.

Modern science and industry as well as basic ideas of the French Revolution have transformed our world. These transformations cannot be separated from their Western European origins. All other countries were placed in the position of follower societies. Even countries that retained their political independence developed a sense of backwardness in comparison with the advance of "the West." And that reaction is related to the worldwide diffusion of idea of progress.

The scientific, industrial, and political revolutions of the seventeenth and eighteenth centuries brought about transformations of world-historical significance, comparable in their global effect to those initiated by early Christianity. As discussed earlier, Christianity introduced a universalist ethic based on a common faith, which was ultimately incompatible with the moral particularism of the pre-Christian era. When the Apostle Paul wrote (Gal 3:28) that after faith has come, "there is neither Jew nor Greek, there is neither bond nor free, there is neither male nor female: for ye are all one in Christ Jesus," he put the new creed in place of distinctions that are taken for granted by most people from the ancient Romans down to the present.

Something like this is also true of the secular universalist ethic that has spread throughout the world since the seventeenth century, partly through persuasion and partly through the massive use of force. Modern science and industry as well as the idea of liberty have led to major redefinitions of the human community. For the quest for scientific knowledge, the pursuit of economic gain and the desire for "liberté, égalité, fraternité" do not want their advance hindered by national, religious, or familial affiliations, any more than Christianity did. The sciences want total freedom for the pursuit of truth wherever it may lead. Economic man wants total freedom for the pursuit of gain on the ground that this is in accord with human nature and enhances the "wealth of nations." Advocates of liberty and equality fight against all constraints that would limit man's "natural rights." Down to the present we are affected by Rousseau's idea that man is good, but has been corrupted by social institutions. This original goodness of man (rather than his original sin) is at the base of all striving without limits, whether it is in pursuit of knowledge, gain, or equality. Infinite striving assumes the possibility of infinite progress.

The revolutionary significance of Christianity had consisted in the change from a moral particularism based on kinship, language, or locality to an ethical universalism based on faith. By way of analogy, the revolutionary significance of the modern creed consists in rejecting any ultimate limitation of human endeavor. Apparently, this modern creed involves an undertaking as contradictory as that of early Christianity. Then, people of the faith encountered the continued existence of religious and cultural as well as social and sexual differences, which put the universal ethic of Christianity into question. Today, the modern belief in infinite progress has to cope with the fact that fields do not advance simultaneously. The origin of early science, industry, and political liberty in Western Europe meant that from the beginning all people outside that perimeter were placed in a position of backwardness, a situation hard to cope with, both emotionally and politically. In addition, the belief in progress must come to terms with the fact that each step forward creates new problems in the very process of having solved old ones.

Progress means the intrinsic universalism of the quest for truth, wealth, and liberty. Hence, the modern state faces the dilemma of having to establish a political order with its institutional limits in a culture dedicated to progress without limit. Christianity claimed recognition for the universality of the faith despite the continued existence of particular loyalties. Similarly, the advanced countries of Western civilization have spread the enlightened creed to the rest of the world despite the relative backwardness of countries. Then as now, ethical dualism limits all universalist claims. The Christian missions could not deny that their success remained partial, since some people declared Christian universalism null and void. The advocates of science, liberty, and economic development cannot deny that their success remains partial, because new, unsolved problems arise with every advance. Spokesmen of the modern state cannot deny that its success in establishing a political order must remain partial, because that order depends on people who want to do things for themselves and thereby frequently test the limits of the state's authority.

A mixture of idealistic zeal and crass materialism has prevailed in ethical dualism as much as in ethical universalism, whether we consider the Western religious tradition or the modern belief in progress. We must try to take that burdensome legacy into account as we formulate basic concepts like state and civil society for our time.

A Concept of the State

In Webster's we find the state defined as "the power or authority represented by a body of people politically organized under one government, especially an independent government, within a territory having definite boundaries." In the equivalent German *Duden* we read: "the totality of institutions whose collaboration should guarantee the enduring and orderly living together of people who are residing within a state-territory with definite boundaries." The Anglo-American definition emphasizes people, the German one institutions, though not too much should be made of dictionary definitions. Both have in common that the people who reside within definite boundaries constitute communities by virtue of their political organization. As such, they are distinguished from people outside that organization. States comprise those institutions that supervise these politically constituted communities, and if need be defend them.

It is useful to think of the state as a modern phenomenon, roughly dating from the era of absolutism and mercantilism culminating in the French Revolution. This restricted meaning conflicts with common usage which refers to all political entities as states if they have identifiable territories and heads of government. The ancient Greek polis, the Roman Empire, the Holy Roman Empire of the German nation, the Ottoman Empire, the England of William the Conqueror, the Mongol empire under Ghengis Khan, the Inca empire can all be referred to as states. One can use the word that way. But if we call all governed territories states, we will be unable to distinguish landed property from cities, counties from provinces, or colonies from empires. Some prior classification is needed that enables us to distinguish between governed territories of different kinds.

Max Weber's emphasis upon the centralization of authority over a territory together with Ernest Barker's emphasis on the separation of political authority from family, property, and rank provide a useful vantage point. Weber suggests that the concept of the state has reached its full development only in modern times. It is, therefore, advisable to define its formal characteristics in terms that accord with contemporary experience. The modern state

> possesses an administrative and legal order subject to change by legislation, to which the organized activities of the administrative staff, which are also controlled by regulation, are oriented. This system of order claims binding authority not only over the members of the state, the citizens, . . . but also to a very large extent over all actions taking place in the area of its jurisdiction. It is thus a compulsory organization with a territorial base. Furthermore . . . the use of force is regarded as legitimate only so far as it is either permitted by the state or prescribed by it.[2]

This ideal type of the state can be traced to Machiavelli, Bodin, and Hobbes, while the development of state institutions had its inception in a process of depersonalization. Ernest Barker has made us aware that premodern political orders in Weber's sense derived their rationale from an identification of public office and political affairs with family, inherited wealth, and social rank.[3] Of course, family relations, property, and social prestige still play a role in the modern state. But contemporary influences of this sort do not compare with the former significance of inherited privileges. Hence, Weber's ideal type remains useful, provided we keep his reservation in mind that all conceptual simplifications are initial orientations that require examination of the evidence.

This reservation applies to what Weber called the "full development" of the modern state. Presumably there is agreement that the state's monopoly of the legitimate use of force becomes operative at the following levels:

1. Legislation, including administrative rules
2. Maintenance of order
3. Defense
4. Control of currency
5. Taxation
6. Adjudication of disputes
7. Public works maintaining the infrastructure of the economy
8. Public relief as in disasters, unemployment, etc.

Each of these functions is a center of controversy, not a static attribute. Each of them also requires an administrative organization (or bureaucracy) ideally operating in accordance with laws and rules rather than as a consequence of personal possession.

These functions are attributes of the state because their operation depends upon the government's monopolization of authority. That is, the government bears responsibility for such functions and neither monopolization nor responsibility are diminished by the fact that each function is also a center of political controversy. Suppose there are demonstrations against a regulation issued under the state's authority. In the end people must still turn to the state and its administration to annul or modify the regulation. As long as the state remains intact, its authority cannot be appropriated by private persons or agencies, even if parts of it are on occasion delegated to them.

Definitions of the state always remain incomplete because the highest authority, whether in the hands of a powerful dictator or a body of lawmakers, cannot act unaided. Even parents need help once the household exceeds a certain size. Charismatic leaders call upon their disciples to spread the message. Traditional rulers depend on the work of servants or retainers. Legal authorities depend on the rule-abiding behavior of judges and administrators to implement legal enactments or executive orders. Accordingly, the definition of the state must be related to the administrative implementation of decisions.

***

All exercise of power implies difficult choices. Whether policymakers are one or many, they usually find that every possible decision involves liabilities of its own. Frequently, it seems easier to postpone a decision than to make it. Postponement may be wise wherever change by itself resolves the difficulty that seemed insurmountable at first. In either case, the administrative assistance needed to get the work done becomes political. For the evasion of "tough choices" by policymakers strengthens the bureaucratic tendency of turning issues of political decision making into problems of administration.[4] When those in charge do not make up their mind for whatever reason, their subordinates are ready to "decide" for them, though this shift is easily obscured by administrative technicalities. This is one instance among many why the relations of decision makers with administrative subordinates is always troubled, although the work of governance cannot be done without them.

In a technical sense, bureaucracy provides the best available solution for getting the work of government done, wherever the rule of law prevails. Under these conditions bureaucracy establishes an impersonal relationship between legal authorities and their subordinate officials. Written regulations define the organizational structure in terms of:

1. Rights and duties of each position as a full-time occupation
2. The authority relation between positions
3. Rules of appointment and promotion
4. Technical training or experience as a condition of employment
5. A fixed salary scale
6. Safeguards against the private appropriation of office by appointees.

Modern bureaucracy contrasts with administration by feudal vassals and retainers, or by officials who circumvent the rule of law with impunity.[5] Like all ideal types, this specification simplifies and exaggerates the evidence. Weber pointed out that the rule of law and this type of administration are the more fully realized, "the more completely [they] succeed in eliminating from official business love, hatred, and all purely personal, irrational and emotional elements which escape calculation."[6] This qualification is essential if an impersonal rule of law is to prevail.

Weber was well aware of the unwritten attitudes that lie at the core of all administration. His definition of bureaucracy fails to stress the point at which these attitudes become most significant. For political control over an administration cannot be extended to technical training or experience, however much written regulations circumscribe the conduct of officials.[7] To be sure, the qualification of officials is tested by examinations. They must use these qualifications if they act responsibly on the job, and that means they exercise their best judgment. After all, technical training or experience are required precisely because the official's competence is to benefit the implementation of decisions that have been made higher up. Competence implies the power to choose between good and bad courses of action. The people concerned want to benefit from that choice. If it is really based on expertise, it is beyond the reach of regulations and, to a lesser extent, of political oversight.

Critics have been unable to provide a better defintion of bureaucracy, even if Weber's concept was modeled on the Prussian civil service. They probably overlooked that this ideal type does not make all bureaucracies alike. They differ from one another in the way officials use their judgment—despite the similarity of formal bureaucratic attributes. This critical role of judgment is already evident in the common pejorative meaning of the term. Bureaucracies are said to apply rules rigidly with little consideration of the individual case, to "pass the buck" and operate at a snail's pace, to duplicate effort and give conflicting directives, to concentrate control in the hands of a few, and to expand the staff in inverse proportion to the amount of work accomplished.[8] To the extent that these pathologies occur, bureaucracy becomes illegitimate and is not to be trusted. However, each of the critiques also refers to an aspect of organization that is highly valued. Rules are imposed in the name of equity. Slow operation and even "buck-passing" can be a by-product of orderly procedure. Conflicting directives may result from ambiguous or contradictory policy choices at higher levels. Duplication of effort reflects redundancies needed to try to get things right. Concentration of control is the other side of supervision. Expansion of staff cannot be isolated from the ever-increasing demands for governmental services. In other words, each critique refers to some prized attribute of bureaucracy and raises the question of how much is too much, ultimately a question of judgment. Bureaucracy should not be assessed by an overall condemnation of its possible flaws, which are the other side of judgments, indispensable for the enterprise of administration. Of course, those defects get out of hand when wrong administrative judgments accumulate. Nevertheless, judgments are still needed every time a decision has to be implemented.

Such judgments tend to form bureaucratic culture patterns. The Prussian civil service and its modern derivatives are certainly cases in point. German officials tend to practice an "administrative fetishism" that gives pride of place to their legal training. They adhere to the idea of the *Rechtsstaat*, which was a by-product of the monarchy's struggle against the estate assemblies and their inherited privileges during the seventeenth and eighteenth centuries. That struggle was successful in replacing inherited privileges with the principle of equality before the law. Since then, German judges and administrators have subscribed to a code of professional "objectivity" in their application of the law. In effect, they have carried forward into the modern era a monarchical rather than a revolutionary destruction of inherited privilege. In their view, law embodies the highest decisions of the body politic, whether these emanate from the monarch's personal decisions or from Parliament's collective deliberations. For in both versions law as the equivalent of justice is interpreted as the carefully considered order of the community.[9] Accordingly the official commits himself to the impersonal performance of his duties in the belief that he is acting properly, regardless of what those duties are.[10] This literal compliance with the law, "letting the law speak for itself," does not mean that German officials adhere to Weber's formal criteria of bureaucracy without due deliberation. After all, their legal training and experience entails the exercise of judgment every step of the way. Instead, their belief in the law as justice leads them to judgments that under the guise of objectivity facilitate the intrusion of personal and political prejudices.[11]

Bureaucratic culture patterns in Germany and America are both legitimate exercises of authority, but the contrast between them exemplifies the role of judgment in administrative behavior. Since the destruction of the spoils system, American officials must adhere to the law and to political decisions just as much as German officials. Yet the difference between them remains. American officials are heir to a constitutional tradition that originated in a revolution against the British Crown. The main principle of that tradition is government by popular mandate. Hence, the rule of law is the guideline of official conduct in the United States only insofar as it serves that overarching principle. Elected and appointed officials vie with one another in representing their proposed actions as a response to public demand, even though it must also be in accord with enacted law.[12] In the German case, there is a greater hiatus between input from the people and the actions of officials; for the latter have lifelong tenure and their adherence to the law puts them at a greater distance than their American colleagues from direct contact with the public.[13]

***

The initial statement that in modern politics membership in the human community is defined by the state has proved to be a complex matter. That complexity is due in part to the underlying belief in human agency, of which the state is a comprehensive organized expression. Granted, the modern state is the unanticipated by-product of many antecedents. The state's monopolization of the legitimate use of force could not be sustained indefinitely if we did not believe that by organized collective action we can improve our condition. That belief underlies the development of modern constitutionalism as the basis of political order, even if particular constitutions have remained inoperative. Why would we have an impersonal state if we had not recoiled from the consequences of concentrating all power in the hands of one ruler? Why would we have government under law if we did not think it preferable to a government by arbitrary will based on inherited privilege? The controversies and dissatisfactions that center on most activities of the modern state too often obscure the basic choices underlying the statist definition of the human community.

Administrative implementation under the rule of law is confined to societies in which the separation of public office from family, property, and rank has taken hold. Where this is not the case, premodern political orders remain intact because the rule of law is virtually canceled out by access to public office based on personal influence or political orthodoxy. Society is difficult to distinguish from the state where purely personal influence prevails. And the state is difficult to distinguish from society when all organized activities are preempted by centralized supervision. In the latter case, people either join or withdraw so that the human community becomes internally bifurcated. Recent events in Eastern Europe show that under these conditions the separation of civil society from the state can become a meaningful political demand. Under modern conditions social relations within the human community can remain distinct from the conduct of public affairs, even when they acquire political significance.

A Concept of Civil Society

During the late 1980s, as the Soviet Union withdrew from its commanding position in Eastern Europe, the political slogan "civil society" expressed the desire to free all social interaction from the organized intrusion of a one-party dictatorship. This most recent concept of civil society derives its meaning from the measures taken by a single-party regime to control or even destroy civil society.

In eighteenth-century England "civil society" referred to all people actively engaged in public affairs. William Blackstone declared that the "civil state" consisted of the aristocracy and the clergy. Adam Ferguson had a kindred idea when he related civilization to the effects of the political establishment, calling forth man's intellectual and moral powers. "It is in conducting the affairs of civil society, that mankind find the exercise of their best talents, as well as the object of their best affections."[14] In this interpretation, the adjective "civil" is used in the sense of polished or refined in contrast to rude or uncivilized. In other words, a civil or civilized society is an aristocratic one in which the best men govern. In such a society the "sense of self-esteem [among the privileged few] rests on their awareness that the perfection of their life pattern is an expression of their underived, ultimate, and qualitatively distinctive *being*."[15]

This aristocratic meaning of the civil order was destroyed by the *Déclaration des droits de l'homme et du citoyen* of 1789, which annulled all inherited privilege by proclaiming the legal and political equality of individuals as citizens. With the abolition of hereditary masters went the abolition of hereditary subjects. Both were to be equals before a law that emanated from the national will of all citizens, and that will is always right (Sièyes). In this view, government edicts are valid or legitimate only insofar as they are constitutional and in accord with enacted law. But an assembly of representatives is required to pass such edicts since the nation cannot act as a whole. Though each elected member only represents his district, laws can be arrived at through discussion and compromise that express the "general will."[16]

The modern, Western meaning of "civil society" can be derived from the reservations concerning private assemblies, which were expressed early on by Rousseau and have been reiterated on both sides of the Atlantic ever since. Rousseau distinguished between the selfish will of the individual and the general or communal will of all. He proposed educational measures aimed at cultivating in each human being the devotion to the general good. In his view, communication among citizens was hazardous and should at least be limited because it would lead to private associations and hence to the promotion of particular, at the expense of general, interests.[17] This idea corresponds to the suspicion with which leaders of the American Constitutional Convention regarded factions and parties, as in Federalist 10. Democratic constitutions proclaim the right to assembly, but most of them do not explicitly recognize the formation of political parties.

In late eighteenth-century France, action was taken against particular associations. The Jesuits had controlled the educational system (until they were prohibited from doing so) on the grounds that the education of children should be entirely entrusted to the state. Subsequently, the same principle was applied against the autonomy of Jewish community organizations, the "mutual aid" societies of workers, religious bodies, academic or literary associations, as well as the organization of women.[18] As the Abbé Sièyes put it,

> The main difficulty arises from the interest through which the individual citizen associates only with a few others. Such interest leads to conspiracy and secret agreements; antisocial plans are made thereby; and by these the worst enemies of the people mobilize.[19]

Yet, the fact is that just such private associations give meaning to the term "civil society."

In modern Western democracies civil society refers to personal interactions that are unencumbered by governmental controls, even if they depend on legal provisions only the government can provide. In this respect the French Revolution proved to be a major turning point in modern political history. The subjects who had obeyed their masters became citizens who were themselves masters, at least theoretically. Subjects had belonged to countless jurisdictions, each having hereditary rights and obligations that were abolished. In place of the king and his officials all exercise of authority was placed in the hands of the state, a term often used interchangeably with the people or the nation.

The general will of all citizens was to be expressed through representative bodies and agencies of government, subject to the constitution and a system of laws. Nothing should be allowed to stand in the way of that general will, because the citizens of the country are the source of all authority, hence the suspicion with which Western democratic thought (as well as laissez-faire theories of economics) have always regarded parties, factions, and other "conspiracies against the public."[20]

In fact, voluntary associations have proliferated despite this anti-associational bias. As a result, civil societies have developed, aided by the legal protection of freedom of contract and the constitutional provisions safeguarding freedom of speech and assembly, hence the paradox. On the one hand, the modern state has operated continuously, based on its exclusive jurisdiction over a territory that includes the legitimate use of force. On the other hand, this development has been accompanied by the growth of a civil society in which "private associations put into effect certain rules of particular interest to them in some special area of social and political life, *but without seeking direct responsibility in public affairs.*"[21] To be sure, civil society extends beyond organized interests. In principle, the law supports all activities that do not infringe upon the activities of others, though what constitutes infringement is often disputed. For present purposes it is sufficient to stay with civil society as the aggregate of organized interests, leaving to one side the large number of activities from friendships and families to common interest associations like recreational clubs, or philanthropic foundations that may depend upon the state to an extent but have no discernable effect upon it. To what forces in modern society is the proliferation of associations to be attributed? In raising this question I focus attention on those movements within civil society that, paradoxically enough, also help to account for the centralization of state institutions.

There are three closely related constellations within civil society that enhance the centralization and compulsory jurisdiction of the state. Tocqueville identified one of these when he wrote that in an age of equality "everyone is at once independent and powerless." Independence fills us with pride and promotes the competitive spirit, but lack of power makes us associate with others in joint efforts to enlist the assistance of government. According to Tocqueville,

> Such persons admit, as a general principle, that the public authority ought not to interfere in private concerns, but, by an exception to that rule, each of them craves its assistance in the particular concern on which he is engaged and seeks to draw upon the influence of the government for his own benefit, although he would restrict it on all other occasions.[22]

For Tocqueville this was a speculative truth that followed from the destruction of inherited privilege and the establishment of equality before the law. For us it is an all too familiar reality.

The acquisition of skills lies at the heart of industrialization, itself a basic condition of economic growth. Skills include not only technical expertise but procedural experience in marketing and administration. The obsolescence of these skills is also a consequence of economic growth. For anyone who has acquired skills develops an interest in preserving their economic payoff, the more so the longer the training has lasted. Note that the acquisition of skills involves the investment of time, a form of capital accumulation. It follows that time invested in the acquisition of skills makes a person more independent, whereas the obsolescence of skills makes a person increasingly dependent and powerless. By joining forces people will defend the economic assets that their acquired skills represent. It is a mark of civil society that, by doing so, people can diminish their lack of power, either in the private sector or by pressuring government to give assistance. Note that these two kinds of association, for the promotion of "novel undertakings" and for the defense of "acquired skills" have a common basis in the rights to property, free speech, and assembly.

The third relation between the state and civil society involves public goods. The term commonly refers to air, water, and all other nonrenewable resources, but this is too narrow a definition. Public functions like lawmaking, the maintenance of public order, defense, control of the currency, dispute settlement, tax assessment and collection, the provision of public necessities, and social services are also public goods. These functions are performed by centralized governments financed by public revenues, because no property owner is interested in doing so, or capable of it, but could not pursue his own interests without them. This is the main reason for calling the continuous operation of the state modern, because prior to the seventeenth century public functions and services were in the hands of those possessing inherited privileges. Aristocrats, the clergy, and the urban patriciate not only enjoyed the rights of their social rank, they also performed official functions, while imposing all menial public services on their subjects.

The organized interests of modern Western democracies cannot appropriate public functions however much they succeed in enlisting government assistance to enhance their own interests. The distinction remains significant, even where such groups exert major influence on public policy. After all, they can only serve the interests of their members as long as the government, whose aid they seek, functions well enough to yield to their demands. It follows that wherever public functions are privately appropriated, the continuous operation of the modern state is in question. In several Latin American countries military forces control all political decision making; in the oil-producing Middle East some family dynasties monopolize the leading positions of state and society; and in many African countries government office is used primarily for family advancement in the absence of a viable economy. In these and other cases the rule of law does not apply because forces within society have overwhelmed the state, the separation between public office and private appropriation has become problematic, and the idea of a public interest has been destroyed.

The Concept of Public Interest

Phrases like "the general will" or "the public interest" are in bad repute because we are unable to define them. Jeremy Bentham made this skepticism respectable when he wrote that "the interest of the community" is so general an expression that its meaning is lost:

> The community is a fictitious *body*, composed of the individual persons who are considered as constituting as it were its *members*. The interest of the community then is—what? The sum of the interests of the several members who compose it.[23]

Bentham concedes that interest is one of those words "which cannot in the ordinary way be defined," a reservation that applies to individual interests as well. If taken literally, Bentham's statement seems to "explain" one unknown by another, but his case is much stronger if we take him to mean that the term "interest" is ambiguous at the individual level and undefinable at the collective level. He did not consider that ambiguous and undefinable terms are indispensable: we use them all the time in order to communicate with one another. Complex terms are not in fact devoid of meaning just because they reveal their sense only upon investigation and interpretation, as in the case of legitimation examined earlier.

Still, Bentham's scepticism about the "interest of the community" was justified. Why else would Rousseau have demanded educational reforms and the sacrifice of the individual will in order to give meaning to the general will? Why else would Marx have identified the interests of humanity with those of the working class and then construed a class consciousness in line with the historical development as a whole? These theories seem dated, but the problem of public interest is as current as the last debate in any representative assembly. Superficially, these debates seem futile and self-serving because they only reflect the divided opinions among the people at large. However, they also reflect a common aspiration to articulate the sense or goals of the community, and that aspiration remains despite inconclusive debates and ambiguous policy outcomes. Efforts to articulate "the public interest" should be seen together with the institutional structure of the state which rests on the hope that human agency can make a difference, that decisions are needed and can be implemented. This is the foundation of politics in the modern era in which the concern with the public interest will not vanish as long as these beliefs prevail.

We are probably readier to explore the meaning of public interest now than when doctrines of self-interest and "the invisible hand" or of the class struggle and its complete termination in the future held undisputed sway. Consider the contemporary relevance of Edmund Burke's statement of 1790:

> Society is indeed a contract . . . it is a partnership. . . . As the ends of such a partnership cannot be obtained in many generations, it becomes a partnership not only between those who are living, but between those who are living, those who are dead, and those who are to be born.[24]

This is a motto, it seems, for our growing concern with pollution and global warming, which are the drawbacks of economic growth. Modern industry has a long and sorry history of exploiting public goods like air or water for the sake of private gain and this exploitation has been abetted by communities and jobholders whose livelihood depends upon it. The centrally planned economies of one-party dictatorships are even worse off because in the absence of public protest they are free to devastate the environment in their pursuit of centrally determined goals. In either case, our inability to define the public interest does not preclude that we know when environmental devastation potentially affects everybody. In ordinary speech, the common good is served when governments distinguish between tolerable and intolerable levels of pollution or control the manufacture of dangerous subsances, even if in particular cases groups in the community contest the measures taken to preserve that good.[25]

There is also behavioral evidence for the practical significance of public interest. We proceed on the assumption that the laws will be upheld even though we are disappointed too often. We rely on the police and under many circumstances this proves as reliable though we are periodically disappointed here as well. We depend on government to see to the defense, the currency, public health, and other public services. Our daily activities presuppose all this even though there is malfeasance on defense contracts, illicit currency speculation, and the countless dishonesties that go with every function of the modern state. In fact, millions of people rely on the continuous operation of the state on the implicit assumption that on the whole honest service prevails over dishonest manipulation. As discussed earlier in terms of the banking analogy, the public's unspoken assumption of good will is the precondition of any institutional structure. True, that assumption includes elements like apathy, half-formed beliefs, longing for "the good," the trust in accustomed practice, and other rather inchoate feelings. These subjective conditions must be present to a "sufficient" degree because no institution can withstand a mass challenge to its authority. Developments in the Soviet Union since the late 1980s exemplify such a challenge; the withdrawal of trust has grown apace with the policy of *glasnost*, which could be defined as the opportunity to express distrust. As I see it, good will in some rudimentary sense is a precondition of state institutions.

Individual or group interests are not as unconstrained as muckraking rhetoric would have it. Perhaps we should take a cue from Francis Bacon who wrote of kingship and aristocracy in a manner that provides analogies for a viable relation between a state and the organized interests of civil society:

> A great and potent nobility addeth majesty to a monarch, but diminisheth power; and putteth life and spirit into the people but presseth their fortune. It is well when nobles are not too great for sovereignty or for justice; and yet maintained in that height, as the insolency of inferiors may be broken upon them before it come on too fast upon the majesty of kings.[26]

Might we not say that a "great and potent" civil society with its capacity for economic growth adds majesty to a country even as it diminishes the power of government? That such a society puts life and spirit into the people even as its organized interests press down on their fortune? That it is well for these interests not to be too great for sovereignty or for justice? And that the capacity to organize for common purposes be free and well developed so as to contain mass challenges before they "come on too fast" upon the capacity of the state to function? Is the very ambiguity of these formulations not a reasonable approximation of the "public interest" even though such ambiguity reflects our inability to define that interest?

To go back to the terms I have used, civil society and the state are based on a balance between too much trust and too little. Organized interests must not be so weak that our freedom is endangered or so strong that the continuous operation of government is in jeopardy. These notions defy precision and hence do not command attention in the social sciences. Ideas like these are the daily preoccupation of politicians, whose success depends upon dealing with imponderables and an optimism which in the face of uncertainty ventures to engage in the art of the possible. It is the task of political philosophy and middle-range theories to deal with the conditions of political action, and in retrospect how trust and distrust have waxed and waned. It is the task of politicians to stake their political fortune on decisions (or their avoidance) that may help them to advance their career and define the public interest as they see it.

This hiatus between theory and practice will not disappear, but momentous consequences have followed from Marx's assertion that through a unity of theory and practice "*one* class [can be shown] to represent the whole society."[27] He claimed that only workers and their allies comprise that class. In their name, Communist parties have claimed a monopoly of historical truth, the inevitability of a proletarian revolution and the socialist reorganization of society. That is the rationale for subjecting state and civil society to the "dictatorship of the proletariat."

Totalitarianism or the Destruction of Civil Society

One-party dictatorships establish tyrannies in the name of popular sovereignty. Where the people are the sole source of law and legitimate rule, the party that claims to speak in their name brooks no interference with the will of the community. As the party defines that will, nothing can limit its reach, and all those who oppose it are ostracized or killed. Such regimes were labeled totalitarian in the 1940s, but then doubts arose whether the term was appropriate.

On the one hand, Hitler and Stalin seemed to rule their countries as if their every command was fully implemented. On the other, inefficiencies were rampant and different factions struggled for power even as each claimed to implement the leader's will. Accordingly, two views hardened into schools of thought. One maintained that because nothing could explicitly occur contrary to the directives of the party, everything happening in the country resulted from them. The other emphasized struggles among competing power groups, forcing the leadership to maintain its domination through compromises, or by initiating new measures as a means of bringing recalcitrants into line.[28] The second interpretation seems more persuasive.

The effects of one-party dictatorships on people's interactions with one another are more important. The phrase "destruction of civil society" refers to the suppression of the ability to freely associate with others in the pursuit of common goals. It is not a synonym of physical coercion. However, one-party regimes would not be able to achieve their political ends without making expropriations, imprisonment, torture, or death a credible and ever-present threat. By steps to be outlined below, the Nazis destroyed the civil society of the Weimar Republic in 1933. And, in 1945, the communists of East Germany quickly eliminated the possibility that people could join together in the independent pursuit of common ends. These two phases of the German development allow a comparison of a fascist and a communist rise to power in the same country. The rise of National Socialism followed the rapid political decline of the Weimar Republic under the impact of the Great Depression. The communist conquest of power in East Germany occurred under the auspices of the

Soviet occupation forces, following the military destruction of German society and the division of the whole country into spheres of influence by the occupying powers. In 1933, the threat of force came from the National Socialist party organization and its many affiliates. In 1945, the threat of force came from the Soviet sponsorship of German communists who had been exiled in Moscow during the war and returned under Soviet auspices in April and May of that year.

The background was different, but the technique of establishing a one-party regime was much the same, either by destroying civil society or by preventing it from reemerging. Under the Nazis,

the term used to describe this process was *Gleichschaltung*—literally, 'putting into the same gear'—a word so cryptic and impersonal that it conveys no sense of the injustice, the terror and the bloodshed that it embraced. Specifically, *Gleichschaltung* meant in its first stage the purging of the Civil Service, the abolition of the Weimar party system, the dissolution of the state governments and parliaments and of the old Federal Council (*Reichsrat*), as well as the co-optation of the trade union movement. Before it had run its course, it led to a disciplinary blood-letting within the National Socialist party, an event which, by compromising the army leadership, marked the beginning of the *Gleichschaltung* of the armed forces that was to be completed in February 1938.[29]

This general description may be supplemented with two instances of *Gleichschaltung*, under the Nazi regime in 1933 and under communist East German rule after 1945, so that the totalitarian method of ensuring political control is understood. These analogous examples will show that in the two cases civil society is either destroyed, or prevented from emerging, by a party claiming to speak for the interest of the whole community.

In 1932–33, experts were persuaded that the worst of the depression was over, a conviction borne out by the decline of German unemployment from 6 to 3.7 million during the first year of the Hitler regime. Early in 1933, at a meeting with industrialists, Hitler promised a quiet future, rearmament and no more elections for the next ten, perhaps one hundred, years. He received a donation of 3 million Reichsmark for his party's (NSDAP) election campaign. He did not commit himself to any economic policy, declaring that the government needed some 18 to 19 million votes, and that no economic program in the world could receive the consent of that many voters.[30] Achieving political control had priority.

In the field of labor relations, Social Democrats and trade unionists were lulled into believing that the destruction of their organizations was not intended. The NSDAP had established a National Socialist Work Council Organization (NSBO) in open competition with the existing trade union structures. There had also been negotiations concerning the establishment of a united front. Then, in the March 1933 work council elections, the NSBO obtained one-quarter of the votes cast, which was a big numerical gain, but hardly overwhelming. The Hitler government quickly reacted to the disappointing result by a law authorizing the instant dismissal of all employees showing the faintest trace of "treasonous activity," and by prohibiting any further work council elections for the next six months. The threat to the trade unions became palpable, but their reaction was restrained in what appeared to be an effort not to jeopardize the survival of the whole trade union movement. Its destruction had been secretly planned for 2 May, but first came the "carrot." The traditional, internationalist labor holiday of 1 May was suddenly declared a national holiday, the "day of national labor." Before meetings of hundreds of thousands, Hitler and Goebbels proclaimed that the class struggle had been replaced by the folk community (*Volksgemeinschaft*), that millions of people previously kept apart by different occupations and artificial status distinctions would now find the way to understand each other again. The slogan was "Honor Work and Respect the Worker." The French ambassador François-Poncet commented that a sense of reconciliation and unity was wafting over the Third Reich.[31]

On 2 May, only twelve hours later, units of the party's paramilitary formations, under the leadership of NSBO functionaries, occupied trade-union buildings throughout the country. All leading functionaries of the trade unions including their banks and newspapers were taken into "protective custody," while all middle- and low-ranking trade union employees could remain at their posts under NSBO auspices.[32] The aim was not to destroy trade-union organizations, but to take them over through an action committee, headed by Robert Ley and charged with reorganizing labor under Nazi auspices (*Deutsche Arbeitsfront* or DAF). Within three days most employee organizations with some 8 million members had subordinated themselves to that committee. By 19 May, a law establishing "trustees of labor" (*Treuhänder der Arbeit*) in effect replaced the earlier collective bargaining. Now, labor conditions were formulated and enforced by the state, completing the destruction of the country's trade union movement that had only begun on 2 May. By July the Nazi's general monopolization of political power had been completed. And by the fall that completion was symbolized in an "Appeal to all Productive Germans," declaring that in the DAF "the worker would stand next to the employer, *no longer separated by groups and associations serving separate economic or social interests.*"[33]

The Nazi regime did not rule by force alone. For a time, it enlisted a very large following that supported this invocation of the national community. The methods used to achieve that support in effect destroyed German civil society by centrally organizing and supervising all social activities, not only by suppressing them.[34] I shall only refer to a few incentives designed to appeal to workers, but these must be seen against the background of general appeals since a regime that monopolizes power must demonstrate that it exerts power.[35]

During the first years of the Hitler regime, the economy recovered rapidly, but working conditions were only allowed to improve slowly. Wage increases were reduced by compulsory deductions for various party organizations and campaigns. At the same time, the regime increased nonmonetary incentives, thereby providing from above for the whole country what collective bargaining between employers and workers was no longer allowed to achieve on its own. Hygienic measures, sports facilities, and recreation rooms were introduced; workers became entitled to two, three, or even four times the vacation time they had previously enjoyed. Production campaigns served the triple purpose of increasing productivity, providing the DAF with inside information, and providing the work force with a communal sense of sports-like competition. Through its "Strength through Joy" (*Kraft durch Freude*) organization the government also provided opportunities for organized tourism. Though many middle-class people participated in these organized vacations, many workers did too, probably for the first time in their lives.[36] To this should be added courses in tennis and riding, theater evenings, dances, and extension courses, all organized by the DAF in the name of national solidarity. However deceitful the official acclamations of the folk community were, it is also true that status differences were reduced as workers participated in ways that had been barred to them before. Of course, this whole gamut of activities was undertaken by agencies of the party and the government, a tactic that Goebbels labeled "organized spontaneity."[37] Chances are that people other than true believers were not fooled by the rhetoric of "the folk," but one can hardly blame workers for enjoying amenities not previously available to them. This made it easy to overlook that all leisure time activities were centrally directed, so that people could no longer freely interact with others in their pursuit of common interests.

The Nazi destruction of the Weimar Republic's state and civil society in 1933 differs in kind from the absence of a civil society in East Germany in 1945. The country lay in ruins at the end of the war and people were preoccupied with survival. Besides, they were emerging from twelve years of dictatorship, in which all joint activities had been tightly controlled. A civil society did not have to be destroyed, as it had been when the Nazis came to power. Instead, when political activity resumed after the defeat, supreme power lay in the hands of the German Communist party under the general direction of the Soviet military authorities.

Between 1933 and 1945 the leadership of the German Communist party had remained intact in its Moscow exile where it was officially encouraged to prepare for the resumption of political activity in Germany after the war. In exile many other parties also organized for the day when they would return to Germany. But much depended on the official attitude of the host countries. In the Western democracies, political exiles were consulted occasionally, but mostly they were left "on hold" until they might or might not serve a useful political purpose. By contrast, the German communists in exile were employed by Soviet authorities to organize German prisoners of war politically. The German Communist party had been subordinated to the dictates of Soviet policy since its foundation in the early 1920s and one can ask to what degree the party had been a part of Germany's civil society during the Weimar period.[38] Subordination to Soviet authority was reinforced during the years of exile in Moscow and obviously remained in place in East Germany under the Soviet Military Administration (*Sowjetische Militäradministration* or SMAD) after 1945.

The Central Committee of the German Communist party (under the leadership of Walter Ulbricht) set up a commission charged with outlining a political action program. The second and third point of this program are relevant here:

2. The party's aim is to complete the "bourgeois-democratic transformation"; an immediate revolutionary transition to socialism is not in the interest of the Communist party.
3. The party must strive to collect all "anti-fascist forces" in one "block."[39]

These programmatic points pose a puzzle. What sense did it make to renounce a revolutionary goal when the country lay in ruin, or to speak of a "bourgeois-democratic transformation" and "anti-fascist forces" when people struggled for sheer survival and political activity was only permitted with the approval of Soviet authority? The short answer is that in 1945 the German Communist party had to assist the Soviet commandant in normalizing conditions for the population as a whole. This meant that the party helped to recreate a civil society at some rudimentary level. But once political activities were permitted again, the party proceeded to organize that society under its own direction by establishing "anti-fascist" mass organizations, a "united front" of all people against the Nazi past. Walter Ulbricht commented: "It has to look democratic, but we must have everything under control."[40]

At the end of the war, both parts of Germany were confronted with a paradoxical situation. The whole country had suffered a military defeat and wholesale destruction. The bulk of the population had collaborated with the Nazis. Some prominent Nazis were tried and convicted. Denazification proceedings against the middle ranks were largely unsuccessful, more so in West than in East Germany. The need to reconstruct the country was palpable and many former Nazis had administrative experience and were allowed eventually to continue in prominent positions. Whereas in 1933 the Nazis had destroyed civil society, in 1945 civil society needed to be built up, and that included the still existing personnel network of former Nazis.[41] Moreover, to the population at large the occupation authorities represented the conquerors, which undermined the credibility of harsh measures against former Nazis. As the reasoning went at the time, the Hitler regime had been bad, but ordinary people had had no choice and should not be punished for what they had been forced to do. Also, the refugees from Hitler's Germany, who were allowed to return, appeared tainted by their association with the victorious Allies and, after a prolonged absence, had to reestablish their credentials with the people. A murky accounting took place: who had suffered more, the people who had been expelled from the country or the people at home who had been subjected to the cruelties of the regime and the devastations of war?

The German communists returning from their Moscow exile faced a similar task of reestablishing their credentials. Subordination to Moscow had been the declared policy of the party under the Weimar Republic and during the Moscow exile of the leaders during the Nazi period. From 1945 on, the newly established Communist party collaborated with the Soviet occupation of East Germany. In East Germany, that subservience cannot have made communist claims very persuasive when the country was occupied and exploited by the Soviet army. But then, communist regimes for the most part have to organize recalcitrant or indifferent people, whose collaboration they enlist by co-optation.[42]

The following chronology of decrees in the first months of the Soviet occupation of East Germany exemplifies the well-coordinated speed with which a kind of civil society was both reestablished and destroyed in short order. The qualification is needed to remind ourselves that the measures taken under tight party control were only made to appear democratic. After all, Soviet occupation ensured the predominance of the Communist party, which followed the Soviet model of claiming the party's monopoly on truth and power.

1945

April/May	German Communist exiles return from Moscow, the Ulbricht group to Berlin, the Ackermann group to Saxony, the Sobottka group to Mecklenburg/Pomerania
June 9	Establishment of Soviet Military Administration in Germany (SMAD)
June 10	SMAD Command No. 2: admission of antifascist parties and trade unions
June 11	Appeal of Central Committee of Communist party to prepare and issue a new constitution
June 15	Appointment of party committee to prepare the organization of antifascist democratic trade unions in Berlin (*Freier Deutscher Gewerkschaftsbund* or FDGB)
June 15/17	Reconstitution of the Social Democratic party
June 19	Collaborative agreement (literally action community or *Aktionsgemeinschaft*) between KPD and SPD and formation of a working group composed of central committee members of both parties
June 26	Foundation of the Christian Democratic Union
July 5	Foundation of the Liberal Democratic party

| July 8 | Convention organized on the initiative of the SMAD to found a Cultural Federation (*Kulturbund* or KB) for the democratic renewal of Germany |
| July 14 | Formation of a block of antifascist, democratic parties, consisting of Communists, Social Democrats, Christian Democrats and Liberal Democrats |

The organization of the Social Democratic party was followed within two days by the proposal of collaboration with the Communist party, whereas the foundation of bourgeois parties (CDU and LDPD) were not followed by a similar proposal. In short order, a series of other organizations (peasants, youths, women, various cultural activities) were established and co-opted in similar fashion.[43]

Normalization of East German society after the defeat consisted therefore in institutionalizing a "civil society" in all its organizational variety, provided this was done with the consent of the Soviet Military Administration, which in turn guaranteed the control of the Communist party. Every association established under these conditions had a public purpose first and common private purposes only if these proved compatible with the policies of the Communist party (SED). Nevertheless, Ulbricht's cynical remark that it must "look democratic" is not to be dismissed. For in the decades to follow it remained communist policy to support other parties (and organizations) financially and to allow them their own activities at local and district levels, as long as supervision remained in communist hands. These local activities under nominally noncommunist auspices helped to mobilize those parts of the population that would not have yielded as easily to direct approaches by communist functionaries. This principle applied to all organizations with one notable exception. The Social Democratic party (SPD) was maneuvered into unification with the Communist party by the establishment of the Socialist Unity party in April 1946. In effect, the SPD was destroyed less than a year after it had been reconstituted in June 1945. This action foreclosed resumption of party activities by the SPD at the local level.[44]

The communists had regarded the Social Democrats as their greatest enemies before the Nazis came to power, and they continued to do so after 1945. Acceptance of the SPD as a "legitimate" party, even in the subordinate position of the so-called bourgeois parties, was impossible from the standpoint of Leninist doctrine and practice. For a Communist party that claims to be the sole representative of the working class must anathematize the Social Democrats who make the same claim. Once again we see the Manichaean principle at work, within the same society. For the communist definition of the community, like other definitions by one-party dictatorships, distinguishes between the party faithful who reap the benefits of their loyalty (real or faked), and all others who are cast out as suspects, if not traitors, and who are thought to justify detailed supervision by the security apparatus.[45]

***

This brief comparison between the Nazi rise to power in 1933 and the communist rise to power in East Germany after 1945 suggests that the totalitarian claims of one-party dictatorships have a family resemblance. Whether the appeal is to race or to the working class, the party claims to be the mouthpiece of the general will, the only authentic representative of the whole country. And by making this claim, the single party justifies the subjection of all common-purpose organizations to the commands and orthodox doctrine of the regime, which are subject to instant change within the confined jargon of the party line. Civil societies are suppressed in varying degrees in a peacetime simulation of combat readiness, though the demand for unity of the country goes together with much strife in the top echelons of the party regimes. As a result, fascist and communist regimes are undermined in the long run from a break in the social contract. As I have suggested earlier, they become illegitimate to the degree that their organizational strategies concentrate all decision making at the top while pushing all responsibility downward. The effect is that decisions on membership in the human community have become the exclusive prerogative of the state, which treats all unsupervised association as conspiracies that must be rooted out. The destruction of civil society is the bureaucratized equivalent of tyranny in the twentieth century.

Notes

1. Fluctuating attention, different contexts, and varied meaings of the same term are the subject of *Geschichtliche Grundbegriffe* (Basic Historical Concepts), ed. Otto Brunner, Reinhart Koselleck, and others. The *Archiv für Begriffsgeschichte* (Journal

for the History of Concepts) has been published for twenty years, suggesting that preoccupation with the history of concepts is a German specialty.

2. Max Weber, *Economy and Society*, trans. and ed. by Guenther Roth and Claus Wittich (New York: The Bedminster Press, 1968), 56. The definition is more comprehensive than it seems, when one considers that many modern dictatorships have formally representative bodies in which laws and rules are passed by acclamation. Where purely personal rule prevails instead, one can speak of "neo-patrimonialism," as Guenther Roth does in *Politische Herrschaft und persönliche Freiheit* (Frankfurt: Suhrkamp, 1987), 115-22, although the absence of property ownership as the basis of rule presents definitional problems.

3. Ernest Barker, *The Development of Public Services in Western Europe, 1660–1930* (Hamden: Archon Books, 1966), 4-5. The premodern development of state institutions is traced in Otto Hintze, "Die Entstehung der modernen Staatsministerien," *Staat und Verfassung* (Göttingen: Vandenhoeck & Ruprecht, 1962), 275-320.

4. Karl Mannheim, *Ideology and Utopia* (New York: Harcourt, Brace & Co., 1949), 105.

5. Weber, *Economy and Society*, vol. 1, 217-26 and vol. 3, chapter 11.

6. Ibid., vol. 2, 975.

7. Weber's stress on specialized knowledge and the secretiveness of administrative procedures comes closest. But secrets, or the "undisclosable" knowledge of the specialist, are an intrinsic part of expertise itself, which can be used for the subversion of policies as well as for their implementation.

8. Goodwin Watson, "Bureaucracy as Citizens See It," *Journal of Social Issues* 1 (1945), 4-13 and C. Northcote Parkinson, *Parkinson's Law and other Studies in Administration* (Boston: Houghton, Mifflin & Co., 1957).

9. The German term *Recht* can mean law as well as justice (*Gerechtigkeit*) so that the language itself obscures the distinction between specific enactments and general principles. See the comparison between *Rechtsstaat* and rule of law in Franz Neumann, *Die Herrschaft des Gesetzes* (Frankfurt: Suhrkamp Verlag, 1980), 203-10.

10. Note that this was the argument of Nazi officials before the denazification tribunals. One can relate the ideas and behavior of German officials to the Lutheran tradition as Richard Münch suggests in *Die Kultur der Moderne*, vol. 2 (Frankfurt: Suhrkamp Verlag, 1986), 686-99, but that derivation violates the rule of parsimony. The relation of the *Rechtsstaat* to the struggle against the estates is more direct. See p. 825.

11. See the analyses of these prejudices in Ludwig Bendix, *Die irrationalen Kräfte der zivilrichterlichen Urteilstätigkeit* (Breslau: Schlettersche Buchhandlung, 1927) and *Die irrationalen Kräfte der strafrichterliche Urteilstätigkeit* (Berlin: E. Laubsche Verlagsbuchhandlung, 1928).

12. A case study of such competition is contained in Reinhard Bendix, *Higher Civil Servants in American Society* (Westport, CT: Greenwood Press, 1974), 89-120.

13. See the detailed analysis of this contrast by Ernst Fraenkel, "Freiheit und politisches Betätigungsrecht der Beamten in Deutschland und den USA," in *Deutschland und die Westlichen Demokratien* (Stuttgart: W. Kohlhammer, 1964), 155-90.

14. Adam Ferguson, *An Essay on the History of Civil Society*, (Edinburgh: Edinburgh University Press, 1966 [1767]), 155. For the changing meaning of "civil" see Oxford English Dictionary (1933), vol. 2, 446. The Blackstone quotation is taken from this article.

15. Weber, *Economy and Society*, vol. 2, 490-91.

188   Unsettled Affinities

16. Cf. Reinhard Bendix, *Kings or People* (Berkeley: University of California Press, 1978), 366–72. For a critique of these assumptions see Carl Schmitt, *Die geistesgeschichtliche Lage des heutigen Parlamentarismus* (Berlin: Duncker & Humblot, 1961).
17. The relevant passage from Rousseau's *Social Contract* may be found in Bendix, *Kings or People*, 366.
18. Ibid., 370–77.
19. Emmanuel Joseph Sièyes, *What is the Third Estate?* (New York: Praeger, 1963), 159. Sièyes was a priest, a freemason, and an active member of the national convention of 1789.
20. "People of the same trade seldom meet together . . . but the conversation ends in a conspiracy against the public." See Adam Smith, *The Wealth of Nations*, vol. 1 (New York: Dutton, 1964), 117.
21. Heinz J. Varain, "Verbände," in Hermann Kunst and Siegried Grundmann, eds., *Evangelisches Staatslexikon* (Stuttgart: Kreuz Verlag, 1966), 2322. My italics.
22. Alexis de Tocqueville, *Democracy in America*, vol. 2 (New York: Vintage Books Inc., 1954), 311 n.1.
23. Jeremy Bentham, *An Introduction to the Principles of Morals and Legislation*, reprinted in E. A. Burtt, ed., *The English Philosophers from Bacon to Mill* (New York: The Modern Library, 1939), 792.
24. Edmund Burke, *Reflections on the Revolution in France*, Gateway edition (Chicago: Henry Regnery Co., 1955), 139–40.
25. The overstatement that everybody is affected seems appropriate. After all, the national policy of providing governmental assistance to disaster areas or unemployment insurance enjoys general consent, even though people outside the affected areas or groups are not involved. We pay taxes for these purposes and a host of others, though naturally agreement varies with different kinds of public interest.
26. Francis Bacon, "Nobility," in *The Complete Essays of Francis Bacon* (New York: Washington Square Press, 1963), 36.
27. Karl Marx, "Critique of Hegel's Philosophy of Right," in Tucker, *Marx-Engels Reader*, 21.
28. For the National Socialist period this controversy is summarized in Norbert Frei, *Der Führerstaat* (München: Deutscher Taschenbuch Verlag, 1989), 235–36.
29. Gordon Craig, *Germany, 1866–1945* (New York: Oxford University Press, 1978), 578.
30. The following discussion relies on Frei, *Der Führerstaat* chapter 2, part 1, where the sources will be found for the quotations used in the text.
31. The idea of *Volksgemeinschaft* had had a long German history before it was appropriated by the Nazis. Their innovation consisted not only in the effective propagation of their message, but in making themselves into the sole representative of that *Gemeinschaft* so that all traces of opposition were instantly identified as treasonous. Carl Schmitt's theory of politics, *Der Begriff des Politischen* (Berlin: Duncker & Humblot, 1963), depicting the encounter between enemies rather than opponents or antagonists, was published in 1932, an intellectual gloss on the wartime experience of Hitler and his followers.
32. Offically, "protective custody" meant that the individual being arrested required the regime's protection against the wrath arising from healthy public feeling (*gesundes Volksempfinden*), a menacing verbal intimation of lynching that could not be put off lightly.

33. The declaration represents the Nazi formulation of the General Will, indicating the anti-associational bias going back to Rousseau. It was preceded by the destruction of all property belonging to political parties and a law declaring that the formation of new parties was high treason. But *Gleichschaltung* did not only mean destruction. Many organizations were allowed to continue under the supervision of party functionaries. This included daily routines (like the greeting "Heil Hitler"), periodic attendance at mass rallies, and compulsory, closely supervised participation in new and frequently repeated mobilization campaigns initiated by the party.

34. These methods proliferated especially in the cultural field, starting with the burning of "un-German" and subversive books in May 1933, extending to the control of all media and churches, and providing for national plebiscites in which over 90 percent of the voters endorsed the regime. The party contrived to make nonvoting an undesirable option.

35. The start of a freeway network for the whole country served military purposes and fired up people's imagination. Several hundred thousand subscribed to a project of building an affordable car for the masses at a time when cars were the luxury of a few. Interest-free loans to young married couples to establish their households could be reduced by a quarter with each birth. Universal conscription and a half-year labor service obligation were introduced, the Hitler youth was enlisted in harvest labor, and so on. These and many other measures mixed incentives with obligations in an effort to reduce unemployment, prepare for war, increase the population, as well as stimulate and symbolize the *Volksgemeinschaft*.

36. By 1939 over 7 million Germans went on "Strength through Joy" vacations, not counting the 35 million who went on organized daily excursions.

37. This cynical phrase combined organization with what was made to appear like spontaneity. By means of supervised mass mobilization Nazi functionaries arranged at suitable intervals for applause and shouts of "Heil Hitler" by the party faithful. The technique has become widespread since the 1930s, for example in advertising campaigns, but it remains a distinctive feature of one-party dictatorships that use it to ensure political approval by acclamation. Other variants of this technique have developed among religious fundamentalists.

38. The same question had been raised under the Wilhelmine Reich about the subordination of German Catholics under the papacy, the so-called *Kulturkampf*. The difference between a religious affiliation and a political subordination to a foreign power would require a separate discussion.

39. The first point attributes collective responsibility for the war to the German people; communists are exempted from this responsibility because they opposed the Nazi regime. The fourth point proclaims the unity of the working class, for which the party is the only legitimate spokesman; hence, all deviations from the party line are "excommunicated." Quoted from the article on the Socialist Unity party (*Sozialistische Einheitspartei* or SED) in Hartmut Zimmermann, Horst Ulrich, and Michael Fehlauer, eds., *DDR Handbuch*, vol. 2 (Köln: Verlag Wissenschaft und Politik, 1985), 1161.

40. Based on the eyewitness report of Wolfgang Leonhard as discussed in Hermann Weber, *Geschichte der DDR* (München: Deutscher Taschenbuch Verlag, 1989), 56–57. A detailed study of these and later claims to communist legitimacy is contained in Sigrid Meuschel, *Legitimation und Parteiherrschaft* (Berlin: Habilitationsschrift, Freie Universität Berlin, 1990).

41. Germany has experienced a turnover of official personnel, or its obstruction, four times in the twentieth century. Monarchist officials continued in office after 1918

and helped to undermine the republic. In 1933, the Nazis destroyed civil rights and dismissed or imprisoned all public officials not belonging to the party. In 1945, Allied occupation forces tried to deal with former Nazis, but the bulk of them retained some public office. And in 1989–90, an emerging democracy in East Germany and the newly unified country must deal in one way or another with former communist functionaries and their collaborators. The topic would require a separate treatment.

42. The techniques of communist co-optation are analyzed in Philip Selznick, *The Organizational Weapon* (New York: McGraw Hill Book Co., 1951).

43. On 21 April 1948, with the consent of the SMAD, the National Democratic Party of Germany (NDPD) was founded and given the task of enlisting former middle- and low-ranking Nazi officials to support the SED regime similar to the CDU and LPDP. Cf. Zimmermann, Ulrich, and Fehlauer, eds., *DDR Handbuch*, vol. 2, 927. The chronology in the text is taken from the *DDR Handbuch*, vol. 2, 1560–61. Soviet and Communist party policy toward leading Nazi officials, while thorough, was initially flawed by a simultaneous repression of prominent anticommunists, so that Nazis and their opponents found themselves in the same prison camps. Later, NDPD membership was tantamount to amnesty of former Nazis, provided of course that this new party submitted to SED controls.

44. The details of this forced co-optation and quick suppression of the SPD are set out in an unpublished paper by Beatrix Wrede-Bouvier, "Die Vereinigung von SPD und KPD 1946 in der SBZ," made available by the Friedrich Ebert Stiftung, Bonn. This "unification" resulted in good part from the pressure of the Soviet military author- ities. It is estimated that some 20,000 Social Democrats were censured, imprisoned or even killed between December 1945 and April 1946.

45. In the elections of 18 March and 15 October 1990 we have witnessed the long-run effects of this policy. The Christian Democratic Union (CDU) of East Germany had collaborated with the Socialist Unity party (SED) for decades, but it won the elections by close to 50 percent. It had been supported financially by the SED and allowed to build a grass-roots organization so that it could reach people who would not respond positively to direct communist appeals. On the other hand, the Social Democrats obtained only 22 percent of the March vote and won a majority in only one out of five Länder in October. Part of the reason was that the forced unification of Social Democrats and communists in 1945–46 prevented any Social Democrats from rebuilding at the grass-roots level. Unification in the SED meant that the Social Democratic party had ceased to exist for over forty years. The fact that the CDU was allowed to continue with SED assistance and under its supervision was obviously not the first time that collaboration with a one-party dictatorship paid off once that regime was overthrown.

8

A Country Divided: Germany after 1945

The Paradox of Unity

There is no preestablished harmony between what a political economy provides and what the forces in civil society demand. By the mid-eighteenth century, a "revolution of provisions" had begun in England, leading to great increases of wealth but also to a depersonalization of human relations. In 1789, a "revolution of entitlements" was initiated by the overthrow of the French monarchy, leading to a constitution guaranteeing the rights of man but also to a proliferation of organized demands upon the state.[1] Modern states in the industrialized countries of the world have had to cope with the ever-shifting incompatibilities between the gross national product created and the political demands for its redistribution.

I want to examine the paradoxical assumption of the French Revolution that the desired political unity can be achieved by a system of laws.[2] In our daily affairs, we rely on governmental regulations when we call the police or prepare tax returns. We are made aware of conflicts of interest when we vote or call for public assistance. We become conscious of our country's unity when we witness a presidential inauguration, travel abroad, or respond to national emergencies. The French Revolution provided the metaphor of the general will for such collective modes of awareness. I want to consider that metaphor because it turns states and nations into communities, though one should guard against the implication of a general consensus. Communities exist without total agreement; to assume otherwise involves the fallacy of misplaced concreteness. This is especially evident when one deals with a country that has undergone as many transformations as Germany has during the last century.[3]

The paradigm of the "general will" consisted of three interlocking assumptions: that all citizens were equal before the law; that the law was based on constituted authority rather than sanctified but arbitrary will; and that the people were united by a common historical continuity between past and future. An earlier meaning of nation, which referred to place of birth, language, and cultural heritage, has continued down to the present. To this the French Revolution added the idea of national citizenship, initially in polemical fashion. As discussed earlier, Abbé Sieyès declared in 1789 that now the Third Estate, which had been nothing, was to be everything. In a nation of some 25 million people with a tiny minority of aristocrats and clergymen who either did nothing or had their religious vocation, it was only proper for the Third Estate to represent the nation and its people.[4] The first institutional expression of this sentiment consisted in the abolition of the estates and the establishment of the National Assembly (17 June 1789). The third article of the *Declaration of the Rights of Man and of the Citizen* states the basic principle that "all Sovereignty resides in the Nation." What was the nature of its "imagined unity"? The answer has material and ideal components.[5]

In the ancient hierarchical community of the king and his subjects, "imagined unity" was aided by the ease with which a whole population could identify with the single person of the ruler. Such collective identification became more abstract and difficult when kings were replaced by a national community of citizens. The country they inhabited had territorial boundaries that established a zone of sovereignty exercised in the name of the people. Legal boundaries defined the rights and duties of a population of individuals, governed by an authority based on a constitution. In addition, one can speak of a psychological boundary that made the nation a communal symbol of membership and allegiance. Modern nations arose when the people curbed, or overthrew, the hereditary prerogative of royalty in the name of popular sovereignty. This new principle of rule had to be defended against foreign enemies. Next, the principle of a popular mandate was generalized by renouncing the use of force against the liberty of other people, who had the right to self-defense, which alone justified a war. Yet eventually, the French Revolution also turned the self-defense of the nation into a struggle against internal enemies. What had begun as an attack upon persons of privilege ended with attacks upon conspirators against the people.

Unity or fraternity arose from these definitions of the community. First the kingdom and then the Republic were declared "one and indivisible."

Soon, a national mystique was attached to symbols of unity: the National Assembly, the constitution, the flag, the hymn, the motto, and the festival. The annexation of Alsace, Savoy, and Corsica, the disappearance of internal boundaries, and the acceptance of a freely chosen authority by popular consent were publicly celebrated. The diversity of ancient jurisdictions gave way to a central government, weights and measures were standardized, and a new Republican calendar was introduced, though it did not last. Finally, the country's unity was greatly enhanced by the *levée en masse* against foreign enemies, although the terror against domestic enemies was probably divisive.

Ethical universalism was added to "imagined unity" discussed previously. The idea of France as the "elect among nations" had been inspired by the military and cultural dominance of France on the European continent, as well as by the Enlightenment. Now it inspired the ideal of liberty, which became linked with the country's life-and-death struggle against foreign aggression but also served as a symbol for liberation movements against oppression. The "imagined unity" of the nation was universalized by using the principle of national self-determination as a defense of the revolution against France's European enemies.[6] The worldwide aspiration for liberty and nationhood can be considered a repercussion of the French Revolution.

This complex of actions and ideas was reinforced in turn by a theoretical construction of consent, variously called general will (Rousseau), public spirit, or patriotism.[7] Here again we face the paradox of unity and diversity. According to Rousseau,

> So long as a number of men in combination are considered as a single body, they have but one will, which relates to the common preservation and to the general well-being. ... The first man to propose [the necessary laws] only gives expression to what all have previously felt, and neither factions nor eloquence will be needed to pass into law what everyone has already resolved to do.[8]

This and similar passages assert a tautology: where everybody agrees, men can be considered a single body with one will, or where consent prevails, the general will of the society is assured. Elsewhere, Rousseau refers to a "purely civil profession of faith" arising from "sentiments of sociability, without which it is impossible to be a good Citizen or a faithful subject." He was prepared to make such faith and sentiments mandatory.[9] His solution was to sacrifice particular interests in the name of unity, a theoretical construction that gave way soon enough to the actual proliferation of individual and collective interests, which were protected by the law and the constitution.[10]

For neither political theory nor revolutionary practice can undo the coexistence, and partial incompatibility, of unity and diversity. Where all unity is sacrificed, anarchy prevails, or political order is reestablished on a smaller scale, by federation or secession. Where unity is made total, political order is unstable, at least in the very long run. Modern totalitarian rule seeks to realize such "unity" and, with the aid of modern technology, can last for generations. While it is possible to destroy civil society, it is impossible to prevent conflicts of interest among the followers of a dictator, or to avoid the psychological repercussions of illegitimacy among the people at large.

These theoretical considerations are derived from ideas that came to the fore during the French Revolution. They are relevant for an understanding of recent German history.[11] My purpose is to show how the human community is defined and redefined in a state and nation of the twentieth century. The case of Germany is especially suitable in this regard. It has encompassed many types of political community, including the division between the Federal Republic and the German Democratic Republic since 1945. The reunification of Germany in 1989–90 has put the country on the current political agenda, and is the most recent example of "unsettled affinities."

Recapitulation

In 1871, Germany was united under one government for the first time in a thousand years, the direct result of the German victory over France in the Franco-Prussian war (1870–71). Public reaction was divided, especially in intellectual circles. One side, probably the majority of the *Bildungsbürgertum* among officials, the military, and the professions, was chauvinistic, convinced that Germany had a worldwide cultural mission. The other side, first a minority of intellectuals influenced by Nietzsche but growing in size and cultural resonance after 1900, claimed that military victory had jeopardized German culture for the sake of empire.

In 1914, the outbreak of World War I was initially greeted with enthusiasm in many countries. The war appeared as a release from the confines of materialism, partisan bickering, and the decline of moral values. Patriotism and the readiness to die for an ideal triumphed over the trading and shopkeeping spirit.[12] The war of attrition that followed dispelled this euphoria everywhere. However, Germany was probably unique in that a minority of writers idealized the community of officers and men in battle as the model for eradicating the money-grubbing, competitive spirit of society in peacetime.

In 1918, Germany was defeated, the monarchy was overthrown, a revolution broke out partly in response to the Bolshevik Revolution of 1917, and by August 1919 the new Weimar Constitution was formally enacted. Monarchist judges and officials remained in office and helped to create a republic without enough republicans. Soon, the country experienced a devastating inflation. Weimar was politically polarized between right and left extremists as well as divided among some thirty political parties. Cabinets changed in rapid succession. After a few years of economic recovery, the Great Depression set in, resulting in some 6 million unemployed. The wartime idea of an embattled community of frontline soldiers became increasingly popular, both as the symbol of the National Socialist party and as the model for a reorganization of the country.

In January 1933, the Nazis came to power and made short shrift of their opponents; within months democracy had given way to a one-party dictatorship. The economic recovery of the later 1930s was made to look like a Nazi achievement on behalf of the people, and was exploited by Hitler to rearm the country and prepare for war. The bulk of the population benefited economically in the short run and embraced the regime more or less enthusiastically, except for those who withdrew as best they could and the few who actively resisted. Mostly, people looked the other way as they benefited not only from the preparation for war but from the organized destruction of synagogues and Jewish enterprises. In the short run, they benefited psychologically as well from the calculated secretiveness concerning the death camps, while arbitrary arrests and displays of brutality frequently reminded them that it was better to play it safe and not ask any questions. In the long run, this combination of opportunism, passivity, and fear was to become the unmasterable past (*unbewältigte Vergangenheit*) of the postwar era.

In 1945, Germany lay in ruins. Some Nazi officials committed suicide, some were brought to trial, most were allowed to continue in positions equivalent to those they had held before. More of this was tolerated in

West Germany than in East Germany. In the Federal Republic, Allied denazification proceedings were discontinued, as the Marshall Plan of economic reconstruction (June 1947), the change of wartime alliances, and the anticommunism of the cold war (March 1948) took hold. In May 1949, the new Basic Law (*Grundgesetz*) of the Federal Republic was promulgated. Under its aegis, West German governments could pursue a policy of economic reconstruction with some degree of political independence as well, partly because this complied with the democratic creed and partly because the Western occupying powers did not impose uniform policies on the defeated country. In East Germany, the Soviet Military Administration imprisoned, sentenced, or deported not only many Nazi functionaries but also many anti-Nazi opponents of the German Communist party, so that former Nazis and liberal anti-Nazis found themselves in the same concentration camps. The steps by which the Socialist Unity party established a one-party dictatorship have been reviewed. The Soviet Military Administration imposed heavy reparations on East Germany. Although the German Democratic Republic was formally established (1949), the Communist party leadership remained under Soviet tutelage emanating from Moscow.

In 1989, the Soviet Union under the leadership of Mikhail Gorbachev withdrew direct political supervision of satellite Eastern Europe. In the German Democratic Republic this resulted in the overthrow of the one-party regime in November 1989, and the establishment of interim governments until October 1990 when the country was formally unified and for the first time in fifty-seven years free, nationwide elections were held.

These six dates mark drastic political and cultural transformations of this German center of Europe: 1871, 1914, 1918, 1933, 1945, and 1989. Looked at from the vantage point of 1990, Gordon Craig has declared that

> the West German Republic is a success story. Its crises were overcome pretty well by democratic procedures. There is grass-roots democracy there. On the whole I am very optimistic about it. I keep telling myself that the Germans have changed and that it cannot be reversed. But then I remind myself that unification will change them again.[13]

Momentous changes have occurred. But the future remains uncertain and our imagination of possible futures is too limited. It is not a question of a return to a Nazi dictatorship, but of the possible reactions of this

German center of Europe to new and unforeseeable international constellations. Like other people in modern history, the Germans are formally the citizens of a state and tend to think of themselves as a nation
in cultural and historical terms. They are thereby distinguished from
people who belong to other states and nations. People constitute a
community where such institutional membership and cultural identification prevail, and the question remains open as to how they react if and
when the setting of their country changes once again, perhaps as drasti-
cally as it has before. Comparative historical studies are not a form of
prophecy, but they can illuminate the assets and liabilities of conditions
as they develop. That remark goes together with Tocqueville's observation, quoted earlier, that the distinctive character of a country results from
"an education that has lasted for centuries."

Notes

1. Ralf Dahrendorf has formulated this contrast in *The Modern Social Conflict*
   (London: Weidenfeld & Nicolson, 1988), 13.
2. Bernhard Groethuysen, *Philosophie der Französischen Revolution* (Neuwied: Hermann Luchterhand Verlag, 1971).
3. In reverting to the French Revolution before analyzing the recent history of
   Germany I adhere to Max Weber's cryptic remark that "the appeal to national
   character is generally a mere confession of ignorance." Max Weber, *The Protestant
   Ethic and the Spirit of Capitalism* (New York: Charles Scribner's Sons, 1958), 88.
4. The argument of the Abbé Sieyès is set out in Reinhard Bendix, *Kings or People*
   (Berkeley: University of California Press, 1978), 365-69.
5. I have referred previously to Benedict Anderson's important study *Imagined Communities*, but I want to add that one does not cope with the paradox of unity by
   making it solely a product of the imagination. Difficulties mount when the nation
   and national sentiment are treated entirely apart from the state, although states exist
   without being nations and there are nations that do not have a state. The division
   between East and West Germany is an example of the first, the Kurds divided
   between Iran, Iraq, and Turkey an example of the second. It is useful to remember
   that in human affairs all types of unity depend upon many existing differences being
   set aside for purposes of analysis. Otherwise, concepts would be perfect fits, ideal
   types would not be needed, and modern totalitarian regimes would not have to go
   to such lengths in order to maintain unity.
6. The preceding discussion is indebted to Pierre Nora's article on "Nation," in
   François Furet and Mona Ozouf, eds., *A Critical Dictionary of the French Revolution* (Cambridge: Harvard University Press, 1989), 742-53.
7. The earlier discussion already referred to the idea that both individual liberty and
   national unity could be enhanced by a system of laws under a constitution, which
   accounts in part for the revolutionary opposition to all factions and voluntary
   associations.

8. Jean-Jacques Rousseau, *The Social Contract*, ed. Charles Sherover (New York: New American Library, 1974), 175. Where these conditions are absent, states are ill-constituted from the beginning. "When the social bond begins to be relaxed and the State weakened, when private interests begin to make themselves felt and small associations to exercise influence on the State, the common interest is injuriously affected and finds adversaries; unanimity no longer reigns in the voting; the general will is no longer the will of all; opposition and disputes arise, and the best counsel does not pass uncontested." P. 177.

9. See ibid., 237. The passage quoted continues: "Without having power to compel anyone to believe them [faith and sentiments], it may banish from the State whoever does not believe them; it may banish him not as impious, but as unsociable, as incapable of sincerely loving law and justice and of sacrificing at need his life to his duty. But if anyone, after publicly acknowledging these dogmas, behaves like an unbeliever in them, he should be punished with death; he has committed the greatest of crimes; he has lied before the laws."

10. Rousseau was not alone. There was widespread agreement that the "particular" rather than the "private" was the opposite of the "public," that public opinion was advanced by the enlightened few who would reeducate the unenlightened many. The high regard for public opinion in terms of its visibility, impersonality, and intrinsic merit arose from the common opposition to the secrecy of royal decisions, their personal arbitrariness, and their association with inherited privilege and court intrigue. Cf. the article on "Public Spirit" by Mona Ozouf in Furet and Ozouf, eds. *A Critical Dictionary*, 771–80.

11. These eighteenth-century ideas are applicable well beyond the German case. They are relevant today because they set the agenda with which modern "nation-states" have to deal. The frequency with which formal constitutions are adopted only to be ignored in practice is a symptom of that relevance. After all, why bother? The answer is that the idea of a system of laws is alive in people's minds and can result in liberation movements against dictatorial rule.

12. Carl Zuckmayer has vividly described the "inner liberation of the whole nation from its obsolete conventions," induced in good part by a sudden decline of the caste spirit, the exhilarating solidarity of young middle-class men with their working-class comrades. Carl Zuckmayer, *A Part of Myself* (New York: Harcourt Brace Jovanovich, 1970), 148–49.

13. Interview with Gordon Craig quoted in *The New York Times*, 25 September 1990.

Part IV

Epilogue

9

Unfinished Thoughts on German Unity

John Bendix

My father died at the end of February 1991, having just revised the first eight chapters of this book. He had originally planned to write a final chapter that would deal with the new process of legitimation and the reestablishment of authority in East Germany after 1989

> in a country which for the forseeable future will be divided into an advanced and a backward part, not only economically but socially and politically. My particular interest is in the ways in which people will now come to terms with being part of the "German nation."[1]

But a return visit to his native Berlin in 1990 and discussions with colleagues and friends, as well as the prospect of working together with a specialist on East Germany, Dr. Sigrid Meuschel, provided the impetus to reconsider the final chapter. He had decided to split his consideration into two chapters, first examining the dual German histories from 1945 on, and then turning to a consideration of what was tentatively entitled "Two Germanies into One (1989–)."

Germany's new situation demanded new perspectives—personal, historical, sociological—even as it provided him with an opportunity to reconsider his earlier work. To one friend he noted that "a generation ago I wrote about the DDR regime as illegitimate, and now I cannot resist the temptation to take a look at current developments. . . . I want to (see) what it means to reemerge as Germans after 'all that.'"[2] To another colleague he wrote that he found "it a mixed and dubious pleasure to have been proven right."[3] In what follows I have tried to provide some indications of where my father's thoughts on Germany were heading.[4] He always liked to explore intellectual territory, and I think it in his spirit

to suggest ways others can continue the exploration and not leave his last
project unfinished.

* * *

The distinction between those who belong to a community and those
who do not was the point of departure for my father.[5] The distinction
itself was made by the intellectual leaders of the community and their
followers, which meant that each community necessarily had to order its
affairs. Moral and political theory had tried to provide answers to how
this *should* occur, but at issue for him was how communities *were*
actually constituted and maintained.

The German national community was a particularly interesting case
because the problems of national identity (or community) and state
legitimation seemed so unresolved, if for different reasons in West
Germany than in East Germany. Unification, after decades of living
apart, meant that ambivalent attitudes about community would be over-
lain with a formal state unity. Intellectuals played a particularly important
role in this process, not only in their definitions of belonging but also in
their contributions to the order of the nation-state and hence the community. Legitimation on the part of the people was also fluid, most explicitly
in the transition from the slogan "Wir sind *das* Volk" (we are the people)
to "Wir sind *ein* Volk" (we are one people) during the demonstrations in
Leipzig. Yet the transition from the delegitimation of the East German
regime to the legitimation of the commonalities with West Germans
occurred without an intermediating discussion of what the new and
unified state and society were to be like. The regime legitimation (or
delegitimation) brought about with the end of Socialist Unity party (SED)
rule in the East raised the same question that was posed by the end of the
Nazi era and by the end of party rule in the Soviet Union: what should
one do with those who collaborated with the old regime?

The reunification problems had to be seen as well in historical perspective within the context of the reference societies, the United States
and the Soviet Union, which had shaped the two Germanies in the
postwar era. Reference societies provided external models of how—or
how not—to order the community as well as yardsticks by which to
measure one national community against another. Those yardsticks
meant judgments about relative backwardness as well. Identity and a

redefinition of community were also inward-looking, and had to be analyzed in terms of what was internally possible. Finally, political transformation was related to the nature and strength of civil society.

One plan for how to examine the dual history of the two Germanies (which was discussed with Dr. Meuschel) included:

1. A demographic contrasting of West and East Germany with a comparison of the costs of the Second World War in both[6]
2. A comparison of revolutionary changes in Europe; the creation and collapse of dictatorships[7]
3. Who was "taken-in" by the SED and how the language was politicized[8]
4. A review of the 1990 elections:
   (a) the discussion about electoral type and the extent to which West German parties "took over" the East and
   (b) the intellectuals' "splitting-off" from the populace[9]
5. "Mastering the past" in West and East Germany:[10]
   (a) administrative practice relative to foreigners—"it is not the political asylees that are the problem but the economic refugees whom one does not want to deport—shadows of the Nazi era"
   (b) on top of this now comes the antagonism toward foreigners, especially in East Germany
6. The *Kulturnation* (culture-nation) in the East in opposition to the Western capitalism of West Germany and the United States.[11]

A different version of the last chapter, entitled "Between Reference Societies and an Unmasterable Past," was to have had a discussion of individualism and communalism at the turning points of German contemporary history,[12] a discussion of the differing "cultural missions" of West and East Germany, the subsequent "creeping cultural crisis," ending with "communal and personal redemption," and "reactions to disillusion."[13]

Clearly there were various approaches that were being considered, and a number of familiar themes from his earlier work that my father wanted to reconsider: revolutionary change, political authority and legitimation, the role of intellectuals, the idea of the reference society.[14] These were among the themes that received greater attention, and the direction of the discussion is noted below. It was in the analysis of the cultural aspects, such as language politicization, the "culture-nation," differing cultural missions, and the "cultural crisis" where the branching out and explorations were to have occurred, particularly in their relationship to national identity.[15] In what follows, I have tried to group the themes under reference societies and relative backwardness, regime legitimation and collaborators, the role of the intellectuals in the national community, identity, and transformations and civil society. There is, however, some overlap in the discussions of these nominally discrete categories.

Reference Societies and Relative Backwardness

Both Germanies had received new "reference societies" after the war, now no longer England and France but rather the United States and the Soviet Union. The impact was quickly evident in the postwar period, with the Marshall Plan in the American zone and the removal of factories from the Soviet zone. In both East and West, the reference societies permitted a turning away from Nazism, allowing each to claim that in its own way, they had stood on the side of the victors against fascism. In national terms, it permitted both Germanies to break with the apolitical tradition of a cultural self-definition of what it meant to be German.

At the same time, in the immediate postwar era, each Germany also perceived itself as relatively backward vis-à-vis the superpowers. The particularism of the contrast between West and East Germany was contrasted to the universalism of the U.S./USSR difference.[16] A further complication was added by having each Germany use the other as a reference society, though more for the negative than for the positive contrasts.

East Germany, tied to the USSR, was aggressive toward a West Germany it regarded as a forward post of America. Yet East Germany lacked any real possibility for an independent existence, caught as it was between the far larger superpowers. That in turn led to continuous efforts at legitimation on the part of the SED regime in an attempt to unsuccessfully assert an independent existence for the country.[17]

West Germany, tied to the United States, was soon involved in the American confrontation with the Soviet Union, and hence played the "forward post" role vis-à-vis the Soviet Union, and for a generation defended the Atlantic tie. This meant a fundamental rejection of the historic antimaterialism that had characterized Germany (described in an earlier chapter), though it lived on in the anti-Americanism of protest against the West German establishment, which was seen as having wholeheartedly sold out in the cultural and material Americanizing of West Germany. West Germany's relationship to East Germany was divided, however, because while it recognized that the East served Soviet interests, the familial and cultural ties made it difficult to entirely reject East Germany. West Germany also initially lacked the possibility for an independent existence, and was granted sovereignty largely due to the cold war.

Both Germanies were hindered in their creation of separate identities, for both found themselves "denationalized" through the reference societies. "In the bipolar system," Marion Gräfin Dönhoff had written, "the Germans seemed to be the East of the West and the West of the East."[18] The ideological divergences between a West proud of its freedom and stance against totalitarianism and an East proud of its triumph over capitalism and stance against fascism also hindered the creation of a unified German identity. Germany, with dual external reference societies, until 1989 also had a bifurcated internal reference system of East contrasted with West.[19] It remained unclear how one could measure the impact of the external reference societies, however, other than by using cultural data.

Regime Legitimation and Collaborators

My father wrote several times that he was interested in establishing a "demography of turncoats"[20] in East Germany in order to establish who or how many were "taken in" (*vereinnahmt*) by the SED in ideological terms or "occupationally disabled."[21] A further interest was to establish the extent to which SED practices paralleled those of the Nazis.[22] He wanted to know if there was a list of people who had to be watched in order to conduct

> an analysis of the ideology of the implicit dangers perceived by the DDR regime . . . the efforts at dealing with an individual author such as Erich Loest is wholly disproportionate to the danger he or she poses, even if one ranks ideological factors very highly. Keeping files on 6 million people in a country with only a few more households than this is also hard to understand, even when one takes the bureaucratic hypertrophy of security forces into account.[23]

The party membership of 2.3 million also led him to speculate: "suppose all the others were secret opponents: what was the support-mentality of those who benefitted? Probably a mixture of sentiment, benefit and doubt—but not among intellectuals."[24]

The question was then what one did subsequently with those who had indeed been "taken in." The situation in East Germany was analogous to earlier German transitions (from the monarchy to Weimar, from the Nazi era to the postwar period) as well as to other countries (the *nomenklatura* in the Soviet Union after Gorbachev, Franco's functionaries in the new Spanish democracy). My father wrote to a German colleague that

> it may not be just, but rather than moral outrage one should consider whether it wouldn't be better to symbolically destroy the old regime through trials conducted against the old leaders such as Honecker and Mielke. Afterwards one could employ both old and new people together, with the old ones well-supervised and subject to disciplinary proceedings if they did not act in accordance with the new order. It wouldn't after all be so pointless to put the old snoopers under surveillance themselves, and besides, it was the old Leninist solution to put tried and trusted revolutionaries at the side of the tsarist officers.[25]

The claim to legitimacy made by the regime also was not legitimacy itself, he felt, despite the use of socialist and antifascist ideology to try to promote it. The SED insisted on conformity to (Soviet) norms and structures because of its dependent status, while it at the same time tried to ensure a measure of independence within the Eastern Bloc.[26]

Socialist unity had the advantage of tying into older, classic-humanist ideals of education or self-cultivation (*Bildung*) in the German population, as well as into nationalistically tinged communitarian ideals.[27] Yet this was also a severely depoliticized model, for it held up an ideal almost completely divorced from public life, captured by Thomas Mann during the First World War in his "Reflections of an Unpolitical Man":

> *Geist* (or *Bildung*) is *not* politics. . . . The distinction . . . (is) that of culture and civilization, of soul and society, of freedom and the franchise, of art and mere literature; and being German means culture, soul, freedom, art and *not* civilization, society, the right to vote, literature.[28]

The identification in this era was with a superior culture, seen—albeit not explicitly—in the comradeship of soldiers in war, a camaraderie that combined the ideal community with an emphasis on a leader. The ideal of *Geist* or camaraderie, and the connection of ideal community and strong leadership was not entirely surprising, since the realities were very different: a country divided between an agricultural east and an industrialized west, a Protestant north and a Catholic south, large cities (27 percent of the population in towns of 100,000+) versus rural countryside

(36 percent of the population in villages with less than 2,000), a polarized political Left and Right virtually unable to speak to one another.

Particularly after the events of 1989, it was quite evident to what extent the language itself had become politicized and deformed by the SED— "party talk" as opposed to "everyday talk"—indicating the domination that the party was able to exercise. The East German regime certainly provided social security, full employment, housing, educational chances for all, albeit in a heavy-handed manner, but rather than enhancing regime legitimacy, the result was a retreat by individuals from the state into what was called the *Nischengesellschaft* (niche society). "In a state that regulates everything," my father wrote, "East Germans learned to adapt and become inconspicuous. Their expectations became modest and it has been said that they became consciously old-fashioned."[29] Perhaps they were being equally old-fashioned, in light of previous historical transitions, in their desire after 1989 to both take revenge on the former SED regime agents *and* try to reintegrate them in the new society.[30]

Regime legitimation in West Germany was complicated by what amounted to a co-optation by the Western Allies. The economic reconstruction made possible through outside support meant

West Germans identified not only with American economic success, but also with democratic institutions, a counterpoint to restitution payments to Israel and the sporadic soul-searching that was expressed concerning the Nazi past.[31]

The contempt for the decadence of the West that had existed in earlier eras was replaced by pride in prosperity and a growing cosmopolitanism: with it came affluent life-styles, fads "and all the other practices which critics deplore in modern culture, especially in America." The result was that younger Germans were no longer nationalistic, but also no longer as distinctively German. Instead, they began to take Westernization and democracy for granted.

Intellectuals and the National Community

Intellectuals in both Germanies were uncomfortable in the postwar era, though for rather different reasons. West German intellectuals felt uneasy about what appeared to accompany or be the price of democracy, while East German intellectuals craved the freedoms denied to them and detested the Western marketizing individualism and lack of social cohesion. The result was that

> the West Germans are smug and uneasy, [and] the East Germans are hurt in their pride and seek to buttress it by claiming moral superiority while wanting the benefits [of the West]. In favor of freedom, the DDR intellectuals deplore the implications.[32]

As already noted, the classicist educational ideals fostered either a narrow view focused on German culture or a worldly and open cosmopolitanism. The antimaterialist tradition created a depoliticized intellectual milieu, which regarded political conflict, interest groups, or bargaining as not really appropriate to their social situation.

Intellectuals in East Germany were in a particularly troubled position. The party maintained that it possessed privileged knowledge that allowed it to know what the interests of society were. Yet intellectuals, because they were claiming an impartial pursuit of truth, were also claiming to investigate in a manner that was in the interest of society, though perhaps at a greater distance from it. Such competing claims put intellectuals into the dilemma of being loyal to the party or resisting it. Loyalty was rewarded by the party, at the cost of societal suspicion of intellectual claims to impartiality, and was reinforced by the party's appeal to the prejudices and ambivalences intellectuals held toward their own society. Both the party and intellectuals were stating implicitly (and sometimes explicitly) that society was incapable of managing its own affairs and that the public interest was better represented by elite groups.[33] Resistance to party claims by protesting or by using religion as a vehicle carried a high cost, including the possibility of forced emigration. The alternative of "inner emigration" only served to reinforce the depoliticized *Innerlichkeit* already long present in the German intellectual tradition.

As reunification proceeded, it was clear that cooperation had its costs. Until 1989, intellectuals had had a leading role to play, but afterwards found themselves relegated to a secondary position by professional politicians; their problem was to maintain their dignity after reunification.[34] More fundamentally, however, under SED rule, the question of community or belonging had been posed by the regime itself.

In the West, the heritage was more diffuse. Questions of community and belonging were often a matter of individual choice rather than regime orientation, though one colored by the influence of the reference society. The possibility of expressing ideological opposition or support of the regime led to polarization over West German politico-military and economic policies, with the political Left opposing German rearmament and the treatment of workers, and the political Right opposing Ostpolitik and concessions to the workers. The *Bildung* heritage led to the same choice as in the East between nationalism and cosmopolitanism, though with left-wing intellectuals particularly suspected of not having any real attachments, and hence not really belonging, to the national community.[35] This suspicion was mitigated by the decline of importance of the humanities, the changing values of the younger generation in the 1960s, as well as the sporadic debate about the Nazi past. Changes in the West produced uncertainty about the continuing role of intellectuals in the community, not made any easier by the ambivalence many intellectuals felt about West Germany's material success.

The consequences of this for unification were difficult. An older antimaterialist orientation, whether in its Eastern or Western guise, mitigated against wholehearted support for the Western economic "colonization" of the East and guaranteed critical intellectual commentary. Indeed, a number of West German intellectuals were rather taken aback at the "clear-cutting" approach taken with East German university institutes by West German education commissions, regardless of the institutes' quality. It always seemed to mean a reaffirmation of the West German model, never a chance to reform German higher education. Unification thereby introduced professional insecurity and bitterness for the East German intellectuals beyond what they already felt as collaborators with or resisters to the old regime.[36] The distance of intellectuals from the population at large in both Germanies was evident in the events surrounding unification, whether in the rapid replacement of the interim governments staffed by intellectuals in the East by professional politicians from the West, the relative lack of any far-reaching constitutional discussion (other than about reconciling abortion policies), or the election results that indicated very weak support for the "citizens' movements" begun in the East.

Indeed, the question of the role of intellectuals as objective seekers after universal truths became compromised by those intellectuals who function as handmaidens and legitimizers of the regime—as in East Germany—or as regime opponents in both East and West. Most serious is the perception that intellectuals belong to no national community at all but only to a community of their own, for that sets them at odds with or even opposed to the idea of national unity.

Identity

The question of East German identity was crucial to reunification: "what does it mean in East Germany today to be German?"[37] The East Germans could claim a kind of moral superiority, not only for bearing the brunt of the consequences of the Hitler years and of the Russian occupation after the war, but also for having eliminated the SED regime after having suffered under it for forty-five years. East Germans could then say that the West Germans owed them assistance as a matter of right: *we* bore the main burden of wartime reparations, *we* overthrew the hated regime while you stood on the sidelines. Of course, this moral superiority was constructed since the "revolution" was made possible by the Russians, as de Mazière had acknowledged, but it was the best means to retain self-respect, particularly after the wave of anti-SED and anti-*Stasi* (secret police) sentiment swept over East Germany once the old regime fell.

Yet whether self-respect or even self-righteousness were a sufficient basis for a sense of national identity was questionable in both East and West; commentators were talking of the "confused nation" rather than the German nation.[38] At heart there were only two themes that were of particular relevance to the East German situation: how do the East Germans (now) distinguish between themselves and those who don't belong? and what do such distinctions mean?[39]

West Germany had, since the mid-1980s, been struggling with the question of national identity as well, trying to reconcile a national consciousness originally formulated in terms of a German "culture-nation." That notion, in turn, was the creation of intellectuals concerned about the relative backwardness of Germany at the time when France and England were the reference societies. Unification now raised the issue whether a new sense of the "culture-nation" could be created out of two separated political entities.

At one level, West Germany had provided an example of how a country could be a state without having a nation, which helped explain why nationalism was barely evident during unification.[40] But at another level, the West German sense of national identity was heavily infused by (if not confused with) wealth, Americanization, and marketization, making it hard to know what was specifically German about it. In this climate, the revival of German traditions in an attempt to forge a new identity raised the troubling specter of reviving precisely those aspects—nationalism, isolation, inwardness—that had proven so fateful in the past.[41]

The statement about the priority of community over party contained in the protest slogan "wir sind das Volk" was soon transformed into a statement about the underlying cultural continuities between all Germans in "wir sind ein Volk." In that sense, the objection to the misappropriation of community by the SED became a more positive affirmation of a common cultural nationalism. And yet the unequal nature of the affirmation was not fully realized in the East: they were more interested in the efficiency and higher standard of living in the West but lacked knowledge of the society and politics in the West.

Transformations and Civil Society

The reconstruction of "civil society" was also problematic, as a German colleague pointed out, since there was not only no semantic equivalent for the idea in German but there wasn't even a proper word for "community":[42] "here one sees at every turn the antagonism towards politics of our classical political theorists as well as the old, fatal dispute over *Gesellschaft* and *Gemeinschaft*."[43] In response, my father noted that it was not surprising that a society that for fifty years had had no experience with autonomous action would have difficulty in immediately developing the kind of organizational competence and political personalities necessary for a multiparty system, whether in the old government or in the opposition. The reconstitution of parties, associations, and even families in the East, as well as the rediscovery of local patriotism were clearly manifestations of the attempt to shape a new identity, one which was difficult to do under conditions that approached colonization.[44] Not only that, but also the functional necessity of maintaining the old state administrators, suspect though they were, because of their knowledge of how to administer the system dictated keeping them until such time as they *could* be replaced. The sending in of West German administrators to run East Germany indicated just how far the West German government was prepared to try to replace the old order as quickly as possible with the new.

Yet what had happened in East Germany was not a revolution, because it was the result of the withdrawal of a hegemonic power (the Soviet Union) and it had been replaced by another power (West Germany). It was not a revolution in the sense previously considered.[45] In Habermas's sense it was a "catching-up revolution" (*nachholende Revolution*), one that was neither innovative or teleological. That very lack of utopia meant that "the utopia of a classless and hence just and harmonious society had failed, but the social and democratic questions remained open."[46] Unlike other revolutions, it appeared that interest groups and civil society would be created as the *result* of the revolution rather than being its cause.

Finally, there was a generational issue that was much more severe in East than West. A gap had developed between the older generation that had a nostalgia for socialism and what East Germany had tried to do, and a younger, more politically marginalized generation that demanded a more democratic path to socialism. This in turn made civil society more difficult to establish: there was no political elite, middle class, or independent intelligentsia, hence no leaders to manage the transition, let alone social groups to support it. There was also no experience in democratic process and certainly no preparation for belonging to "a complex, differentiated, formal-rational, regulated and conflict-ridden society."[47]

It is clear that my father was far more concerned about what would happen in East Germany than in West Germany. He was not sanguine about postreunification Germany, and quoted Hegel to the effect that the future was the object of hopes and fears, not of knowledge. In Germany, he wrote,

> Prospects for the long run are much more uncertain. They will be a compound of West German materialism and self-righteousness and East German moral indignation and the quest for moral renewal. . . . Moral superiority in the West, hurt feelings in the East. I do not know the outcome, but 20 years from now it can be quite explosive, not just in terms of a nationalistic revival, but in the political exploitation of Germany's new economic power in the center of Europe.[48]

In the new Germany, he saw reflected the paradoxes of unity and the difficulty of creating unified community after so many decades of separation. He found echoes as well in the paradox of universalism.

Both Max Weber and Goethe had used the idea of "elective affinity" (*Wahlverwandschaft*) in their work, and my father, in differing ways, felt his own affinities with these figures. He often said that the only real community that he belonged to was the university, and he recognized how fragile and intermittently social that intellectual community was. The profoundly unsettling refugee experience made him want to remain anchored to one location, but even that was not entirely satisfactory. He belonged to an America that he often regarded from a bemused distance, and no longer belonged to a Germany to whose heritage he owed a great deal. The desire to build bridges between these heritages characterized a great deal of his intellectual work; the later work he did on German-Jewish identities attempted to bridge the gap between personal and social experiences of a particular generation. His elective affinity was an unsettled one, but it was a price he was willing to pay to gain the distance needed to be able to express concern about communities he could not join.

Notes

1. Letter to Karen Beros, 24 May 1990. In a letter to Richard Buxbaum, he suggested that the means to study this process would be through intellectual articulations (as well as opinion polls) that would show how East Germans began to define their new community. Letter of 7 May 1990.
2. Letter to Gordon Craig, 12 May 1990.
3. Letter to Conrad Wiedemann, 30 December 1989.
4. The materials used here include correspondence, particularly with Dr. Sigrid Meuschel, Dr. Conrad Wiedemann (both of Berlin), and Dr. Rudolf von Thadden (of Göttingen), notes from lectures given in 1989 and 1990 at Berkeley and at Portland State University, a manuscript and notes he wrote in conjuction with his visit to Berlin in the summer of 1990, and other, more ephemeral jottings. Book references in this section are to works he had consulted or was considering using.
5. From lecture notes, March 1990.
6. See Lutz Niethammer, *Posthistoire—ist die Geschichte zu Ende?* (Reinbek: Rowohlt, 1989) as well as Niethammer's chapter in Charles Schüddekopf, *'Wir sind das Volk.' Flugschriften, Aufrufe und Texte einer deutschen Revolution* (Reinbek: Rowohlt, 1990). "If we want to deal with the national problem of the New Germany," he wrote to Sigrid Meuschel in late 1990, "we have to first describe the 'denationalization' of the two halves first."
7. The comparison was to be between 1918, 1933, 1945, and 1989, based in part on Plock's work. A later set of notes included 1871 and 1914 as well, indicating that he was not thinking of Europe as much as of German history. Works that were to be considered included Detlef and Klaus Megerle, *Politische Identität und nationale Gedenktage* (on Weimar), Martin Broszat's *Nach Hitler*, and Hans-Ulrich Thamer's *Verführung und Gewalt.*
8. The thought was to make an explicit comparison with the Nazi era, using Norbert Frei's *Der Führerstaat* and Martin Arend's *Allseits Gefestigt.*
9. For (a) the position of the West was that "we will finance things and we have the proven institutions," while in the East the position was "we will not allow ourselves to be 'taken-over' and we insist upon having our own valid contribution." For (b)

the relevant work was Dietz Bering's *Die Intellektuellen: Geschichte eines Schimpfwortes.*

10. *Vergangenheitsbewältigung* is the German term, to be discussed with reference to Charles Meier's *The Unmasterable Past.*

11. One empirical proposal was to work up what one could glean from the manner in which history was presented in schoolbooks and at teachers' conferences in East Germany.

12. One suggestion was to compare the antiforeigner attitudes to attitudes toward unification.

13. Another question was contained in the converted West German phrase "wir sind wieder wer" (we are someone again) to the query "Wie sind wir wieder wer?" (How are we someone again?) with the note that it did not apply in the same manner to East Germany. Notes from 2 July 1990.

14. He described the context of the German material in a letter to Gordon Craig (12 May 1990):

> The center piece is a sweeping discussion of definitions of community in Western civilization. . . . Then comes an essay on nationalism. . . . And then I present this case-study of Germany as one of the earliest "follower societies," an idea I have discussed earlier. . . . I try to show how this familiar evidence fits into a larger, comparative framework.

15. Hermann Glaeser's *Die Kulturgeschichte der Bundesrepublik Deutschland,* 3 vols. (Frankfurt: Fischer, 1990) was to be used for exploring the nature of the "culture-nation" in West Germany.

16. Notes from 2 July 1990. This was probably meant with reference to Tocqueville's statement in *Democracy in America* that the future destiny of the world would depend upon America and Russia. Letter to Sigrid Meuschel, 1 May 1990.

17. Letter to Sigrid Meuschel, 5 January 1991. The orientation of East Germany to the Soviet Union and against West Germany as a "forward post" of U.S. capitalism was crucial here.

18. The passage, from an article in *Die Zeit* of 7 December 1990, was underlined. The "in-between position of Germany in the territorial sense" was a German theme with considerable history. Lecture at Portland State University, November 1990.

19. The historical background for such "questionable allegiances" were to be found for the Weimar period in the works of Walter Lacquer, Gordon Craig, Karl Dietrich Bracher, Horst Moeller, and Detlef and Klaus Megerle; Hans-Dieter Schaefer's *Das gespaltene Bewusstsein* was also to be used. For the contrast between the two Germanies, Werner Weidenfeld, Zimmermann's *Deutschland Handbuch,* and Plock's work seemed promising.

20. In another formulation, he spoke of a "demography of decrepitude."

21. More precisely, he wanted to know "which occupational groups were, owing to their education, susceptible to the SED?" Notes of 19 July 1990.

22. Here he was particularly interested in Norbert Frei's chapter on ideological mobilization in his *Der Fuehrerstaat.*

23. Letter to Sigrid Meuschel, 1 October 1990.

24. Notes from 16 June 1990.

25. Letter to Conrad Wiedemann, 19 January 1990.

26. See Sigrid Meuschel's "Wandel durch Auflehnung. Thesen zum Verfall bürokratischer Herrschaft in der DDR," in Rainer Deppe, Helmut Dubiel, und Ulrich Rödel, *Demokratischer Umbruch in Osteuropa* (Frankfurt: Suhrkamp, 1991).

27. See Ulrich Engelhardt, *"Bildungsbürgertum": Begriffs- und Dogmengeschichte eines Etiketts* (Stuttgart: Klett-Cotta, 1986).

28. From a public lecture on "Moral Legitimacy and the Collapse of German Democracy," UC Berkeley, 11 November 1989.

29. Lecture at Portland State, November 1990.

30. Notes from 19 June 1990.

31. Lecture at Portland State, November 1990.

32. Notes from a discussion with Christine Schoefer, 25 May 1990; notes from July 1990.

33. This discussion owes a great deal to Dr. Meuschel's detailed knowledge of the East German developments.

34. Notes from 19 June 1990.

35. The term "homeless journeymen" (*vaterlandslose Gesellen*) was once again being used to refer to intellectuals, and had its similarities to arguments about the *trahison des clercs* that had been made in the Weimar era. See also Günter Grass, "Wider den Einheitsstaat: Kurze Rede eines vaterlandslosen Gesellen," in Ulrich Wickert, *Angst vor Deutschland* (Hamburg: Hoffmann und Campe, 1990), 61–72.

36. Letter from Sigrid Meuschel, 28 November 1990. The ambivalence was created in the rapid change from the euphoria of liberation from the old regime to the realization that its cost was exclusion from comparable influential roles in the new society. Notes from 16–17 June 1990.

37. Notes of 19 June 1990.

38. Wolffson's characterization, cited in a letter from Conrad Wiedemann, 4 March 1990.

39. Notes from July 1990.

40. Letter to Sigrid Meuschel, 5 January 1991.

41. Letter to Rudolf von Thadden, 9 February 1991.

42. *Bürgerliche Gesellschaft*, Hegel's term, referred to a rather different social order and conceptualization of the state.

43. Letter from Conrad Wiedemann, 12 April 1990. Wiedemann noted that the process of coming of age would likely last and there was "a great deal of undigested Rousseau at work."

44. Letter to Conrad Wiedemann, 23 April 1990.

45. Letter to Sigrid Meuschel, 5 December 1990.

46. See Sigrid Meuschel, "Revolution in der DDR," in *Die DDR auf dem Weg in die deutsche Einheit*, Edition Deutschland Archiv (Köln: Verlag Wissenschaft und Politik, 1990), 4. See also her contribution on the same question to the conference volume produced after the twenty-fifth *Soziologentag* in Frankfurt.

47. Letter to Meuschel, 5 December 1990.

48. This is the conclusion of the Portland State lecture, November 1990.

10

Endangered Affiliations

Rudolf von Thadden, translated by John Bendix

In the last years of his life Reinhard Bendix's thoughts turned more and more toward problems of identity. In personal conversations, letters, and lectures he was increasingly concerned with how individuals became members of groups and how such memberships or affiliations developed or were historically created. He felt, seismographically, the resurgence of national conflicts in Middle and Eastern Europe, and felt compelled to reexamine the driving forces behind them. It is thus no coincidence that his last academic contribution in German was on the topic of the "Structural Preconditions of National and Cultural Identity in the Modern Era." "Modern science and industry," he began, "as well as the basic ideas of the French Revolution have changed our modern world throughout the globe; this development cannot be divorced from identities which had their origins in Western Europe." Every country outside of Western Europe had been affected and made into followers. "The perception of backwardness relative to 'the West' was of fundamental importance in the development of national and cultural identity, even in countries which had maintained their political independence."[1]

When a segment of the population or even a nation became conscious of its backwardness, that consciousness became a factor that left its mark on the sense of identity of people and societies. It made clear how much historical experience and politico-social values were bound together.

This worldview led him to emphatically reject monocausal explanations for individual and collective behavior. In an unpublished manuscript from his last visit to Berlin in the summer of 1990, he cautioned against a too simple interpretation of the lack of resistance by Germans to Hitler, which would attribute it to the tradition of the authoritarian state.

It was not enough to know that German history was full of cumulative liabilities and that the German people were especially prone to submit to higher authority. For five years (1933–38) I had witnessed the seduction and coercion of a whole country, and I felt unsure that other people would be vastly superior in resisting such massive pressure once it was brought to bear upon them.[2]

With this background it is not surprising that Bendix felt uneasy in the discussion surrounding the *Historikerstreit*. He neither liked the comparative tabulation of atrocities committed under Hitler and Stalin, nor did he think the historico-theological and exorbitant elevation of German guilt helpful.

The German discussants were preoccupied with the question how such well-organized atrocities could have occurred in a country in which the term "a culture-nation" is a fairly common expression. It is not that they cannot cope with the past—they deal with it very well. It is rather that they cannot resolve for themselves the moral dilemma which their subject poses for the foreseeable future.

In such judgments his personal experiences played a significant role. As a student in Berlin he had experienced how differently people could behave in threatening situations. Social and cultural influences on identity were certainly important factors. Yet they were not so determinative as to cut off the possibility of individual responsibility. He drew the necessary conclusion: "We should not call upon history to answer existential questions."

But Bendix was not only thinking about a German predilection to making too many demands on history in the context of discussions over personal or collective guilt. Rather, he extended his reflections to Western self-righteousness in seeing a connection between fortuitous history and personal accomplishment. "Without thinking we enjoy the benefits of a fortunate past. But we should not claim as personal virtue what is in fact past virtue and good fortune for which we cannot take any credit."

These sentences were not written with reference to the past alone, but were also applicable to the present, tremendous changes in Germany and Eastern Europe. He saw that with the collapse of the Communist regime in East Germany the question of how historical determinants and personal responsibility were linked would once again be posed. The success of reunification, he felt, would depend upon that connection. "There is a link between the dilemma of what to do with the Communist hardliners of East Germany today and the Nazi hardliners of yesterday," he wrote. If, as in Nuremberg in 1946, only the victors would pass judgment on the vanquished, then the decisions would lack conviction and the sense of law would suffer. The tension between formal law and substantive justice would be overstrained.

But he was just as concerned with the socio-psychological consequences of German identity as with the juridical problems of German unification. In the discussion in mid-1990 about the future German capital, he argued for Berlin in light of the self-esteem of the weaker East Germans in the new Germany. The status of Berlin was extremely important, "not Berlin itself, but what the city is made to stand for is at issue." He sensed the danger for the inner stability of Germany arising from the imbalance between a successful, self-righteous West Germany, and a deeply insecure East Germany with a damaged sense of self-esteem. If decisions that took account of the sensibilities of the East Germans and that countered further shifts of power to the West were not made, then long-term cultural damage would result. "By making Berlin the capital, East Germans can be made to feel that they are also making a contribution to German unification."

In this plea for Berlin as the new capital, Bendix showed no sympathy for old nationalist ideas: he had experienced nationalist excesses too personally to fall into Wilhelminian dreams. Rather, from the day the Berlin Wall fell, he thought about the intellectual and political forces that, in the area devastated by communism, could have the power to progressively shape the future. His last letters worried about the inner direction of the reunified Germany, and asked whether it would lead to a "reawakening of many parts of the German tradition, in particular an 'anti-foreigner sentiment' to replace or revise the old nationalism." He feared that in the long run it would lead to a cultural division of the country, to a combination of isolation and *Innerlichkeit* that, in light of "the needs of the rest of the world," could lead to international reactions and possible military reactivation of Germany.[3]

The needs of the world were no less of a concern than those of Germany. He asked himself, with German anxiety, whether European integration had enough inner bonding force to match the new challenges.

Could it be that the post-war easing of tensions between Germany and France is not as permanent as Chancellor Adenauer and General de Gaulle had envisaged? That German-Russian relations, composed as they now are of German economic strength and the demise of Soviet power, may resume where they left off over fifty years before? That England is as aloof from the Continent as before?

And how would the world develop if America retreated entirely from Europe?

Bendix knew, from a life filled with change, how brittle political and social order could be in the world, "in 1938, I came to America with a profoundly troubling sense of the fragility of civilization." This sensibility toward the tremors in the world had a deeper basis not confined to the experience of twentieth-century catastrophes, but rather in the heritage of his family in Judaism.

Since the publication of his autobiography *From Berlin to Berkeley*, Reinhard Bendix had thought with greater and greater intensity about the intellectual roots and problems of Jewish identity. He researched cultural and religious history in connection with early Christianity and the interpretations of Paul; the origins and effects of Christian claims to absoluteness run like a thread through this work.

But he did not become a theologian. He remained what he had been: a historically minded sociologist who always considered political, social, and cultural structures within the compass of human ethical behavior. He was concerned with the conflict-ridden coexistence of Jews, Moslems, and Christians in the Middle East against the background of the centuries-long tensions between the three large monotheistic religions. He wanted to know the connection between belief and culture, and did not ignore the place of political interests, a factor that was usually determinative. In this sense, in his last letter, he expressed his care-filled thoughts about the Gulf War:

> The Middle East will, I fear, also preoccupy the next generation. It is the unresolved inheritance of European colonization, of a thousand-year confrontation of the West with Islam and in the end with Judiasm—now transformed into a "völkisch"-national version which I have never been able to accept.

In these sentences the central themes reemerge. The conflict between a modern, colonialist, Western world and a world of Islam in its backwardness and need for emancipation along with the problem of a Judaism that was becoming entrenched in its national form in Israel. There was also sorrow at the lack of human understanding. As important as the themes, such as the reflections on affiliations of all kinds, is the spirit in which they were treated: trust in an—embattled—reason to have a lasting effect on the way life was organized, and this despite all the skepticism about the chances that reason would triumph, in a world full of irrationalism. In his conversations he sought an exchange of views and ideas, never demanding anything but the individuality of his conversation partner. For him there was no objectivity without humanity.

Notes

1. Reinhard Bendix, "Strukturgeschichtliche Voraussetzungen der nationalen und kulturellen Identität in der Neuzeit," in Berhard Giesen, *Nationale und kulturelle Identität. Studien zur Entwicklung des kollektiven Bewusstseins in der Neuzeit.* (Frankfurt: Suhrkamp, 1991), 39.
2. This and subsequent quotes are from Reinhard Bendix, "Reflections: A Summer's Visit (Berlin, 1990)," unpublished manuscript.
3. Letter to Rudolf von Thadden of 9 February 1991.

Index

DATE DUE